rsity of

CRITICAL IRELAND

Critical Ireland

New Essays in Literature and Culture

ALAN A. GILLIS & AARON KELLY
EDITORS

FOUR COURTS PRESS

Set in 10 on 12.5 point Caslon for
FOUR COURTS PRESS LTD
Fumbally Lane, Dublin 8, Ireland
e-mail: info@four-courts-press.ie
and in North America
FOUR COURTS PRESS
c/o ISBS, 5824 N.E. Hassalo Street, Portland, OR 97213.

A catalogue record for this title
is available from the British Library.

ISBN 1-85182-597-5 hbk
ISBN 1-85182-598-3 pbk

SPECIAL ACKNOWLEDGMENT

This publication received a grant in aid of publication
from the Arts Council of Northern Ireland
and the Queen's University of Belfast Publication Fund.

Printed in Great Britain
by MPG Books, Bodmin, Cornwall

Foreword

Academics often take a long time to publish conference papers. Not so with the two 'New Voices in Irish Criticism' conferences held in Dublin (1999) and Belfast (2000). The speed with which the proceedings have been assembled by the young editors (in both cases, also the conference organisers) is waking up Irish studies to the ideas and enthusiasm of a new generation.

The title *Critical Ireland* may imply several things. First, it emphasises the critical thrust of Irish literary and cultural studies. Second, it invites us to consider how Ireland figures in that critical mirror. Finally it suggests that the country is in a 'critical' condition, and so might benefit from the critique on offer here. Indeed criticism, literary and otherwise, has not always been highly regarded by Irish people. Ireland is notable for strong communitarian values, and such values tend to equate the critic with the heretic or traitor. Again, Ireland has a small population. Ernest Boyd, a neglected ancestor of contemporary Irish criticism, wrote in *Ireland's Literary Renaissance* (1916):

> Impartial criticism is a more than usually delicate task where a small country like Ireland is concerned. When the intellectual centre is confined within a restricted area, personal relations are unavoidable, and the critic finds discretion imperative, if he is to continue to dwell peaceably in the midst of his friends ... The effect ... of this absence of critical judgment, publicly expressed, has been that honest criticism prefers to be silent where it cannot praise.

After the Easter Rising, Boyd found that another problem of Irish criticism had become more acute. In a preface to the 1922 reprint of his book, he wrote: 'Irish criticism is too largely the monopoly of the patriotic whose unimpeachable sentiments concerning Ireland are regarded as entitling them to pass judgments upon questions of aesthetics.'

Not everybody might agree with Boyd. But the problems he identifies are still relevant to Irish literary (and now cultural) studies, although they have assumed new guises. At 'New Voices' 2, a panel on reviewing showed that the difficulty of 'honest criticism' abides. And the issue of how to read the relation between literature, history and politics continues to be probed in the more theoretical essays here. Yet *Critical Ireland* conveys a refreshing sense of moving on: in particular, from what the editors – with an evident yawn – call 'the revisionist-nationalist debate'. All kinds of new debates are brewing in these pages. At the same time, the essays gain force from the critics' self-consciousness about the historical context in which they write, from their awareness that wider questions are at stake. *Critical Ireland* is vitally in touch with contemporary Irish literature and culture in their changing forms.

Attention to the world outside the academy comes centre-stage in the discussion of reviewing. If literary and cultural studies are to influence Irish society, the media must be involved. And, with the exception of the *Irish Times*, whose literary editor spoke at the conference, Irish media are not doing much. The British media, too, have become less interested in literature. Nor is it necessarily the case that other kinds of 'culture' are seriously discussed instead, or that the Internet will fill the gap. The dictates of the market mean that criticism suffers all round. The academy is not immune from similar processes which especially affect the humanities – both the job and job-prospects. Some contributors boldly analyse their own position as apprentices in a profession that is undergoing various transformations. Their resistance to 'market-driven' priorities seems not only a mark of youthful idealism but the product of intelligent reflection on the purposes of a humane education. Their elders should take note.

Also questioned in *Critical Ireland* is the disciplinary category to which it subscribes: Irish literary and cultural studies. This too could become a stifling institution if not aerated by the sceptical as well as idealistic young. David Cotter puts the matter most subversively when he says: 'We are likely to lose something if lines of enquiry are determined by help-wanted ads in the *Guardian*, the MLA or the *Times*. Literature should not be portioned out between various fields of national studies.' Other contributors change the lines of enquiry in a range of thematic, theoretical and methodological ways. I notice that as 'Ireland' is less often treated as an exceptional case – as Belfast and Barcelona come into critical proximity – greater literary and cultural complexity is being disclosed. It is not only the thinking of young critics from continental Europe or America which advances such discovery and moves the horizon. I sense that 'theory' has come of age in Irish criticism and is being deployed more variously, flexibly and interrogatively. At the same time, the editors rightly claim a lively 'miscellaneity' rather than an empty 'pluralism'. Not only lines of enquiry but lines of argument or battle are on display, and a close reader might note that the joint sponsors of the first two conferences, Declan Kiberd and myself, do not escape the critical eye.

It seems important that the second conference was held in Belfast. The North has been the undeclared subtext of much that has happened in, and between, all branches of Irish studies during the last three decades. The lively atmosphere of the conference suggested that the new generation is creating a generous intellectual space where everything can be declared.

Edna Longley

Contents

CONTENTS

CONTENTS

Introduction

The pleasure of this text resides in its miscellaneity. The essays it contains cover a vast terrain, written by emerging graduate students of that indeterminate discipline: Irish literary criticism. When first presented at a conference (*New Voices in Irish Criticism*, held at the Queen's University of Belfast in February 2000), these papers were arranged into sections. Yet each themed panel was transcended by the speakers' refusal to be homogeneous, and by the broader, multi-level echoes and continuities that began to emerge as the conference unfolded. Indeed, perhaps the sole point of agreement amongst the essays is the necessity of challenging conceptual stereotypes and historical certainties. Therefore, the thematic structure of the conference has been dropped: unlike most books which present the proceeds of a conference, the papers here have been arranged by the alphabetical order of contributors. This allows essays on poetics to mingle with those on gender, lets an essay on D.P. Moran be followed by one on Samuel Beckett, and so on. No doubt, something is lost in replacing the comfort of categories with the alphabet's arbitrariness. Instead of a smooth drive through mapped territory, one is forced to go cross-country, as it were, creating a mental file of the essays' fields of investigation as one proceeds, without the surety of defined directions. But the hope is that the book will facilitate the conception of new sign-posts, cross-cuts, directions to be explored further, and dead-ends to be avoided. And if this effect is achieved, the individual works within will have been presented in a spirit that properly befits them.

The *New Voices* conference in Belfast was the second of its kind; this book also follows the publication of the inaugural conference's proceedings.[1] A third conference is to be held in Galway, hopefully confirming *New Voices* as an annual event. Thus postgraduate students of Irish Studies throughout the world (the event's

---

1 *New Voices in Irish Criticism*, ed. P.J. Mathews (Dublin: Four Courts Press, 2000).

internationalism, to date, has been notable) owe a debt of gratitude to the drive and success of P.J. Mathews, who initiated, co-ordinated and edited its successful beginnings. Mathews wrote: 'Prior to the inaugural *New Voices* conference, there existed no forum ... where students at an advanced stage in their doctoral research could present their work or engage in debate with their colleagues in other universities and colleges.' He also pointed out the 'extent to which graduate students were largely ignorant of the work being carried out, and the challenges faced, by their peers elsewhere', and he remarked upon the 'palpable sense of frustration among emerging scholars that opportunities to introduce new ideas into the public domain and to make an impact on wider scholarly or cultural debates were relatively few'.[2] It is this scenario that *New Voices* is designed to remedy; its absence would create a vacuum at the heart of Irish studies. This book is thus a showcase for new ideas from new scholars: a delta in which readers can engage with emergent scholarship. In this sense, it carries a burden of expectation. Here was a conference at which speakers could at last refer to the twentieth century in the past tense (the thrill of which will hopefully be felt for some time) in the context of previously unknown Irish economic prosperity. Most contributors were experiencing prolonged peace in Northern Ireland for the first time. The only theme that was actively courted was one on 'literary reviewing';[3] otherwise, the doors were left open in hope of surprise and innovation. But scholarship, of course, is not a media event, and proclamations of radical departures and intellectual revolutions within the discipline of literary studies (interminably made by experienced 'pros' who should know better) almost always turn out to be empty promises. Rather, these essays look to the new from the vantage-point of established traditions of criticism. They are dialectically engaged with contemporary theory and interpretative practices; many of them look to the past in trying to redefine the present. Yet they do emit a welcome absence of anxiety with regard to the bugbears of Irish Studies: a dissatisfaction, lingering on the threshold of boredom, with the revisionist-nationalist debate; a resolve to historically interrogate current postcolonial paradigmatics; an interest in texts outside the established cannon. The essays thus mix disciplined scholarship with innovative perspectives, and it is the complex signals generated by their accumulated propinquity, throughout this book, which constitute its most distinguishing feature.

The transition from one essay to the next is often abrupt. We begin with Nicholas Allen's detailed interpretation of George Russell's little-known text, *The Interpreters*, and then move immediately to Steffi Bachorz' critical review of

---

2 Mathews, *New Voices* xii. 3 The three essays in the book on this subject probably suffer most from the eradication of themed sections. The conference panel on reviewing was conceived to pit two postgraduates with an interest in the subject together with two people involved with the practice. Thus Stephen Hull and John Kenny were joined by Caroline Walsh, the literary editor of the *Irish Times*, and David Wheatley, co-editor of *Metre*. Wheatley's paper is included here, although he is not an emerging PhD student, because *Metre* as a publishing venture is young, fresh and innovating: thus aligned with the ethos of *New Voices*.

postcolonial theory. From there, one is led to Rachael Buxton's comparative paper on the poetics of Robert Frost and Paul Muldoon, followed by Ester Carrillo's comparison of Juan Marsé's Barcelona and Maurice Leitch's Belfast, then on to Brian Cliff's investigation of the Irish Literary Theatre's publicity in 1899. What we hope is communicated through such plurality is a subliminal, indefinite, yet nevertheless discernible narrative redefined in the form of a webbed network: Ireland is not an isolated entity, its culture and aesthetics are intertwined with America and Europe; nationalist idealism in the 1890s and 1930s hit different but affined complications in different but affined circumstances, etc., etc. The potential that the book thus proffers—the creation of multiple links across genres and epochs—might then indicate a new kind of metanarrative for Irish Studies: one that is neither predetermined nor monological; one that is multi-textured, variformed, and performatively (rather than constantively) polyphonic. Such a form is demanded by the rich array of work currently undertaken within the rubric of Irish studies.

The book is certainly proof of this multivocality, as evidenced by the rest of the essays. Paul Delaney traces the shift from nation to state through the writing of Daniel Corkery. James Heaney provides an alternative reading of Russell's *The Interpreters* in the context of the civil war period, whilst Katy Plowright's paper echoes Brian Cliff's, looking back to the influence of Yeats on the 1890s. Michael McAteer's essay, meanwhile, suggests a new methodology for destabilizing the mainstream placing of the Irish text in accordance with national and postcolonial paradigms and its negotiations with modernism and postmodernity. Aaron Kelly's Marxist study questions the allochronic rewriting of the historical specifics of Irish literature by the metacodes of the Metropolitan Left. Other essays examine the construction of national subjects and movements within literary texts and enterprises, with reference to D.P. Moran in the piece by Bernie Leacock, and George Moore in the contribution by Brendan Fleming. Elsewhere, contributors investigate the effect upon poetic form of social upheaval, particularly urbanity and modernity in the essays by Alan Gillis and John McAuliffe. Christian Huck considers how poetic forms textualize history and myth, whilst Adrienne Janus demonstrates how poetic language offers a liminal space that brings texts to the limits of standard genre and form. Further papers offer comparative studies of Irish texts, including Hanne Tange's evaluation of the influence of Joyce upon a dialogic tradition of twentieth-century Scottish writing, and Diana Garcia's interesting imbrication of Defoe and Joyce. Also, as mentioned, the practicalities and the politics of literary journalism and academic practice in Irish literature are examined in essays by Stephen Hull, David Wheatley and John Kenny. In another field of interest, Karen Vandevelde analyses the function of theatre in projects of national identity, whist Julie Anne Stevens examines the staging of Protestant identity in the work of Somerville and Ross, and Noreen Doody suggests the influence of French Symbolism on Yeats and Wilde. Yet more essays examine the interrelation of gendered identities with those of region, the city, and religion in exposing Irish culture as a conflictual terrain. Robbie Meredith elucidates a Northern consciousness in the work of Alice Milligan, Ana Rosa Garcia studies an urban aesthetic in Eavan Boland's poetry, whilst Jarlath Killeen redraws the usage of gender and Catholicism in Wilde. Further, Gareth Joseph Downes retrieves the largely ignored theme of Catholicism in Joyce's fiction, whilst Des Fitzgibbon traces the infusion of urbanity and city dialectics in contemporary Irish fiction, and Francesca Lacaita examines the production and reordering of national narratives within the novel form.

There has been a slippage, in this introduction so far, between the terms 'Irish literary criticism' and 'Irish studies'. We do not mean to imply that they are identical; merely that they intersect. And this intersection is questioned by David Cotter's highly idiosyncratic essay, written in a style conceived to upset academic expectations and intellectual decorum. Cotter asks: 'What is it that we expect to learn from gathering historical and sociological detail?', adding that, increasingly, 'markets make us value literature for the support it can offer to surveys in which people have ticked the tag that fits them best.' He suggests that Art contains 'Vision, with a capital V', and that its utopian kernel should provoke us to more radically question our contextualizations of it; our perpetual resort to 'stable things'. Art's capacity to challenge precipitant contextualisations, in such a manner, demands that criticism should be aware of its own methodological premises. Moreover, some of the more didactic essays mentioned above serve to question the idea of a webbed, essentially non-directional postmodern metanarrative. Many of them bring to light the fractious themes of class, gender, or urbanity and global capitalism in relation to both nation states in Ireland. In terms of such cultural fracture, perhaps some self-reflexive consideration of the material placing of the young critics in this book is necessitated.

In deliberating the determinant and institutional locations and directions of criticism, Jean-Paul Sartre's definition of the intellectual as 'objective traitor', precariously suspended between class affiliations and class guilt, has two profound implications.[4] Firstly, it serves as a reminder that any committed social consciousness and insight, whether in terms of class, gender or race, must be intellectually achieved and formulated through an engaged and critical reading of a culture and its products. It consequently dismisses the paradoxically elitist condescension that just because someone is, for example, working-class or female they will be intuitively revolutionary. However, Sartre's model and its fundamental guilt are geared towards an understanding of the bourgeois intellectual and his/her need to egress the limitations of that class. For the second and more negative ramification of the Sartrean 'objective

4 Jean-Paul Sartre, 'des rats et des hommes' *Situations* 4 (Paris: Gallimard, 1964) 38-84. See also *Critique of Dialectical Reason*. Trans. Alan Sheridan-Smith (London: New Left Books, 1976).

traitor' is that it can therefore foster an image of the intellectual as a heroically solitary or withdrawn figure. This formulation becomes increasingly dangerous and politically debilitating within the fractious specializations and professionalizations of late capitalism, which historically modify and perpetuate the conventional enthronement of literary criticism within the sacral and distanced realm of Academia. For despite its avowedly ironic and sceptical relation to knowledge and to the social itself, the postmodern mainstream of contemporary thought provides a constitutive ideology for the putatively emancipatory free-play of textual relationships within our culture and society, and their celebration within increasingly self-referential scholarly institutions. Indeed, Aijaz Ahmad considers the supposed apolitical or post-political liberation of postmodernism and late capitalism to be the apotheosis of bourgeois mystification:

> It suppresses the very conditions of intelligibility with which the funda-
> mental facts of our time can be theorized; and in privileging the figure of the
> reader, the critic, the theorist, as the guardian of the texts of this world,
> where everything becomes a text, it recoups the main cultural tropes of
> bourgeois humanism—especially in its Romantic variants, since the dis-
> missal of class and nation as so many "essentialisms" logically leads to an
> ethic of non-attachment as the necessary condition of true understanding.[5]

Antonio Gramsci posited saliently that everyone is a potential intellectual but, most crucially, that not everyone is permitted the social function of the intellectual.[6] Our own positioning within structures of governmental institutionality demands a large degree of self-reflection. The industrialized tertiary education systems of the Western world have of necessity incorporated more and more people previously excluded from the university system, whether on the grounds of class, gender or race. But this process is by no means entirely reducible to a top-down economic imperative and also bespeaks the capacity of human agents to change their society and to regalvanize the social institutions which they inherit. In turn, a new and more radical range of perspectives have infused the academic mainstream. In Louis MacNeice's 'Eclogue from Iceland' (a particularly apt form of poem given that our introduction is itself a dialogue between this book's two editors), Grettir enthralls: 'do not avoid the ambush, / Take sly detours, but ride the pass direct'.[7] The essays in this book similarly ride the historical pass direct and, in doing so, offer alternative, untrodden pathways of analysis. MacNeice himself, neglected by English literary history in the shadow of W.H. Auden and seemingly failing the litmus test of Irishness for the national canon, proffers a telling antinomy in the conventional

5 Aijaz Ahmad, *In Theory: Classes, Nations, Literatures* (London: Verso, 1992) 36.   6 See Antonio Gramsci, *Selections from the Prison Notebooks*, ed. and trans. Quitin Hoare and Geoffrey Nowell Smith (London: Lawrence and Wishart, 1971) 5-23.   7 Louis MacNeice, *Collected Poems* (London: Faber, 1966) 46.

problematics of Irish literary criticism. The task of doing justice to his poetry is the task of imbricating the vast imaginative and historical scope of his writings within the challenges of the 1930s, of circumnavigating Fascism and Stalinism, of confronting modernity and urbanity, of remapping place, regionality and religion in the face of convulsive historical process. We are ultimately arguing that Ireland is not a deviant anomaly or self-contained entity but an integrated constellation of social and historical forces and relationalities simultaneously fractured and affiliated by the global dynamics of capitalism, class, gender, religion, the city, regionality and so on. Literary criticism, then, as with the primary texts which form the object of its study, should concern itself, in confronting the determinate historical problematics encoded in Irish cultural production, with the imagining and legitimization of new currents and areas of thought in an attempt to construct a hegemonic project that will produce real social and cultural change. Literary and cultural criticism offers a method through which to deliberate upon the material conditions of a text's production, upon how texts are received and in what context. In short, it can afford the instigation of a vast historical tribunal in which to judge the failings but also the conditions of possibility contained within our present. In a way, the disparate collection of essays comprising this book are a form of Benjaminian constellation. The essays could be considered a series of critical snapshots forming a set of what Walter Benjamin terms 'dialectical images', wherein the past collides with the present in a reciprocal illumination so that not only the historical context of the past but also the accurate understanding of the present are revealed.[8] We hope that the range of historical perspectives proffered by this book itself will relate the historical multiplicity of Irish writing and offer a critical awakening from the perpetually nightmarish concussion of the unitary national problematic.

We wish to thank a number of people who contributed greatly to the success of the Belfast *New Voices* conference, and to this publication of its proceedings. We would like to acknowledge the financial assistance of the Queen's University of Belfast Publications Fund and the Arts Council of Northern Ireland, and the helpful encouragement of Brian Caraher and John Brown respectively in securing that funding. The unfailing support of Declan Kiberd, Edna Longley and Eamonn Hughes was central to the project. Particular gratitude is due to P.J. Mathews for his instigation of the whole *New Voices* venture and for the kind and invaluable assistance that he granted to us. Thanks also to Karen Vandevelde for ensuring the continuation of the conference at NUI Galway in 2001. We are also grateful to Keith Connolly for the production of the original conference programme and to many of our postgraduate peers for their invaluable assistance

---

8 See Walter Benjamin, *Gesammelte Schriften* Vol.V.ii. Ed. Rolf Tiedemann and Hermann Schweppenhauser (Frankfurt: Suhrkap, 1972-89).

in the running of the conference, and to Caroline Walsh, Literary Editor of the *Irish Times*, for speaking at and supporting the event. Finally, we would like to extend our deepest and most heartfelt gratitude to our families and loved-ones for putting up with us and supporting us.

Alan A. Gillis
Aaron Kelly
The Queen's University of Belfast
October 2000

A Political Vision: George Russell and The Interpreters

NICHOLAS ALLEN, TRINITY COLLEGE, DUBLIN

George Russell's *The Interpreters* was published in November 1922, just one month before the first ever sitting of the Executive Council of the Irish Free State. Only ten months had passed since the Dáil voted to accept the Anglo-Irish Treaty on 7 January 1922, but much had changed. Eamon de Valera had resigned as Dáil President, his successor Arthur Griffith was dead and a Civil War that lasted from June 1922 until April 1923 wracked the country. Fought between pro- and anti-Treaty factions, the Civil War was bitter and fractious. Russell himself supported the Treaty side. Published at a critical time in the history of the Irish State, *The Interpreters*, Russell's major prose work of the 1920's, is Russell's proposal for a new, politically decisive, relationship to be forged between the Free State and its intellectuals.

The Interpreters' opening scene pictures one of its six main characters, Lavelle, crossing an unnamed city to take part in an uprising. Lavelle was 'but dimly aware of his fellow citizens' and felt 'raised above himself by the adventure on which he was bent'.[1] But the act of rebellion itself takes up little of the text's attention. The main body of *The Interpreters* is set in a prison cell in its aftermath, an environment with deliberate echoes of the Easter Rising. In effect, *The Interpreters* creates a new myth of origin for post-revolutionary Ireland from a tradition of martyrdom that was crowned by the sacrifice of Pearse and company in 1916. Tellingly however, Russell replaces the sixteen dead of the Easter Rising with six main characters of his own, each of whom has a chapter of *The Interpreters* devoted to an exposition of his individual ideal. Lavelle, the first character we are introduced to, is a poet. Leroy, Lavelle's first companion in the cell, is an anarchist, accompanied by Culain, the labour leader, Brehon, the historian, Rian, the architect and Heyt, an imperial businessman wrongly arrested by state security.

The primary political struggle in the text is between capitalism and what Russell describes as state socialism, a ploy, in part, by the narrator to avoid specific reference to the Irish situation, wracked in schism by 1922. Heyt, the autocratic industrialist, is a symbol of individual character grown dominant over weaker, less conscious individuals. The labour leader Culain is in contrast a modern character, whose power derives from industrial organisation. He is the individual focus upon which 'the workers of the nation had been brought to take part in the revolt'.[2] What is surprising is the system that *The Interpreters* favours. Russell, once a confidant of James Connolly, had been faithfully sympathetic to Irish labour in the previous decade of

1 Russell, G.W., *The Interpreters* (London: Macmillan, 1922) 1.   2 Ibid. 34.

his editorship of the *Irish Homestead*.[3] Similarly, Russell's aversion to Irish capitalism is well registered in his polemic of William Martin Murphy during the 1913 Lock Out.[4]

But in 1922, under pressure of national disintegration during a Civil War, Russell changes sides. *The Interpreters* marks Russell's farewell to radical labour activism. Distrustful of the common mass of the revolutionary army, whose fate it determines, *The Interpreters* is deeply sceptical of what Russell, just six years before in *The National Being*, called the 'general will' for 'good'.[5] The fact that Culain's socialism fails Russell's test of political relevance to the new order is apparent from *The Interpreters'* following observation:

> A silence followed during which Rian watched that prisoner of puzzled countenance who could not understand Culain, and whose expression indicated that now less than ever could he relate the politics of time to the politics of eternity. The sullen eyes, knit brow, and impatient feet grinding on the floor, betrayed the anger of one at home in practical action who finds himself trapped in a web of incomprehensible abstractions.[6]

In contrast, Heyt represents all that Russell was previously against. He is anti-democratic, capitalist and denies the importance of national identity. But Heyt is capable of engendering a sense of social cohesion that the revolutionary characters can not. Heyt is strong evidence of the deep aversion to popular democracy that Russell developed during the Civil War.[7] The capitalist is Russell's alternative to the anarchy he associated with popular activism, the pivotal figure around which Russell's post-revolutionary state can rearrange itself in orderly, efficient corporation. Thus Heyt has the ability to converse with the poet and the other prisoners on their own terms and in their own language. The narrator reckons that

> Everyone in this age sought for the source and justification for their own activities in that divine element in which matter, energy, and conscious-ness when analysed disappeared. It was an era of arcane speculation, for science and philosophy had become esoteric after the visible universe had been ransacked and the secret of its being had eluded the thinkers.[8]

3 Russell's relationship with Connolly between 1913 and 1916 forms the basis of my article 'A Revolutionary Co-operation: George Russell and James Connolly'. *New Hibernia Review*, 4:3 (autumn 2000). 4 See, for example, Russell, G. W., 'A Plea to the Workers: A Speech Delivered in the Royal Albert Hall, London, November 1, 1913'. *The Dublin Strike* (London: Christian Commonwealth Company, n. d.) 1-4. 5 Russell, G.W., *The National Being* (Dublin: Maunsel, 1916) 107. 6 *The Interpreters* 119. 7 Russell's mistrust of democratic society was pronounced during this period. Russell had argued that he would rather have 'one autocrat with good intentions than several millions who don't know what is wise and what is foolish' in the *Irish Homestead* (1 October 1921) 669. This was not an isolated remark: 'one can only pray that Heaven will send us a powerful autocrat with ability to govern and a real desire to lead and educate the people so that they will be able to govern themselves' 'Democracy on Trial', *Irish Homestead* (10 June 1922) 362. 8 *The Interpreters* 70.

This commentary provides the required element in the text by which capitalism, in the form of Heyt, can be made amenable to culture. It shows that Heyt's autocratic vision allows a response to artistic intervention. Such interaction depends on the acquisition of a spiritual dimension by capitalism. Heyt duly insists that he is not a materialist: 'The power I spoke of does not lie in the generation of mechanical force but in the minds which organise control.'[9] It could reasonably be argued that *The Interpreters* is in effect a primer for state sponsored action, with capitalism being trained for an unlikely new master, the intellectual.

The Interpreters exhibits a similar obsession with order in its debate on cultural imperatives, conducted mainly by two characters, Lavelle and Brehon. The narrator describes Brehon as the inspiration of a cultural Revival identical to Ireland's in the late nineteenth and early twentieth centuries. Brehon, like Standish O'Grady, the author of a two volume *History of Ireland* in 1878 and 1880, is accredited with bringing the nation 'forth young and living from its grave'. The historian's achievements were 'followed by creative writers like Lavelle, in whom the submerged river of nationality again welled up shining and life-giving'. This river was 'bathed' in by the 'youth of the nation' who, once cleansed, rebelled against the 'empire, its mechanical ideals, and the characterless culture it imposed upon them'.[10]

Appropriately, Brehon presents the relationship between himself and Lavelle, the historian and poet, as natural, combining two of the main functions of epic authenticity: the exercise of memory and its articulation in the imagination. But Brehon does not concentrate on the fact that Lavelle's cultural revival was inspired by Brehon's work of retrieval. Critically, Brehon details his own achievements after the publication of his history. Brehon became disenchanted with culture and turned his imagination to a discovery of 'that vast life which is normally subconscious in us'.[11] Brehon's interest in the subconscious parallels his growing belief in a universal organisation of human society as 'the lure of national ideals began to be superseded by imaginations of a world state'.[12] To Brehon, the expression of human consciousness and the organisation of political association become one, as a definition of the subconscious will lead to a mechanism whereby human desire can be charted. The expression of Brehon's ideas is arcane but it contains a disturbing political subtext. The historian acted in concert with a number of other mystics and 'the will of many in unison was powerful enough to transcend the bodily life so that in meditation together consciousness rose like a tower into heaven, and we were able to bring back some knowledge of the higher law'.[13]

Meditation results in the perception of a new order. As Brehon says elsewhere in *The Interpreters*: 'The apprehension of law is but the growth in ourselves of a profounder self-consciousness'.[14] Brehon's idea of law binds together the concepts of self-regulation and self-perception in a potentially authoritarian construct. But his idea of order would remain secret without the creative, distributive, power of

9 Ibid. 67.   10 Ibid. 41.   11 Ibid. 138.   12 Ibid. 138.   13 Ibid. 139.   14 Ibid. 131.

Lavelle, the poet. The historian's discussion with Lavelle is Brehon's preparation of the artist for a commitment to a new Revival, this time based on science and international association rather than literature and nationalism. Lavelle questions Brehon's intentions, aware that the historian's ideas will result in the death of 'our nation, its culture and ideals' with its replacement by 'an unresisted materialism'.[15] But as the poet is convinced of the historian's logic, *The Interpreters* resolves itself into a manifesto for a new Revival. All the pre-Revolutionary elements of Irish nationalism, political, cultural and literary, are refined down to the basics of Russell's post-Civil War doctrine of intellectual and Free State authority.

This is the remarkable point of *The Interpreters*. Russell comes to an accommodation in the text with forces deemed necessary to the survival of the new Irish state: with industry, share options and the attraction of foreign capital. This is a change of substantial cultural importance to post-Treaty Ireland as Russell jettisons his Revival rhetoric of national inclusion to create a critical vocabulary partisan in its vision of social equality. The civil war was the definite impetus to the reactionary nature of much of Russell's political theory post 1922. But its lessons mapped a new territory for Russell in the final phase of his literary career, when his increasingly authoritarian cultural polemic was expressed in support of European corporatism and a conservative, even reactionary, Irish polity.

The Interpreters itself ends with a poem, 'Michael', first printed privately for Russell in 1919.[16] Since *The Interpreters* as a whole is concerned with the necessity for intellectual management of the post-Revolutionary state, it is possible to read 'Michael' as Russell's poetic statement of intent. John Butler Yeats compared the style of Russell's poem to Coleridge, but it is Wordsworth, the author of a poem called 'Michael' in his *Lyrical Ballads* in 1800, who overshadows Russell's text.[17] Wordsworth's poem is significant to *The Interpreters* primarily in terms of its subject matter, the effects of capitalism on a previously settled social order. Wordsworth's speaker traces the decline of a rural land-holding family after their only son, Luke, is ruined by a life of dissolution in the city: 'ignominy and shame', Wordsworth wrote, 'Fell on him, so that he was driven at last / To seek a hiding-place beyond the seas'.[18]

Russell's 'Michael' similarly leaves a race of 'fisher folk' to move to the city, to become involved in what Russell calls the 'army of the Gaelic mind'.[19] 'Michael' ends with its character's rebellion in 'the season of the risen Lord', an Easter image to remind us both of Pearse and the resurrection. The speaker describes

15 Ibid. 134.   16 'Michael' was further reproduced in the first series of the *Irish Statesman* (20 December 1919) 622, in *Living Age* (14 February 1920) n.p., and *The Dial* (March 1920) 326-34.   17 In a letter to John Quinn, dated 19 January 1920, the elder Yeats wrote that 'There is not a word in the poem which is not common sense of the sort which Coleridge called the substance of poetry'; cited from Denson, A., *Typescript in Three Volumes of the Collected Letters of George Russell (A.E.)* (n. p., n. d.) 354.   18 Wordsworth, W. 'Michael', *The Poems: Volume One*, ed. J. O. Hayden (London: Yale UP, 1977) 455-68.   19 *The Interpreters* 161; 168.

rebellion as the ascension of 'the Lord in man', freed from the 'dark sepulchre of fear'.[20] In language reminiscent of Russell's earlier poem 'Apocalyptic',[21] the fighters in 'Michael' stand 'wilful, laughing, undismayed,/Though on a fragile barricade'.[22] *The Interpreters* is here exposed in one of its subsidiary aims, to incorporate the heroic tradition of Irish revolutionary nationalism in Russell's own programme of intellectual activism.

As 'Michael' draws to a close, Lavelle, its speaker in *The Interpreters*, now claims that he has added a new gloss to the poem which comprises a further two stanzas, moved to do so 'by what was said in this room'.[23] This final addition is a fiction of *The Interpreters*. Both stanzas are included in the 1919 text and neither contains any new material. Russell's intention is to draw specific attention to *The Interpreters'* final resolution. From the text's earliest pages Lavelle has been ambivalent towards the creations of empire around him; he is described as a potential traitor because of his admiration for a fleet of airships outside the cell window.[24] The airships are perfect examples of the union between power and beauty that underpins Lavelle's attraction to imperial order and, by extension, to Heyt. Lavelle's aesthetic displaces his poem's nationalist sentiments to order a new politics ordered by occult divination. Lavelle suggests that Michael died for an abstract notion other

> Than that grey island he had known.
> Yet on his dream of it was thrown
> Some light from that consuming power
> Which is the end of all desire.
> If men adore it as the power,
> Empires and cities, tower on tower,
> Are built in worship by the way,
> High Babylon or Nineveh.
> Seek it as love and there may be
> A Golden Age or Arcady.
> All shadows are they of one thing
> To which all life is journeying.[25]

As 'Michael' ends, *The Interpreters* draws to a close, with Heyt escaping from a cell whose other occupants will all be executed. The reader alone is privileged to witness the exit of the 'Imperialist' through the words of the narrator. Heyt was 'moved by what he had heard' and was 'understanding' of the fact that 'these

---

20 Ibid. 169. 21 'Apocalyptic' is part of Russell's privately published 1915 collection, *Gods of War*. The poem's speaker observes that in face of revelation 'only those can laugh who are/The strong Initiates of Pain,/Who know that mighty god to be/Sculptor of Immortality' (n.p.). 22 *The Interpreters* 169. 23 Ibid. 170. 24 On seeing the airships, 'One of the prisoners cursed bitterly. But with Lavelle, the poet in him made him for an instant almost traitor to the nation, stirred as he was by that vision of the culmination of human power soaring above the planet', *The Interpreters* 30. 25 *The Interpreters* 172.

men were different from all he had imagined of them'.[26] The interpreters, then, are the intellectuals of the text who, by their imminent death have, like the rebels of Yeats' 'Easter 1916', consecrated their ideal by self-sacrifice. Or, in the language of *The Interpreters*, Lavelle and Brehon have instilled a sense of beauty in Heyt's appreciation of power. As he leaves the cell, Heyt hesitates 'for a moment as if he would have said or urged something.'[27] But instead he shakes 'his head, as if he realised how impossible it now was to effect anything, and he left them without a word and went out to make the world in his own image.'[28] What we are left with is a character properly fit to rule, an archetype against which the future of *The Interpreters'* world will be judged.

Postcolonial Theory and Ireland: Revising Postcolonialism

STEPHANIE BACHORZ,
THE QUEEN'S UNIVERSITY OF BELFAST

The idea of applying postcolonial theory and its insights to the complexities of a society in the aftermath of colonial supression has proved an interesting challenge for Irish criticism. Ireland, as one of the first British colonies, definitely 'qualifies' for the label 'colonial'. However, the problem of applying a framework which has been developed largely within and for the so-called 'Third World' to a 'First World' country remains difficult. Ireland is not India, Bangladesh or part of the African continent. The racial and spatial closeness to its former colonizers sets it apart from many other former British colonies: whereas the so-called Third World is still struggling with economic progress, tribal warfare and starvation, at least in terms of economic growth, Ireland has become one of the most successful members of the European Union. And whereas black people are still confronted with racism in western societies, the Irish themselves have discovered the growing number of Eastern European immigrants as a useful instrument of propaganda, be it to boost newspaper sales or to gain votes in elections. At the same time, the quest for a national identity, one of the core problems in many postcolonial locations, has developed a dynamic of its own in the Irish case: 'Irishness' today has become a trade-mark for unspoiled nature (to sell butter or to promote Ireland as a holiday destination), as well as for musicians and poets like The Corrs or Seamus Heaney.[1]

26 Ibid. 179.   27 Ibid. 179.   28 Ibid. 179-180.

STEPHANIE BACHORZ
1 See Colin Graham, 'Liminal Spaces: Post-Colonial Theory and Irish Culture,' *Irish Review* 16 (1995) 29-34.

The question of identity and national identity, as this essay will show, is not only central to postcolonial theory, it also poses serious problems. The importance of the colonial paradigm, Colonizer-Colonized, Self-Other will be highlighted, and it will be shown how this paradigm becomes reversed in the process of decolonization. This will be illustrated by examples of recent Irish literary criticism. The use of Marxist frameworks in these examples will serve to highlight the imminent dangers of any dialectical approach, namely that it has to be careful not to lead to a simple apportionment of blame. In other words, the binary 'colonizer'/'colonized' is helpful only to a point, namely to describe the exact relationship between the two opposites at the time of colonization and its effects on society in the aftermath, the post-colonial. To simply equate this opposition with 'bad' and 'good' simply replaces the former power structure with a new set of binaries which sets the formerly colonized as being in the morally correct position, whereas the former colonizer is seen as the eternal villain. Instead of pointing out the one-sidedness of power under the colonial system, showing the impact of it on the powerless victim, the colonized, the power-structure is simply reversed: the former victim becomes the morally 'correct', standing in direct opposition to the morally 'incorrect' former aggressor.

One way to overcome the dichotomy between colonized and colonizer, Self and Other, can be found in Homi Bhabha's concept of hybridity. This concept of hybridity cannot only be seen as a way of escaping the binaries—it will also serve to highlight some of the imminent problems within postcolonialism. One of the general debates in postcolonial theory, as Williams and Chrisman point out in their introduction to *Postcolonial Discourse and Postcolonial Theory*, remains the question of which framework to use, Marxist theory or poststructuralism: 'For some post-structuralists, such as Robert Young, Marxism is part of the problem in post-colonial theory, whereas for someone like Gayatri Chakravorty Spivak it is an indispensable tool.'[2]

This essay will argue that Marxist theory can indeed provide a theoretical framework that can both point to the core problems and, at the same time, provide the necessary solutions. Theodor W. Adorno's *Negative Dialectics* will be introduced as a means to reconsider hybridity in terms of a dialectical process rather than a more or less 'stable' concept. The fact that Marxist frameworks are able to examine the political and socio-economic factors which determine any society, and thus its literature and culture, makes this approach indispensable. It is the aim of this essay to show how a Marxist postcolonial theory can overcome the problematic aspects of its binary structure by its very own dialectical nature. Finally it should become clear how this approach could lead to a 'revised' postcolonial theory for Ireland, a notion of postcolonialism which does not depend on the exclusion of the 'Other,' but at the same time can account for the socio-political reality which created post-coloniality in the first place.

---

2 Patrick Williams and Laura Chrisman, eds., *Colonial Discourse and Post-Colonial Theory: A Reader* (New York: Harvester Wheatsheaf, 1994) 6.

At the heart of postcolonial theory lies the concept of a stable national identity. In the wake of imperialism and colonization, many writers have recognized the loss if identity as one of the most traumatizing aspects of the colonial past. The suppression of a 'native' language and culture has been one of the most effective tools of the colonization process. As Declan Kiberd points out, by declaring themselves as the 'norm', British colonizers used the native population as a 'foil to set off British virtues'.[3] Thus the white Anglo-Saxon, being the norm, reduced any other 'race' to a distortion of that norm, a non-identity. This simple paradigm, distinguishing the 'Self' from any 'other' forms of existence, becomes the basis of the ideology of colonialism. Unfortunately, however, it also lies at the heart of de-colonization.

The reclaiming of identity, of a native and thus national language and culture of a colonized people, can be seen as one of the strongest forces in the process of de-colonization. The colonial paradigm is reversed, the former colonial subject discovers his or her own identity. The logical next step is the liberation of the Self from the new 'Other', the colonial oppressor, thus leading to a new ideology of the Self, a new nationalism, this time with the new nation as the norm, and the old colonial power as the distortion. This implies that the ensuing ideology of the new nation—and the new national identity—are nothing but, to quote Ranajit Guha, 'the ideological product' of colonialism.[4] This contradiction can be found in many critical studies concerned with Irish literature and culture. Namely, how can one reclaim a genuinely Irish identity and simultaneously criticize the imperialist framework based on race and nation. Deane, in a well-known quote from his Field Day pamphlet, unknowingly described the dilemma: 'Everything, including our politics and our literature, has to be rewritten—i.e. re-read. That will enable new writing, new politics, *unblemished by Irishness, but securely Irish.*'[5]

The search for a national identity through a national literature can be seen in the 1991 *Field Day Anthology of Irish Writing*, to which Deane, as the general editor, wrote the introduction. He outlines the enterprise as follows:

> [I]n this anthology we take a much wider time-span, embracing 1,500 years, and we avoid the narrow sense of the word 'literature', extending it to cover various other kinds of writing ..., all of which have played an important part in the story which this anthology has to tell.
>
> There *is* a story here, a meta-narrative, which is, we believe, hospitable to all the micro-narratives that, from time to time, have achieved prominence as the official version of the true history, political and literary, of the island's past and present.[6]

---

3 Declan Kiberd, *Anglo-Irish Attitudes* (Derry: Field Day, 1984) 5.   4 Ranajit Guha, 'On Some Aspects of the Historiography of Colonial India,' in *Mapping Subaltern Studies and the Postcolonial*, ed. Vinyak Chaturvedi (London: Verso, 2000) 1.   5 Seamus Deane, *Celtic Revivals: Essays in Modern Irish Literature 1880-1980* (London: Faber and Faber, 1985) 58 (italics mine).   6 Seamus Deane, gen. ed., *The Field Day Anthology of Irish Writing*, vol. 1 (Derry: Field Day, 1991) xix.

In his study *Literature and Culture in Northern Ireland since 1965: Moments of Danger*, Kirkland elaborates the complex theoretical construct that lies behind the project of the Field Day Theatre Company who published the anthology.[7] The Field Day enterprise, he argues, can be seen as an attempt to establish a 'counter-hegemony'. The theory concerning such a challenge was inspired by Antonio Gramsci's *Prison Notebooks*, which provided a construction that allowed the directors and editors of Field Day to legitimize a nationalist agenda in terms of Marxist and postcolonial theory.[8] In the *Anthology*, Field Day thus tries to challenge the traditional modes of historiography by presenting Ireland in its various texts, thus reacting against the dominant or 'official' version of Irish history. However, as Deane's embrace of the word 'story' suggests, as a multi-dimensional counter-hegemonic project, the *Field Day Anthology* was doomed to fail. As Smyth puts it in his review of the *Anthology*:

> [T]he *Field Day Anthology of Irish Writing*, published last year, appears as the most arrogant and challenging example of such a neo-Romantic, totalising vision to be produced in Europe. There is a fundamental absur-dity to the project: in spite of the language of 'discontinuity' and 'rupture' displayed as fashion accessories in the critical framing, there seems to be something primordially continuous about 'Ireland' and 'being Irish' over a 1500-year period.[9]

This is repeated by Longley in a critique of David Lloyd's *Anomalous States: Irish Writing and the Post-Colonial Moment*, when she remarks that 'For all his emphasis on "heteroglossia", Lloyd's subversives, subalterns and hybridised street-ballads often turn out to sing the same old song when their "occluded practices" come to light.'[10] Longley also criticizes the rather eclectic use of postcolonial and other theories of the Field Day enterprise: 'Field Day understandably favours theorists who might help to insert Northern Ireland/Ireland into the colonial/post-colonial frame,' appropriating reality to fit the theory rather than finding a suitable framework to explain what is happening: 'Strange collusions are taking place: holiday romances in a postcolonial never-never land.'[11] This 'postcolonial never-never land' can also be found in Kiberd's 1995 study *Inventing Ireland*, one of the few comprehensive Marxist and postcolonial studies that takes into account some of the more recent developments in Irish literature. Kiberd obses-sion with an Irish 'narrative' which had been supressed during the colonial

---

7 Richard Kirkland, *Literature and Culture in Northern Ireland since 1965: Moments of Danger* (London, 1996).   8 He refers to Antonio Gramsci, *Selections from the Prison Notebooks*, op. cit. For a detailed discussion of the importance of Gramsci for Field Day, see Kirkland 121-48.   9 Damian Smyth, 'Totalising Imperative,' *Fortnight* 309 (September 1992) 26. Quoted in Kirkland 142.   10 Edna Longley, *The Living Stream: Literature and Revisionism in Ireland* (Newcastle: Bloodaxe, 1994) 31; David Lloyd, *Anomalous States: Irish Writing and the Post-Colonial Moment* (Dublin: Lilliput, 1993).   11 Longley 28.

period, leaving 'gaps' which have to be filled, is as limiting as the colonial hegemonic (hi)story.[12]

Kiberd's 'narrative,' as his elaborations show, is still based on a reversal of the colonial paradigm, in his treatment of the present time with the added ingredients 'EEC' and 'capitalism.'[13] This move does not help to overcome the simplicity of the opposition 'anti-colonial Ireland' versus 'imperialist Britain': it has merely been changed into a paradigm based on the binary opposition between pre- or non-capitalist Ireland and capitalism in form of the EEC. To reduce Irish history to moments of resistance does not naturally make *Inventing Ireland* a postcolonial history of Irish culture: although the 'other' has changed (capitalism instead of colonialism), the 'self' remains unblemished and unquestioned.

Kiberd's premises might be challenged by the work of Homi Bhabha. The solution to the postcolonial search for identity, put forward by Bhabha, lies in the principle of 'hybridity'. Bhabha draws on Freud by describing 'hybridity' in terms of a 'metonymy of presence.'[14] This translates Freud's notion of disavowal, the conflict between narcissistic demand and external reality, into the terms of cultural differences. Once freed from the colonialist power, the postcolonial subject reacts by disavowing culture as the culture of the colonialist—culture as a means of oppression. Only in a second step the hybrid object is able to accept difference. 'Hybridity,' in Bhabha's terms, then 'reverses the *formal* process of disavowal so that the violent dislocation of the act of colonization becomes the conditionality of colonial discourse.'[15] Thus by recognising the difference instead of denying it, the postcolonial citizen (and especially migrants and minorities) will be able to achieve a 'double vision'.[16] This means they can actually accept the multiplicity of history, knowledge, and so on, by the very nature of their own existence, being brought up or living in-between two versions of history, culture and knowledge.

'Hybridity', a term derived from the colonial powers' dismissive stance towards mixed people, becomes in Bhabha's writing a space in which oppositions can no longer hold. Intercultural relationships are no longer seen in terms of essentialism or dualism. Instead, Bhabha creates the concept of a 'Third Space', a space in which Self and Other are recognized as an insoluble and inseparable penetration of centre and periphery, colonizer and colonized: 'It is that Third Space, though unrepresentable in itself, which constitutes the discursive conditions of enunciation that ensure that the meaning and symbols of culture have no primordial unity and fixity; that even the same signs can be appropriated, translated, rehistoricized and read anew.'[17] However, this poststructuralist concept of a Third Space is problematic for a Marxist theorist. As Eagleton remarks:

---

12 Declan Kiberd, *Inventing Ireland* (London: Cape, 1995) 587.   13 Ibid. 567.   14 Homi K. Bhabha, *The Location of Culture* (London: Routledge, 2000) 115.   15 Bhabha, *The Location of Culture*, 114.   16 Ibid. 110.   17 Ibid. 37.

Ideologies like to draw rigid boundaries between what is acceptable and what is not, between self and non-self, truth and falsity, sense and non-sense, reason and madness, central and marginal, surface and depth. Such metaphysical thinking [...] cannot be simply eluded: *we cannot catapult ourselves beyond this binary habit of thought into an ultra-metaphysical realm.* But by a certain way of operating upon texts—whether 'literary' or 'philosophical'—we may begin to unravel these oppositions a little, demonstrate how one term of an antithesis secretly inheres within the other.[18]

Although he recognizes the potential of deconstruction as a means of detecting ideologies, Eagleton does not accept the deconstructivists' denial of a materialist and essentialist basis. This would mean a denial of the dialectical nature of our perception of the world: 'we cannot catapult ourselves beyond this habit of thought'. It is at this point that the work of the Marxist critic Theodor W. Adorno can be introduced to provide a means of overcoming the gap between Marxist theory and poststructuralism in a way that does justice to both sides: it remains safely within the bounds of a materialist outlook and dialectical thinking, but at the same time questions the stability of the very binaries upon which any dialectical thought depends.

Adorno's concept of a 'negative dialectics' examines the problem of identity in a way which explains the longing for identity, on the one side, and the immanent problems of the concept itself on the other. This can be seen as running in parallel lines to Bhabha's Freudian conceptualization of hybridity. However, Adorno's approach, due to its Marxist origins, removes the dichotomy between self and other from the psychological level to the political. The binary structure of the paradigm Self-Other cannot be ignored nor can it simply be turned around. Adorno considers the declaring of one side as the truth, the taking of one's own self as the 'norm', and the other side as the 'abnormal,' in political terms, as it represents the basic method of any totalitarian system: 'Totality has to be opposed by convicting it of its non-identity with itself, the non-identity it denies by the very term' identity.[19] This would mean a mere shift of the original totalitarian (or imperialist) nature of a preference of one concept from one side to the other. As soon as one side is declared to represent the truth and the other a distortion of this truth, their dialectical nature is denied. True to the Marxist basis, Adorno's critique of existing oppositions is dependent upon those very oppositions. His solution is a *negative* dialectical process, which leaves the system of oppositions 'untouched'; that is, without the evaluation of its components: a process which takes into account the other side as a possible 'norm', being just as 'normal' as one's own position.

18 Terry Eagleton, *Literary Theory: An Introduction,* 2nd ed. (Oxford: Blackwell, 1996) 133 (italics mine).
19 Adorno, *Negative Dialektik, Jargon der Eigentlichkeit* (Gesammelte Schriften 6), (Frankfurt am Main, 1973) 150 (translation mine).

For Adorno, only dialectical thinking, the acknowledgement of a gap between subject and object, can provide what he terms 'reconciliation'.[20] Reconciliation does not 'solve' the difference, but it accepts difference as necessary. Without this reconciliation, non-identity seems negative; the subject needs the identity with the object, a 'frame of reference', where everything has its place.[21] Adorno accepts the essential need for a stable system as something close to a human instinct. This leads him to the insight that any system, any ideology, is based on this longing for identity: 'identity is the basic form of ideology'.[22]

'Norm' and 'reality' as fundamental categories thus mean a betrayal of the dialectical nature of the world and the human being. At the same time, to simply declare them as interchangeable, as Bhabha's poststructuralist concept of the Third Space implies, would mean an equally damaging denial of the dialectical nature of the world *as we perceive it*. The incommensurability between self and other, for Adorno it must lead to a dialectical process which, as the term 'process' implies, has a temporal, even a 'historical' quality. It is in this sense that Bhabha's Third Space can be removed from its metaphysical position: hybridity, arguing out the existing dialectical nature of human existence, can thus lead to the process of 'reconciliation'.

Adorno's work suggests that any postcolonial approach should take into account not only what happened between the colonizer and the colonized, but also face the fact that a dialectical process is still going on. A historiography, a 'narrative' which is based only on the 'repressed', is doomed to fail because of its one-sidedness. But is a national identity really desirable? The warning example of British imperialism shows what it can lead to. A national identity is a pressing question in any newly formed nation, a question that has to be answered. What has to be borne in mind is that Ireland, like all the other postcolonial nations, is the product of the combination of two systems: in this case of British imperial-ism and original Irish feudalism. The pre-colonial situation of Ireland was not that of an organic community in which everybody was equal. It was not an 'Island ... of the Blest',[23] a heroic nation at the beginning of a heroic era that had merely been hibernating during the eight hundred years of British domination, ready to wake up on the day the last soldier will be withdrawn from their native soil. Any historiography which takes as its premiss a national identity that was stable until the arrival of the non-identical is doomed to fail. The Other had always formed part of what seemed the Self. As soon as such a fixed national identity is postulated, it is taken as the norm; any other form of identity becomes abnormal, a mere distortion of the 'real' identity. Any system that takes the repressed Catholic minority of Northern Ireland as the norm is just as totalitar-

20 'Dialektik entfaltet die vom Allgemeinen diktierte Differenz des Besonderen vom Allgemeinen. Während sie, der ins Bewußtsein gedrungene Bruch von Subjekt und Objekt, dem Subjekt unentrinnbar ist, alles durchfurcht, was es, auch an Objektivem, denkt, hätte sie ein Ende in der Versöhnung.' Adorno, 18. 21 Ibid. 43. 22 Ibid. 151. 23 Derek Mahon, 'MacNeice in England and Ireland', *Journalism*, ed. Terence Brown (Loughcrew: Gallery, 1996) 29.

ian as the system that took a British pedigree as the norm and based eight hundred years of colonial suppression upon it.

Adorno's solution to this is that 'Totality has to be opposed by convicting it of its non-identity with itself, the non-identity it denies by the very term' identity.[24] Any postcolonial approach to Ireland and Irish literature has to bear this in mind. Thus the answer to the question of a national identity is twofold: we are to a certain extent what we are not, the 'self' is determined as much by what we take to be the 'self' as by what we take to be the other. The same applies to capitalism: it is not the 'other', British imperialism or the EEC, which forces it upon the Irish. The threat of capitalism lies in its ideological nature, in that it supplies the human being's longing for happiness with the *ersatz* of commodities. Thus capitalism must not be condemned as being the non-identical *per se*, which can be successfully fought off by being poor or repressed. This means only a temporary solution, one which stands in sharp contrast to the likewise expressed necessity of a free Ireland. If the threat of a capitalist ideology is recognized as what it really is, an ideology, and if its identical nature (man's longing for physical happiness) can be distinguished from the non-identical aspects (the implied alienating result of mass-production and class), only then is a 'reconciliation' possible.

Adorno's political aesthetics, the 'negative' dialectical process, provides a formula with which all the different forces at work can be taken into account: the colonizer and the colonized are part of the problem as well as part of the solution. To take into account this dialectical process as being *still at work* is to overcome a totalitarian anti-colonial practice which blames all shortcomings of the new nation on the colonial past and the capitalist present. Only then can nationalism be productive and be seen as truly having transcended the European nationalism of the British Empire. And only then can Irish nationalism, and Irish national identity, call themselves 'postcolonial'. Irish history has over many hundred years been closely connected to European history, from the beginning of the rechristianization of large parts of central Europe by Irish monks in the sixth century, through the part played by Ireland in the formation of Catholic Europe, up to the role of Ireland in the shaping of the European Community. In this sense Ireland differs from other postcolonial nations in the so-called Third World. There the Irish missionaries made their own contribution to the repression of the 'natives', thus supporting the very imperialist system nationalists detect anywhere else. The cross-fertilization between Ireland and Europe, and that between Ireland and Britain, too, has therefore to enter a postcolonial discourse all the more urgently.

24 Adorno 150.

'Structure and Serendipity': The Influence of Robert Frost on Paul Muldoon

RACHAEL BUXTON, OXFORD

Back in 1930, following a conversation with the Harvard professor and literary critic John Livingston Lowes, Robert Frost penned the following lines:

> A poet need make no apology
> Because his works are one anthology
> Of other poets' best creations
> Let him be nothing but quotations
> (That's not as cynic as it sounds)
> The game is one like Hares and Hounds
> To entertain the critic pack
> The poet has to leave a track
> Of torn up scraps of prior poets.[1]

In writing this Frost had, it seems, been prompted by Lowes' assertion that poetry 'is one texture of quotations' stitched together from all that the poet has read, and that it is the critic's 'pleasure to come after you and trace it to its sources.'[2] Here the poem is of note for a number of reasons. Firstly, it highlights the fact that, for Frost, poetry-writing is akin to playing a game, be it for the poet's own amusement or for the diversion of 'the critic pack'. These same lines—which, despite Frost's pre-emptive denial, are surely to be read on one level as being as 'cynic' as they sound—also indicate that Frost is all too aware of the dangers of writing solely, or at least primarily, for the entertainment of an academic audience.

This is a hazard which Muldoon also heeds: he has, at times, been perceived as 'a poet designed for (and perhaps by) academics',[3] and famously, and quite quotably, has parodied himself as one

> Disappearing up his own bum.
> Or, running on the spot
> with all the minor aplomb
> of a trick cyclist.[4]

1 Robert Frost, *Collected Poems, Prose & Plays*, ed. Richard Poirier and Mark Richardson (New York: Library of America, 1995) 542. 2 Frost 992-3. In reference to Lowes' *The Road to Xanadu*, Muldoon writes that 'If John Livingstone Lowes / is to be believed, Coleridge's turn / of mind was that of a man who's half-shot most of the time'. *Hay* (London: Faber, 1998) 20. 3 Sean O'Brien, *The Deregulated Muse: Essays on Contemporary British and Irish Poetry* (Newcastle upon Tyne: Bloodaxe, 1998) 172. It should be noted that O'Brien is not one of those who views Muldoon in this way—his contention here is that this is the way in which Muldoon is depicted in Tim Kendall's book *Paul Muldoon* (Bridgend: Seren, 1996). 4 Paul Muldoon, *Quoof* (London: Faber, 1983) 47.

The concluding lines of Frost's Lowes-inspired poem could quite easily provide ammunition for those with the inclination to view Muldoon as 'nothing but quotations,' and his verse as little more than an engaging and diverting performance staged for the exclusive benefit of an élite scholarly audience. This is the stance taken by John Carey who, in a review of Muldoon's *Meeting the British*, alleges that the poems 'stand around smugly, knowing that academic annotators will come running'.[5] Yet, regardless of the reader's opinion of Muldoon's 'nonchalant virtuosity',[6] it must be acknowledged that he does have a tendency to scatter throughout his verse 'torn up scraps of prior poets', and that one of the poets most frequently shredded and found littering his work is Frost himself.[7]

In 1986, Muldoon was interviewed for the *Chicago Review* by Michael Donaghy. Towards the end of the interview, the two consider why, in recent decades, a number of Irish poets have looked to America for inspiration. Muldoon's explanation is that 'in terms of writing it seems to me that a lot of exciting things have happened here'—and then declares that 'One of my favourite poets is Robert Frost.' Donaghy notes that 'You've mentioned Frost in other interviews, and so has Seamus Heaney. In a way it seems to suggest that you two see more going on in Frost than a lot of Americans do.' Muldoon's response: 'Well, I think Frost is partly to blame for that.'[8]

Robert Frost is a vital figure for both Heaney and Muldoon. They discuss him at length in their criticism, and the Frostean influence pervades their poetry. One continually encounters imagery, sound postures, diction, and even phrases and rhyme patterns drawn from Frost. The American poet's influence has not passed unnoticed—as the Donaghy interview attests—yet most critics allude to him as just one in a long list of influences on the two poets. In a recent article, Edna Longley tells of a seminar she gave for some graduate students in 1986, and relates, evidently with some astonishment, that 'They were surprised to learn that Frost (who?) had inspired Heaney and Muldoon in differently fruitful ways.'[9]

Yet Heaney and Muldoon are alike in that both perceive in Frost a combination of what Muldoon terms 'knowingness' and 'unknowingness',[10] and Heaney (drawing on Valéry) calls *'les vers calculés'* and *'les vers donnés'*.[11] They both see Frost as a model of how the two elements can be held in productive tension. Each, however, is attracted to, and has been significantly influenced by, a different element. Heaney is drawn to the *donnés*—the given cadence, especially the

5 John Carey, *Sunday Times* (21 June 1987) 5.   6 Alan Jenkins, *Paul Muldoon* (London: Book Trust, 1988) n.p.   7 When tracing Muldoon to his sources in 'The More a Man Has The More a Man Wants', Kendall, for example, writes that 'Muldoon's allusive genius ensures that the shattering of the body is paralleled by poetic splintering, as the passage makes fleeting reference to three poems by Frost.' Kendall 113.   8 Michael Donaghy, 'A Conversation with Paul Muldoon,' *Chicago Review* 35.1 (Autumn 1986) 84.   9 Edna Longley, 'Irish Bards and American Audiences,' *Southern Review* 31.3 (July 1995) 768.   10 Paul Muldoon, F. W. Bateson Memorial Lecture, 'Getting Round: Notes towards an *Ars Poetica*,' *Essays in Criticism* 48.2 (1998) 119-20.   11 Seamus Heaney, *Preoccupations: Selected Prose 1986-1978* (London: Faber, 1980) 61-2.

Frostean notion of the 'sound of sense'.[12] Muldoon, on the other hand, is drawn to the *calculés*—to the studied slyness and wryness.

As Muldoon perceives it, there are two areas in which this Frostean 'knowingness' operates. Firstly, there is the knowingness of a crafted, controlled and controlling, form. Secondly, there is the fact that many of Frost's poems have, built into them, an element of arbitrariness, of playful unpredictability—a quality Muldoon has termed Frost's 'calculated capriciousness', a means by which he can entertain 'the critic pack'.[13] Frost's 'The Silken Tent', discussed by Muldoon in his 1998 Bateson Lecture, is a poem in which we can see this binary in operation. It's a sinewy single sentence of a poem which, to do it justice, must needs be quoted in its entirety:

> She is as in a field a silken tent
> At midday when a sunny summer breeze
> Has dried the dew and all its ropes relent,
> So that in guys it gently sways at ease,
> And its supporting central cedar pole,
> That is its pinnacle to heavenward
> And signifies the sureness of the soul,
> Seems to owe naught to any single cord,
> But strictly held by none, is loosely bound
> By countless silken ties of love and thought
> To everything on earth the compass round,
> And only by one's going slightly taut
> In the capriciousness of summer air
> Is of the slightest bondage made aware.[14]

This is a taut poem, structurally and syntactically, and it draws attention to itself —though certainly not in any obtrusive fashion—as a poem which is carefully, even painstakingly, crafted. Frost wrote the poem while his wife Elinor was still alive but he didn't publish it until 1939, at which time he presented it to Kathleen Morrison with the title 'In Praise of your Poise'—and this is, undeniably, one of the most poised, self-assured poems he composed.[15]

Frost was in many ways a traditionalist, and fond of saying that he would as soon play tennis without a net as write free verse. In 'The Silken Tent', however, the point is made that only occasionally is one conscious of the constraints of form, however rigorously they are observed, and this is mirrored in the graceful, seemingly

---

12 To take a recent example of this, in the introduction to his 1999 translation of the song-cycle *Diary of One Who Vanished*, Seamus Heaney speaks of 'trying to get words that kept close to the [Czech] meanings, but retained an English "sound of sense" and a certain metrical feel'. Seamus Heaney, *Diary of One Who Vanished: A Song Cycle by Leos Janacek in a New Version by Seamus Heaney* (London: Faber, 1999) np.   13 Muldoon, Bateson Lecture 117.   14 Frost 302.   15 William. H. Pritchard, *Frost: A Literary Life Reconsidered* (New York and Oxford: Oxford UP, 1984) 228-9.

effortless, syntax. The tent 'gently sways at ease,' and is 'loosely bound' by 'countless silken ties of love and thought': it is only through the 'capriciousness' of the breeze that one is 'of the slightest bondage made aware.' It is a 'made' thing, yet the impression it gives is of being unfettered by anything external to it. Muldoon touches on this an interview when he concedes that 'of course, all poetry is in a sense artificial: at its root is the idea of artifice ... But at the same time one wants to give the impression that it arises naturally, that it is made, as it were, with natural fibres.'[16] The implication, in 'The Silken Tent', is that freedom does not necessarily conflict with the boundaries set upon it by form. In fact, Frost's lyric 'Bond and Free' goes beyond this and states that there is a case to be made for true freedom—whether one is talking about love or about poetry—being possible *only* in thralldom:

> ... some say Love by being thrall
> And simply staying possesses all
> In several beauty that Thought fares far
> To find fused in another star.[17]

In his critical dissection of 'The Silken Tent', Muldoon notes that the phrase 'in guys'—as well as alluding both to guy-ropes and to Kay Morrison's attractiveness to many of the men (guys) of her acquaintance—puns on 'in *guise*', which, as he observes, 'reminds us again of the formal aspect of a construct in which things are not as they seem.'[18] This highlights the fact that what might at first appear to be confining can, in fact, be liberating, and read in this way the guy ropes are deceptive. Of course this also works in reverse: what at first appears to have no limits set on it is, the moment a slight breeze appears, revealed as being restricted 'by countless silken ties.'

The unpredictable nature of the poem, its unwillingness to be tied down to a single fixed meaning and the uncertainty experienced by the reader as a consequence of this, are qualities which are characteristic of Frost's work as a whole and which have attracted commentary from a number of critics. Richard Poirier, for example, writes of this sonnet that 'Both tent and poem are constructs of comparisons that do not completely settle anywhere; each comparison refers us to others in a self-supporting web of connections.'[19] This lack of fixity can be attributed to a certain capriciousness on the part of the poet. There is an acknowledged appreciation of the necessity of form, but alongside that is evident a desire to buck against those constraints. This is cognate with Frost's approach towards scansion. Consider, for example, his 1913 letter to John Bartlett: 'if one is to be a poet he must learn to get cadences by skillfully breaking the sound of sense with all their irregularity of accent

16 Paul Muldoon, interview with John Redmond, *Thumbscrew* 4 (Spring 1996) 2.   17 Frost, *Collected Poems* 117.   18 Muldoon, Bateson Lecture 118.   19 Richard Poirier, *The Work of Knowing* (Oxford: Oxford UP, 1977) xv.

across the regular beat of the metre'.[20] The poet works from necessity within the confines of form, and these can, paradoxically, provide a sense of freedom. However, this must be held in tension with the need to push up against those constraints, to kick out at unvarying and enforced regulations.

Frost's 'The Silken Tent' is, then, an apposite example of the combination of these two qualities—of that binary of form, and of playfulness within form. Muldoon has described this as the relationship between 'structure' and 'serendipity', two attributes which parallel 'knowingness' and 'unknowingness'. He has discussed these alongside a consideration of the control he has over his own poetry, explaining that

> It's as if I set out to pitch a tent and end up building a garage, if not a cathedral. Then there's a poem called 'The Bangle (Slight Return)' which is a sequence of thirty sonnets ... this poem uses the same rhyme-words, in the same order, as 'Incantata' and 'Yarrow'. This particular constraint ... is extraordinarily releasing for me ... One of the great mysteries for me is that one can actually combine structure and serendipity to great effect, simultaneously knowing and not knowing what one is doing.[21]

What is of interest in this passage is that Muldoon acknowledges that a poem can sometimes take off on its own—it is as if the poet sets up the initial conditions, but after that the poem can 'find its own way organically'—transforming itself, say, from a tent, be it silken or otherwise, into a cathedral.[22] In a conversation with John Haffenden, published in 1981, Muldoon relates how he'd 'become very interested in structures that can be fixed like mirrors to each other ... so that new images can emerge from the setting up of poems in relation to each other'.[23] Again and again, in lectures and in interviews, Muldoon drives home this same point: that, as a poet, he feels as if his role is to put in place certain structures, and then to give the poem free reign to develop within and against those structures as it pleases.

For Muldoon, rhyme is indisputably the structure, or maximal constraint, most commonly utilized. Repeating patterns of rhyme-sounds provide the poet's entire oeuvre with an overarching coherence, a spun web binding poem to poem and collection to collection. For Frost also the specific constraint of rhyme occupies as significant a position within his poetic universe as form in general, and he is conspicuous as a rhymer in an era of free-versers. He is reported as scorning those who would 'forget rhyme', claiming at one point that poetry, for him, began with 'Mother Goose,' when he found himself 'unable to get over rhymes'.[24] For both poets, the

---

20 Frost 665.   21 Paul Muldoon, 'A Drink with Paul Muldoon,' interview with Sebastian Barker, *Long Poem Group Newsletter* 7 (1998) 3.   22 Muldoon, Redmond interview 3.   23 John Haffenden, *Viewpoints: Poets in Conversation with John Haffenden* (London: Faber, 1981) 136.   24 Robert Frost, 'Playing for Mortal Stakes: Mr Frost's Remarks at the National Committee Meeting,' *Amherst Alumni News* 15.2 (Fall 1962) 10.

brilliance of the rhymes is to be associated not solely with artifice and calculation, with the structured knowingness of form, but also with the serendipitous swerve up against these constraints. Their use of rhyming language shows how design and play, structure and serendipity, are to be viewed not as binary opposites but as sides of the same coin, inextricably intertwined in a type of what Frost has labelled 'elevated play'.[25]

Although the critic pack may be entertained by means of these aesthetic games, however, this does not preclude the poet from dealing with weighty, and indeed disturbing, themes. Selden Rodman quotes Robert Frost stating in a lecture that 'Poetry is play. Even *King Lear* is called "a play", isn't it?'[26] Frost's point is not that playfulness and profundity are always analogous, but rather that play does not preclude the profound, or even the tragic. Muldoon reiterates this when he says that 'All poetry has to do with trickery to a greater or lesser extent, and "truth" and "trickery" are not necessarily opposed though they may seem to be in the minds of some lazy commentators.'[27] Trickery is not just a decoration but an indispensable element of the poetry, and, as Randall Jarrell notes, is in part a reflection of Frost's attitude towards life: 'Some of Frost's letters, talk, and later poems methodically joke about serious matters; their argument progresses by plays on words, puns, allusions, as though the writer were determinedly staying on the surface of things.'[28] Take, for instance, this late couplet of Frost's:

> Forgive, O Lord, my little jokes on Thee,
> And I'll forgive thy great big one on me.[29]

This querying of the role of the divine in the affairs of humankind is a stream of thought coursing through Frost's work, and is intertwined with and reflected in his stylistic use of play. The confusing aspects of the world are held at bay by the construction of the edifice of the poem. Robert Pack maintains that 'The play of the poem—the poet's power to create a design—is what Frost summons to contend with this darkness and confusion. He takes delight in the resistance to uncertainty and disorder that humour can provide.'[30]

Both Frost's and Muldoon's approach to metaphysical matters parallels their approach to aesthetic matters. In the composition of a poem, freedom is, as we have seen, most often evident within, and indeed dependent upon, the constraint of a design. Similarly, both poets, when speaking or writing of cosmological or theological issues, profess a belief in external constraints—be they societal,

25 Quoted in Pritchard 182.   26 Selden Rodman, *Tongues of Fallen Angels* (New York: New Directions, 1972) 43.   27 Muldoon, Barker interview 2.   28 Randall Jarrell, 'Good Fences Make Good Poets,' rev. of *Selected Letters of Robert Frost*, ed. Lawrence Thompson, *Sunday Morning Herald: Book Week* (30 Aug. 1964) 10.   29 Frost, *Collected Poems* 440.   30 Robert Pack, 'Frost's Enigmatical Reserve,' *Modern Critical Views: Robert Frost*, ed. Harold Bloom (New York: Chelsea House, 1986) 10.

genetic, or a 'fate' imposed by a deity—within which human free-will might operate. Muldoon discusses the interplay of the determined and the random in his interview with John Redmond: 'On the one hand we're terrifyingly complicated things, but on the other hand, we're very simple creatures, very basic organisms, and so much about us is pre-programmed and determined. It's something which has always been an element in my poems.'[31] Here again, then, though on the meta-physical rather than the aesthetic level, we have the intertwining of structure and serendipity, of knowingness and unknowingness.

The notion that all in the universe might be known, might be predicted—that there be none of what Muldoon terms 'the wonderful chanciness and randomness of things'[32]—horrifies both poets. Their poetry continually resists being tied down to single fixed readings; both relish the mischief of playing games with the reader, of subverting expectations and kicking out against the set design.

Consider, for example, the elegy 'Incantata', which Muldoon wrote in 'a five day frenzy of rage and remorse'[33] after the death, from cancer, of his former partner, Mary Farl Powers. His anger is in part directed at Powers, who, when diagnosed, refused the standard treatments, choosing instead to trust in alternative homeo-pathic remedies. As he explains, the reasoning behind her actions was her quasi-Aquinian, fatalistic view of the universe:

> Again and again you'd hold forth on your own version of Thomism,
> your own *Summa Theologiae* that in everything there is an order,
>
> ... you simply wouldn't relent
> from your vision of a blind
> watch-maker, of your fatal belief that fate
> governs everything ...[34]

Powers' 'vision of a blind / watch-maker' calls to mind Frost's poem 'Stars,' writ-ten after the death of his young son Elliott, which speaks of a universe indifferent in the face of human suffering—of 'stars like some snow-white / Minerva's snow-white marble eyes / Without the gift of sight.'[35] Powers' 'fatal belief that fate / governs everything' horrifies Muldoon as it would Frost.

'Incantata' is itself, however, governed by a pre-determined design, in that it follows a mirrored rhyme-sequence which winds its way up through twenty-three stanzas before turning back on itself and running itself down through the same pattern to the final stanza. In this sense the exact ending of the series is determined from the start by the poet's chosen formal constraint, which lends it

31 Muldoon, Redmond interview 4.   32 Ibid. 4.   33 Paul Muldoon, 'Paul Muldoon writes ...,' *Poetry Book Society Bulletin* 162 (Autumn 1994): 2.   34 Paul Muldoon, *The Annals of Chile* (London: Faber, 1994) 14, 27.   35 Frost 19.

a deadening finality. The pivotal twenty-third stanza of the elegy evidences Muldoon's virtually inarticulate expression of pain and desolation, his absolute inability to make any sense of what has occurred:

> The fact that you were determined to cut yourself off in your prime
> because it was *pre*-determined has my eyes abrim:
> I crouch with Belacqua
> and Lucky and Pozzo in the Acacacac-
> ademy of Anthropopopometry, trying to make sense of the
> '*quaquaqua*'
> of that potato-mouth … [36]

The critic Carol Tell argues that Powers' epistemology—in which the 'omnipotent watch-maker regulates a single rather than multi-narrative'—is diametrically opposed to Muldoon's, for Muldoon's 'is contingent on *maybes*—never the certainties"[37] There can be no play in Powers' uniform universe, therefore no room for creative vision, and the realization of this only increases the poet's anguish, as is conveyed forcibly to the reader through this stammered stanza. That the distressingly uncontrolled incoherence in these lines is paralleled by the repetition of strategic rhyme patterns uncannily echoing across this elegy, across the poems in the volume, and even between volumes, is even more disturbing.

One of the major reasons for both Muldoon's and Frost's pleasure in the play of poetry is that it allows for the holding of several perspectives at once. When space is made for the tangential and paradoxical, a number of outcomes can be juggled simultaneously—as Muldoon manages expertly in, for example, *Hay's* 'The Bangle (Slight Return).' In a deterministic universe, however, there is only one possible outcome, and this accounts for much of the grief in poems such as 'Incantata' and 'Stars'. The manner in which the playful is infused with the tragic is, indeed, one of Frost's most substantial legacies to Muldoon, who has clearly been inspired by Frost in 'fruitful ways,' and profoundly challenged and motivated, on various levels, by his negotiation of and mediation between structure and serendipity. The aim is certainly not always to 'entertain the critic pack,' yet in much of their work structure and serendipity are indeed combined to great effect, and for this, at least, the poets 'need make no apologies'.

36 Muldoon, *Annals* 20.   37 Carol Tell, 'Utopia and the New World: Paul Muldoon's America,' *Bullán* 2.2 (1996) 80-1.

Bleak Cities: Belfast in Maurice Leitch's Novels and Barcelona in the Work of Juan Marsé

ESTER CARRILLO, THE QUEEN'S UNIVERSITY OF BELFAST

Catalan and Northern Irish history are broadly similar in terms of an essentially colonial past, with its impositions of different cultures and languages. The consequences of these impositions are still deeply felt in both areas, and in their deeply divided societies, a fact which provides a basis for comparison. This may not be obvious, given the absence of an armed conflict in Catalonia. Nevertheless, linguistic conflict between Spanish and Catalan is, in fact, every bit as bitter and carries as many enduring political and economic consequences as the religious conflict in Northern Ireland. In this paper I will concentrate on comparing how different depictions of the cultural struggle in Barcelona and of the political/religious struggle in Belfast affect the portraits of these cities offered by just two authors, namely Juan Marsé and Maurice Leitch.

The consequences of these conflicts pervade all walks of life and, of course, a study of literature like this one is therefore affected. Juan Marsé is a good example. He was born in Catalonia, where he has always lived and worked; he has made Barcelona an important part of most of his novels and he defines himself as 'a Catalan novelist who writes in Castilian'.[1] Despite this, most Catalan literary critics would object to Marsé being included in a study of Catalan literature on the basis that he writes in Castilian, that is, Spanish. Due to the fact that Catalan was a forbidden language under Franco's dictatorship (1939-75), official Catalan culture has a protective attitude which denies the possibility of a Catalan literature in Spanish because it would weaken the hard-won status of the Catalan language, always endangered like any other minority language. While such an attitude is under-standable, given the Catalan circumstances, it denies Catalonia a literature which, apart from the language, has every reason to be considered Catalan, and which could be the equivalent of the Irish literature in English.

While there is also a language issue in Irish culture it is not as central to Northern Irish fiction as the sociological one. The political and religious factors that divide the Irish population have given raise to an unofficial but quite widespread critical notion that all good Irish literature belongs in the Catholic, or for some, Celtic, tradition. Consequently, the works of Protestant writers writing about Ireland and the Irish people have been, until recently, often judged either to be of poor literary quality or to belong to the British tradition. This would explain why

---

1 All translations in this paper are my own. The original reads: 'novelista catalán que escribe en castellano.' Maria Dolores de Asís Garrote, 'Universo y sentido en la obra de Juan Marsé', *Última hora de la novela en España* (Madrid: Eudema, 1992) 211.

Maurice Leitch, a Protestant, has received much less critical attention than Catholic authors like, for instance, Brian Moore, though their works are perfectly comparable in terms of quality. Such views are perfectly summarized by one of Leitch's characters: 'The Protestant ruling minority. An ugly face. Inbreeding? No poet will ever sing for them—of them.'.[2]

The practical consequence of such issues in a short essay like this is that the views offered are restricted to one side of the respective divides. Such a broad comparison as this obviously needs to be narrowed to manageable proportions. Among the many different possibilities available, focusing on the city is particularly suitable for two main reasons. Firstly, contemporary fiction in both areas, following a widespread European tendency, is predominantly urban, so materials for comparison are abundant; and secondly, using the city as a focal point actually allows for other important points of comparison (questions of identity and of class, cultural clashes, etc.) to be drawn into the study as part of the urban experience.

For both authors, the city is, on a symbolical level, a battlefield (and literally so in Leitch's *Silver's City*). Therefore, they use Barcelona and Belfast as settings in order to portray conflict, though as we will see Marsé is mostly concerned with class and, to a lesser extent, language issues, while Leitch focuses on religious and political issues.

Nevertheless Leitch, with the exception of *Silver's City*, chooses to set his novels in little villages instead, keeping Belfast in the background as a kind of reference, a shorthand for sectarian hatred: 'Belfast. The old man [Quigley's father] hated Belfast—black, bitter, British Belfast.'[3] According to Kevin Wall, this is due to the fact that sectarian hatred is more pervasive in smaller communities, which would be more narrow-minded: 'I believe Maurice Leitch's objective in setting the novel in the villages of Ballyboe and Slaney is to illustrate the type of constructed communities, plagued with narrow-mindedness that provided a fertile breeding ground for the eruption of violence'.[4] A good example is Tardree, in *Stamping Ground*, whose inhabitants are observed as if they were birds, or insects, by one character, and described as 'half-creatures' by another: 'I was the same at your age. Sensitive. Aware of the finer things, because, never forget, dear Hetty, there is another world outside Tardree and the poor half-creatures who live there and think it is the only world.'[5]

Marsé, on the other hand, chooses to set most of his novels in impoverished districts of Barcelona. The great majority of Marsé's main characters are unemployed immigrants to this city or their children, surviving in 'picaresque' ways, often morally (and sometimes even physically) degraded by their poverty and, most remarkably, male Spanish speakers. This is so, for instance, in *Últimas tardes con Teresa* (Last Afternoons with Teresa), *La oscura historia de la prima Montse* (Cousin's Montse

---

2 Leitch, *The Liberty Lad* (Belfast: Blackstaff, 1985 [1965]) 164.   3 Leitch, *Poor Lazarus*. (1969; London: Minerva, 1995) 111.   4 Kevin Wall, '"The Keen Eye of the Observer": Community and Society in the Fiction of Sam Hanna Bell and Maurice Leitch'. Unpublished dissertation. (Belfast: [author], 1995) 35. 5 Leitch, *Stamping Ground* 18.

Dark Story), and *Si te dicen que caí* (If you are told I fell down/died). Their alienation is echoed in the novels by the ugliness of their surroundings. For instance, the Barceloneta beach, in what used to be one of the poorest districts of the city, is described as follows:

> This is a shrill and overcrowded world that roasts in the sun. This is the industrial debris of the entrepreneurial 'seny' of Barcelona, the tramway-using and factory-working servants and the alien labourers who impose their ugly nudity within a limited free area of dirty sand and cloudy waves where scraps of both food and debased [sexual] intercourses float, a motley and violent and extremely ugly world ... within which it is not easy to stay clean or to keep a dignified posture for a long while.[6]

In such districts violence is often of an economic, even 'moral' kind, exerted by the rich (in these novels, almost invariably Catalan speaking) over the poor, as Paco Bodegas, the first person narrator in *La oscura historia de la prima Montse*, points out: 'Isn't it a form of violence, I asked, the power that the privileged minorities wield over them? Aren't ignorance, hunger, poverty, labour emigration, insufficient wages, organized prostitution, intellectual discrimination, and so on, forms of violence?'[7]

Physical violence, when it occurs, is often presented as a consequence of the deprivation that the working class characters have to endure due to the abuse of power of the upper classes, and also of the excesses of the Francoist regime, whose police is regularly shown torturing those they arrest. The answer to that behaviour is vandalism and, sometimes, terrorism: 'insulting graffiti against the [Franco's] rule in the walls in Hospitalet [a town in the south of Barcelona, so intimately connected to the city that they can hardly be told apart], electricity pylons blown up in the Llobregat area, a bomb at the monument to the "Cóndor" legion. The murder of a policeman in the Joanich square. Another bomb at the cathedral, another one at the Ritz hotel.'[8]

Due to this, and to the already mentioned fact that most main characters in his novels live in poverty, the vision of Barcelona offered by Marsé is consistently bleak.

6 The original reads: 'Es un mundo chillón y superpoblado que se cuece al sol. Son los detritos industriales del emprendedor *seny* condal, la servidumbre tranviaria y fabril y el peonaje foráneo que impone su fea desnudez en una reducida zona libre de sucia arena y turbias olas donde flotan residuos de comidas y de coitos degradados, un mundo abigarrado y violento y feísimo ... dentro del cual no es fácil mantenerse limpio ni guardar una postura digna durante mucho rato.' Marsé, *La oscura historia de la prima Montse* (Barcelona: Planeta, 1993 [1970]) 230. 7 The original reads: '¿acaso no es una forma de violencia, le pregunté, el poder que ejercen sobre ellos las minorías privilegiadas? ¿No es una forma de violencia la ignorancia, el hambre, la miseria, la emigración laboral, los salarios insuficientes, la prostitución organizada, la discriminación intelectual, etc.?' Ibid. 51. 8 The original reads: 'letreros ofensivos al régimen en los muros de Hospitalet, voladura de postes de alta tensión en el Llobregat, una bomba en el monumento a la Legión Cóndor. Asesinato de un policía en la plaza Joanich. Otra bomba en la catedral, otra en el hotel Ritz.' *Si te dicen que caí* (Madrid: Cátedra, 1985 [1973]) 212.

This is true not only in those works which deal with the post war city, still recovering from the bombardments, such as *Si te dicen que caí* or *Un día volveré*, but also in those which portray the city in more prosperous times, even the eighties:

> It was ten past ten and he planned to take the last bus at Universitat square. The illuminated signs blinked, hanging up on the evening mist. Like a faceless shadow, volatile, a young pusher approached him from behind, mate, do you want a little bit of happiness? Some beggars confronted him, chum, would you buy me a sandwich? Behind a kiosk, a young girl on high heels, stiff with cold, called him you handsome, wouldn't you like to fuck me hard?[9]

Even the industriousness for which the city is famed acquires sinister overtones: 'He hated that district with gloomy pubs and well-lit shops selling cleaning stuff, with cobblers crouching down in dark hallways and porter's lodges and with small workshops purring in basements, letting go their chant of milling machines and power saws at all times.'[10]

Barcelona in Marsé's novels is made to embody not only the characters' alienation but also their corruption: 'in this unruly body, in these decayed teeth and in these lifeless eyes the mysterious putrefaction of the city was also operating, that indifference of a muddy puddle receiving successive showers of humiliations and deceptions'.[11] According to William M. Sherzer, Barcelona is actually the adversary of the main character in *Últimas tardes con Teresa*, Manolo Reyes, which makes the city the embodiment of Catalan bourgeoisie. Pointing to a passage in the novel he remarks:

> The scene consists of a description of the view of Barcelona from mount Carmelo, necessarily through Manolo's eyes, but he almost does not appear in the narration ... What matters in this paragraph is not the character, but the city ('unknown city under the distant fog, almost like dreamed of') which constitutes his opponent. In the very structure of the paragraph the word 'he', the only direct reference to Manolo, is completely surrounded by the immensity of Barcelona city.[12]

9 The original reads: 'Eran las diez y diez y pensaba coger el último autobús en la plaza Universitat. Los anuncios luminosos parpadeaban suspendidos en la bruma de la noche. Como una sombra sin rostro, volátil, un joven *camello* se le acercó por la espalda, compañero, ¿quieres un poco de felicidad? Algunos pedigüeños le salieron al paso, hermano, ¿me pagas un bocadillo? Detrás de un quiosco, una muchacha aterida de frío sobre altos tacones le llamó guapo, ¿no te gustaría metérmela hasta el alma?' *El amante bilingüe* (Barcelona: RBA, 1993 [1990]) 34.   10 The original reads: 'Odiaba este barrio de sombrías tabernas y claras droguerías, de zapateros remendones agazapados en oscuros zaguanes y porterías y de pequeños talleres ronroneando en sótanos, soltando a todas horas su cantinela de fresadoras y sierras mecánicas.' *Ronda del Guinardó* (Barcelona: Plaza y Janés, 1995 [1984]) 23.   11 The original reads: 'también en este cuerpo desmedrado, en estos dientes picados y en estos ojos muertos se operaba la misteriosa putrefacción de la ciudad, aquella indiferencia de charco enfangado recibiendo sucesivas lluvias de humillaciones y engaños.' Marsé, *Si* 224.   12 The original reads: 'La escena consiste en una descripción de la vista de Barcelona desde el Monte Carmelo, necesariamente a través de los ojos de Manolo, pero

The most important exception to the aforementioned 'rule' in Marsé´s works that main characters are Spanish-speaking immigrants is to be found in *El amante Bilingüe* (The bilingual lover). Its main character and first person narrator has a split personality which, at a symbolic level, mimics the linguistic and cultural dichotomy present in contemporary Catalan society. As Juan Marés, he is from Barcelona and speaks Catalan, but as his alter ego, Juan Faneca, he is from Andalucia and speaks Spanish. Marsé playfully points at it in the novel, by making Marés attribute his double personality syndrome to Barcelona itself, with mirrors becoming a symbol of duplicity: 'He would go to lavatories to look at himself in the mirrors: in a schizo-phrenic city, with diverse duplicities, he thought, what the helpless citizens must do is to look at themselves in the mirror frequently in order to avoid unpleasant surprises.'[13]

As remarked, Marsé avoids an image of Barcelona as linguistically homogeneous, which gives his negative representation of the city a more realistic feel. However, this is not meant to be a realistic portrayal of the city. According to Maria Dolores de Asís, Marsé 'confesses that what interests him is a manufactured reality, that he adores invented truth, that he writes because of aesthetic motivations, to put order into his internal chaos, the external one and the verbal matter'.[14]

This comment is also true of Leitch's works. Whenever a representation of Belfast appears in his novels the view of the city offered is, like in Marsé's, quite bleak: 'Along narrow back streets, over wet greasy black square-sets, past warehouses and later, squeezed-in stinking houses with the bluish gleam of television in every window ... The long trek through the York Street slum area hadn't cooled my temper any.'[15] Nevertheless, while in the latter author's works the main characters are usually desperate to move to plusher districts within Barcelona, that is, what they want to avoid is poverty, Leitch's characters are desperate to move out of Belfast, what they want to avoid is the city itself, London being often the alternative of choice:

> No, she couldn't face another winter of it, not here in this bleak, black outpost, where the rain buckled the plywood fronts of the shops, while, before their doors, the pot-holes filled steadily, where the bus windows never seemed to get washed except by more rain, where hands pawed you at the

éste casi no figura en la narración ... Lo importante en este párrafo no es el personaje, sino la ciudad ("ciudad desconocida bajo la niebla distante, casi como soñada") que constituye su adversario. En la misma estructura del párrafo la palabra "él", única referencia directa a Manolo, está totalmente rodeada por la inmensidad de la ciudad de Barcelona.' Sherzer, *Juan Marsé: entre la ironía y la dialéctica*. Madrid: Fundamentos, 1982. 75. **13** The original reads: 'Entraba en los lavabos para mirarse en los espejos: en una ciudad esquizofrénica, de duplicidades diversas, pensaba, lo que el ciudadano indefenso debe hacer es mirarse en el espejo con frecuencia para evitar sorpresas desagradables.' Marsé, *El amante* 84. **14** The original reads: '... confiesa que es la realidad elaborada lo que le interesa, que adora la verdad inventada, que escribe por motivaciones estéticas: para poner orden al caos de su interior, del entorno y de la materia verbal.' de Asís, 211. **15** Leitch, *Liberty* 167.

security-checks, and the bars were full of roaring, unhappy drunks. More and more she seemed to be in a frontier town, the men in stained parkas with rabbitskin ruffs, hauling themselves in and out of cars which, like their owners, looked expendable. No, she wanted the grime of this Murmansk of a place scrubbed off for good—just as soon as she could stretch out in a London bathtub.[16]

The reason for so many characters in Leitch's novels to want to move out of Belfast, and of Northern Ireland in general, is the political and religious divide which is generally at the centre of his work: 'The valley had flowered with a bright harvest of hate. *To Hell with the Pope and Remember 1690*. He had often been tempted to add his own *Why?* to walls, sparking off a thunderous chalked correspondence.'[17]

It is this divide, rather than a class-based, economic one, which drives the lives of most of these characters, even of those who are critical of it:

> We drove along past the borders of The Holy land, past Palestine Street, Jerusalem Street, Damascus Street, Cairo Street. We passed a gable-end on which it was scrawled in faded white paint 'TO HELL WITH THE POPE'. The letters had dripped like action painting. It would be lovingly re-painted when the twelve of July came round. God knows how many thicknesses of paint there were. Oh yes, we are a great crowd for writing on walls. Our national bloody pastime.[18]

This does not mean, of course, that Leitch's characters are not aware of the economic divide that Belfast has in common with any other city: 'Trees and lawns and a thick stillness that could only be bought with lots of cash'.[19] Leitch, like Marsé, often focuses his novels in working class (or lower middle-class) male characters, social misfits. Besides, though Leitch does not make poverty and class struggle a constant issue in his work, when he does reflect on it the resulting picture is as gloomy as in Marsé's works. This is so because many working class people, but especially Protestants with hard work ethics, often derive their self-respect, their sense of worth from their jobs. In *The Liberty Lad*, for instance, the main character's father cannot come to terms with the fact that he has lost his job:

> And a memory of a slow, shuffling line of quiet respectable men in washed dungarees, in the dole queue, none of them the cocky brigade of the popular press. Just serious men in clean denim. Those unsoiled trousers were the saddest part ... and the old man taking up the end place, as I waited and watched from the car out on the street. Not looking ashamed; just stunned.

16 Leitch, *Silver's City* (1981; London: Abacus, 1983) 101.   17 Leitch, *Stamping* 34.   18 Leitch, *Liberty* 144.
19 Leitch, *Silver's* 6.

He still didn't believe his working live was finished even when they slid his five pounds eight across the counter at him.[20]

This character's stunned acceptance of his situation is a constant in Leitch's works, whose main characters do not often rebel against their conditions, no matter how unfair, or try to go up the social ladder in the way Marsé's do. The rare exceptions always end in failure: 'There had never been any escape, really, for the likes of him.'[21] The same lack of rebellion is shown to apply to the troubles: the physical scars that they have left in Belfast are mentioned in a matter-of-fact kind of way which conveys the weariness of its inhabitants, resigned at having to live with them:

> A vista of bricked-up doorways and windows stretched for as far as the eye could travel, for it was one of those immensely long, slightly curving streets, artery for all those little side streets which, together on the map, went to make up a defined city-area with its own nickname and loyalties. But all that was dead and done, merely a memory now. They picked their way through sodden debris and drifts of wind-blown rubbish, past the brutal breeze-block facings in the older brick.[22]

Unlike Marsé, however, Leitch does not blame an unfair ruling class for the violence in Irish society that such passages reflect, or the other side of the religious and political divide, as is the rule in real life. Instead, through Silver, he puts the blame firmly on Irish people as a whole, and, as the following paragraph shows, the adjective 'Irish' here includes Northern Irish Protestants as Silver himself:

> 'Who should we blame then? For all the violence?'
> 'That was there all along. We're a violent people. Look at us. Listen to us …
> This country came out of violence. It sits on the brink. Yet everyone's always amazed when it breaks out again—every time.'[23]

In this light, even positive descriptions of richer parts of Belfast do not alter the overall negative impression of the city: 'It was a residential area, the avenue outside was poplar-lined and the neighbours led the quietest of lives. Dogs were walked or rose bushes seasonally pruned. There didn't seem to be any children … Worse than—? But here in this city, there were even things beyond that'.[24]

As Marsé does with Barcelona, Belfast is also made to embody some of the flaws of its inhabitants, like cynicism and unforgiveness, in Leitch's *Silver's City*. It is also interesting that the city seems to be the real adversary of the main character in this novel, as Sherzer comparably pointed out regarding Marsé's *Últimas tardes con Teresa*:

---

20 Leitch, *Liberty* 169.   21 Leitch, *Silver's* 121.   22 Ibid. 92-3.   23 Ibid. 143.   24 Ibid. 51.

He thought of the city and the street-lamps lighting one by one, his city, the city that had made him what he was. Old and cynic He thought of the city and the street-lamps lighting one by one, his city, the city that had made him what he was. Old and cynical begetter, it watched its sons come, it watched them go. Despite dreams, he had been brought back down to the level of its streets, as it always knew he would ... That would be his sentence, for the city always made you pay for your dreams.[25]

Belfast is also blamed for the characters' shortcomings. Nan, a character in *Silver's City*, feels unhappy with her life and, to cope with it, attributes to Belfast a change which up to a point reflects the change she herself has undergone: 'She felt she had a lot of revenge left in her, not just for them and all the other burghers, but for the city itself. It had cheated her, by changing from the innocent slip of a young thing she thought of it as being once upon a time—her time—to the ugly old whore it now was'.[26]

This clearly shows that Leitch, like Marsé, does not intend to offer a realistic portrayal of the city, but a gloomy one which reflects the desperation that his characters feel: '*Is there life before death*? It was a line of graffiti that had originated back home, so he was given to understand. Something Belfast had given to the world, along with Georgie Best, Hurricane Higgins, James Galway—that city of short, dark, driven men.'[27]

This is a very limited study of the authors concerned, since it concentrates in just one point of comparison. Further ground for comparison is in questions of gender, depiction of the past and their approach to madness and marginalization. Bearing that in mind, both authors studied seem to share, where class is concerned, what Sherzer calls 'a social fatalism', that is, a belief that the working classes' lot is unlikely to ever improve.[28] Such bleak vision is mirrored in their portrayal of their respective cities, which is consequently quite dark and grim. Moreover, both of them firmly focus their works on just one side of their respective divides, with no attempt to describe or understand the 'Other' (that is, the Catalan bourgeoisie for Marsé and the Catholic community for Leitch) in depth. This approach offers a quite negative, limited vision of their respective cities, which highlights the difficulties, limitations and choices that a writer faces when representing divided societies. The result is a rather narrow and fragmented picture of Barcelona and Belfast which, as Hana Wirth-Nesher points out, is only to be expected: 'Finally, setting in the modern urban novel, by its provisional and dynamic properties, tends to undermine the quest for a total vision, an ultimate homecoming, or a lasting knowledge.'[29]

25 Ibid. 180-1. 26 Ibid. 101. 27 Leitch, *Burning Bridges* (London: Arrow, 1990 [1989]) 85. 28 The original reads: 'un fatalismo social'. Sherzer 107. 29 *City Codes: Reading the Modern Urban Novel* (Cambridge: Cambridge UP, 1996) 21.

'As Assiduously Advertised': Publicizing the 1899 Irish Literary Theatre Season

BRIAN CLIFF, EMORY UNIVERSITY

With varying degrees of insight, the serial controversies of Irish theatre are generally attributed either to the provincialism of early twentieth-century Dublin or to the fractures engendered by colonialism. Aiming more to supplement than supplant these twin emphases, this essay examines how the Irish Literary Theatre's own publicity contributed to a view of the Theatre, in the words of the Royal University protesters, as having broken 'the contract concluded with the Irish public ...'[1]

Most early press notices for the ILT's troubled inaugural season in May 1899 sustained a highly favorable tone. The constructive Unionist *Daily Express*, widely regarded as Yeats' virtual mouthpiece, published an advance article exemplary in its fluffing: 'those privileged to witness' the rehearsals 'pronounce them excellent in every way, and prophesy that the ultimate result will be a first-rate and perfect production when for the first time these essentially Irish dramas are given before an Irish audience'.[2] In the weeks preceding the season, most of the other major Dublin papers gave the ILT similarly enthusiastic coverage, with a similar emphasis on the anticipated Irishness of the enterprise. The nationalist *Irish Daily Independent*, for example, consistently the least critical Dublin paper, effervesced that the ILT 'aims at founding drama which shall worthily express the thoughts, the feelings, the romance, the poesy which touch the spirit of the Irish race. To do this they must found a school of literature that is in form and substance Irish. Herein lies the greatness, herein lies the value of their movement.'[3] This emphatic connection between usefulness and Irishness, with the ILT subordinate to that connection, lies at the heart of the problems the season encountered.

Neither this connection nor this subordination came into being on their own; in fact, the ILT itself had encouraged them from the very beginning. The famous letter sent to potential guarantors in the summer of 1897 walked a thin line, as Roy Foster has written, 'between its claims of "national" politics, its avant-garde ambitions, and the patronage of the establishment'.[4] In it, Gregory, Martyn and Yeats declare their

---

1 The *Daily Nation* (10 May 1899), cited from Joseph Holloway, theatre clippings book, ms 4374 (microfilm POS 7047), National Library of Ireland, 48. All further newspaper quotations are from 1899 and are taken from this volume, hereafter cited as Holloway. Due in part to the interrelations of Dublin newspapers, many of the letters and articles discussed in this essay appeared in multiple sources, but with the exception of articles that transcribed speeches, little variation occurred. In the interests of space, then, I have focused on the *Daily Nation* and the *Daily Express*, the two major participants in the 1899 season.
2 (3 May), Holloway 3.   3 (6 May), Holloway 9.   4 Roy Foster, *W.B. Yeats: A Life, Volume I: The Apprentice Mage* (Oxford: OUP, 1997) 206. For the dating of the ILT's circular, see *The Collected Letters of W.B. Yeats, Volume Two: 1896–1900*, ed. Warwick Gould, John Kelly and Deirdre Toomey (Oxford: Clarendon, 1997) 123f, hereafter cited as *CLii*.

particular 'desire to bring upon the stage the deeper thoughts and emotions of Ireland' and assert their confidence about gaining 'the support of all Irish people, who are weary of misrepresentation, in carrying out a work that is outside all the political questions that divide us'.⁵ The tension implicit here between expressing the nation and, as Yeats said in an April 1899 talk to the Irish Literary Society, hoping to 'mould and perfect national feeling', would grow increasingly explicit as the ILT's debut approached.⁶

Having officially announced the season in a letter to the Dublin papers two days previously, Yeats' 14 January article in the *Daily Express* both extended and complicated the ambivalences of the Theatre's initial mission statements:

> upon [national feeling], more widely spread among all classes in Ireland to-day than at any time this century, we build our principal hopes. ... Although we have for the moment decided to produce no plays not upon Irish subjects, we know that when Irish literature is more developed, Irishmen will utter the personality of their country, no matter what subjects they write about ... Victor Hugo has said that in the theatre the mob became a people, and ... I have some hope that ... we may help to bring a little ideal thought into the common thought of our times.⁷

With ambitions beyond the page and the stage, Yeats' prescriptive assertions suggest that the entire theatrical project has its basis in expressing and ennobling the nation. Even his closing cautionary note—that it may be the duty of these writers to condemn the vanities of what he calls the 'passing and modern Ireland'—implies that the ILT would represent *only* an essential Ireland.⁸ Additionally, in intriguing contrast to the hieratic scorn of his later *Playboy* and *Plough* pronouncements, rather than emphasizing why a national movement might need the ILT, Yeats here (as throughout the publicity campaign) insistently reiterates the dependence of the ILT on that movement. Some of his various audiences required only a short jump from this acknowledged dependence to seeing the ILT as subservient to the needs and demands of the different national movements, a jump clearly, if unknowingly, encouraged by Yeats.

Controlled by Tim Healy, one of the ILT's initial guarantors, the conservative nationalist paper, the *Daily Nation*, quickly made this jump and began the season's controversy proper. Healy's paper utterly repudiated *The Countess Cathleen* only two days before the premiere, protesting 'in the names of morality and religion, and Irish nationality, against its performance' because the 'production of such a play as "The

5 *CLii* 123-4. The editors note that a 'shortened version of this letter appears in [*Our Irish Theatre*] (20), and it is not known whether the version actually sent out differed from the draft' (*CLii* 123n1).   6 W.B. Yeats, *Uncollected Prose Volume 2*, ed. John P. Frayne and Colton Johnson (London: Macmillan, 1975) 158; hereafter cited as *UPii*.   7 *UPii* 140-1.   8 *UPii* 141.

Countess Cathleen," on the occasion of the inauguration of what was intended to be a distinctively national institution, is nothing short of an outrage'. Although the paper had 'believed that' the ILT 'would be both "Irish" and "Literary",' it concluded angrily that the ' "Countess Cathleen" is, however, neither one nor the other.'[9] The unacknowledged inspiration for this attack came from Frank Hugh O'Donnell's famous *Souls for Gold!: A Pseudo-Celtic Drama in Dublin*, a pamphlet reprinting two of his letters to the press, the first of which had already been published in the *Freeman's Journal* on 1 April, and the second of which, apparently with Yeats' encouragement, had been rejected by that paper.[10] Within the pamphlet, O'Donnell rages in much the same hysterical vein indicated by his title's exclamation mark, asserting that Yeats 'has no right to lay the scene in Ireland, whether of to-day or in the golden days ... Why, why has Mr W.B. Yeats called this thing a "Drama of Ancient Ireland"? If he had called it a "Drama of Colney Hatch" no man living would have protested.'[11] Emphasizing his utilitarian criterion, O'Donnell draws to a close by querying 'the meaning of this rubbish? How is it to help the national cause? How is it to help any cause at all?'[12] O'Donnell's complaint here, like that of the *Daily Nation*, clearly centers on his sense that Yeats was guilty not just of inauthenticity and misrepresentation, but more seriously of violating the promise held out by the ILT's own publicity, the promise to serve the nation.

Indeed, Yeats had made no secret of the ILT's need to lean on national sentiment, and he had continually pitched the project as using Irish subjects to express Irish ideals, Irish essences. With the onset of heavy criticism, most prominently from the *Daily Nation*, and with an increasing awareness that the ILT might not satisfy the very expectations it had helped awaken, this emphasis began to falter. The beginnings of this shift are apparent in the first issue of the ILT's house organ, *Beltaine*, assembled in late April and probably published in early May, that is, long enough after the publication of O'Donnell's 1 April letter for Yeats to have reexamined his rhetoric.[13] Although Yeats, writing in the third person as the 'Editor of "Beltaine",' tentatively affirms the ILT's commitment to Irish particularity, to producing plays 'founded upon an Irish subject', he spends more time here withdrawing to the safer ground of undefined symbols.[14] After ceding that the 'interpretative argument ... for *The Countess Cathleen*' written by Lionel Johnson (and published under the ILT's imprimatur in the same issue) 'places the events it describes in the sixteenth century', Yeats openly overwrites both himself and Johnson by rescinding such historical specificity: 'So Mr Yeats originally wrote, but he has since written' otherwise, for the 'play is not historic, but symbolic, and has as little to do with any definite place and time as an *auto* by Calderon'.[15]

9 From a lengthy article of 6 May, given in Holloway 6-8.   10 See *CLii* 387n1 and 390n4.   11 F. Hugh O'Donnell, *Souls for Gold!: Pseudo-Celtic Drama in Dublin* (London: Nassau Press, 1899) 7-8.   12 O'Donnell 13.   13 In a letter of 15 April to T.P. Gill, who was helping publish *Beltaine*, Yeats indicated a contributor's deadline of 'about the 20th' of April (*CLii* 393).   14 *Beltaine: The Organ of the Irish Literary Theatre* 1 (May 1899) 6.   15 *Beltaine* 8. 'WBY gratefully appropriated' this reference to Calderon from

At the conclusion of an apparently successful season, Yeats was able to qualify this line of argument: 'Literature was the expression of universal truths by the medium of particular symbols,' he told the guests at a celebratory dinner on 11 May, 'and those who were working at the National Literary movement and at all such movements were simply trying to give to universal truths the expression which would move most the people about them.'[16] These 'particular symbols' had indeed moved people, though not generally in the direction Yeats had hoped, for much of his audience seemed to expect that a national theatre should express local particulars before it could express any universals, a prioritization clearly and repeatedly under-written by the ILT's publicity.

Despite having served as a major source of that publicity, even the *Daily Express* began to retreat from its earlier descriptions of the ILT as 'essentially Irish' and 'excellent in every way'. Their review of the opening night concludes that the ILT's 'appeal is "rather to the intellect and the spirit than to the senses," and its first performance has proved the abundant existence of a public intellect and spirit which only require education and encouragement to become the most powerful and dominant factor in the national welfare and progress of our country'.[17] To make this argument about the intellectual vitality revealed by the play's reception, however, the *Express* has to claim that the questions raised by *The Countess Cathleen* have 'nothing to do with politics or sectarian theology', a claim oddly blinkered at best.[18] Two days later, in its retrospective on the season, the *Express* would follow Yeats' line more closely: 'Mr Yeats has told us that his play is an allegory, representing, not human characters, but passions by which the soul of man is moved. It is merely the poet's predilections that give it an Irish colouring. The scene is laid in the human mind, the time is no time, the peasants are not Irish peasants, but simply imaginative symbols.'[19]

But almost all ILT publicity, including that created and covered by the *Express* itself, had in fact encouraged precisely the view of the play's representational status that the paper now decries. Such defenses would lead the *Daily Nation* and others to ask, fairly enough, 'If Mr Yeats' play had so little to do, as we are now asked to believe it had, with Ireland, in what way could it serve as an "expression of the national thought and ideals of Ireland"?'[20]

This question points toward one of the core issues at work in this season, that of expectations and disappointments, contracts and withdrawals. Accordingly, then, the *Daily Nation*'s fiery response to the ILT, *The Countess Cathleen*, and the various rhetorical retreats described above, arguably centers less on the play itself than on the play as a violation of the ILT's apparent promise to reflect Ireland:

the Reverend William Barry, one of the two clergy whose qualified approval of the play cleared Edward Martyn's conscience (*CLii* 383-384n3). **16** *Daily Express* 12 May, qtd. in Robert Hogan and James Kilroy, *The Irish Literary Theatre 1899-1901* (Dublin: Dolmen, 1975) 50. **17** (9 May), Holloway 42. **18** (9 May), Holloway 41. **19** (11 May), Holloway 71. **20** (12 May), Holloway 75-6.

> We say that the theory [of souls for gold] is un-Catholic, unnatural, and ...
> absolutely un-Irish, and the production of a play based upon it for the inau-
> guration of the Irish Literary Theatre appears to us to be gratuitously
> insulting ... Leaving aside, for the moment, all questions of religious truth,
> what is to be said for Mr Yeats' play regarded from the national or patriotic
> standpoint? *As a picture of the habits of thought and action of our people*, in "the
> latter part of the sixteenth century," or at any other time, the "Countess
> Cathleen" is a gross and offensive libel ... It was and is, therefore, necessary to
> protest that Mr Yeats' play is not Irish. It is not even Art![147] [emphasis added]

Ironically echoing the *Express'* attempt to separate religion and nation, this attack
on the ILT's apostasy undermines such a distinction by arguing that the national
offense lies in the depiction of widespread, craven irreligiousness. As so often
elsewhere during this season, despite the occasional rhetorical effort to keep them
distinct, morality, religion, and nationality here appear inseparable in a symbiotically
entangled discourse: the immoral aspects of the play are those which are irreligious,
and the irreligious aspects are those which are immoral, and the un-Irish aspects are
those which attribute immorality or irreligiousness to the Irish. *Contra* Conor
Cruise O'Brien's claim that *The Countess Cathleen* 'shocked not for theological, but
for social and tribal reasons', the play encountered the reaction it did precisely
because of the ways in which these forces depended on each other.[22] Amidst such an
intricate tangle, the expectations shaped by the ILT's publicity could hardly fail to
be disappointed.

Signed 'A Catholic Irishman', an intriguing letter to the *Daily Nation*'s editor
distills these fundamental charges still further:

> We do not so greatly object to Mr Yeats' picture; we do object, and very
> earnestly, to his labeling it 'a portrait' ... It does not 'reflect Irish ideas and
> sentiments'; it is not a 'literary expression of the thoughts and ideals of
> Ireland'; it will not 'serve the higher intellectual and artistic interests of the
> country.' It is in direct contradiction with the whole scope and purpose for
> which the Irish Literary Theatre is supposed to have been founded.[23]

This correspondent, who quotes (and cites) Yeats extensively, points towards the
critical difference between re-presenting and representing; between, as Yeats would
later say in the shadow of the Synge controversies, a photograph and an 'imaginative
image as in an impressionist painting'.[24] As for Frank Hugh O'Donnell and the
Daily Nation, for 'A Catholic Irishman', then, the crowning offense came from the
'assiduously advertised' Irishness of the Irish Literary Theatre and from the related

21 (8 May), Holloway 22-4.   22 Conor Cruise O'Brien, *States of Ireland* (London: Hutchinson, 1972) 60.
23 Holloway 26.   24 *UPii* 366.

claims of portraiture, both of which the ILT and its supporters had eagerly brought on themselves.[25]

The widely published letter of the Royal University students, meant to defend their protest at *Cathleen*'s opening night, illustrates the stakes involved in such claims. Referring to 'the contract concluded with the Irish public' which they felt the ILT had broken, their letter asks whether 'the Irish public and the Irish Press [have] thoroughly considered what their approval of Mr Yeats' picture means from a national and historical standpoint? Why, if this is a true portrait of Irish Catholic character, every effort of England to stamp out our religion and incidentally our nationality is not merely to be justified, but to be applauded.'[26] Clearly, the students see *The Countess Cathleen* as utterly incompatible with national pride and ambition. In its own way, the seemingly blustery confidence about Irish identity here poignantly suggests a real uncertainty behind the students' nationalism and that of the *Daily Nation*. Particularly in its relation to what George Watson has described as the 'explosive gap between Yeats' version of famine and the myth of the Great Famine', this uncertainty gives an emotional force to their claims of misrepresentation.[27] In such a context, the expectations fostered by the ILT led directly to this volatile sense of a contract broken, a sense that would prove enduringly problematic for the ILT's successors.

The 1899 season did, of course, include another play. Perhaps in relief that Edward Martyn's *The Heather Field* allowed them to support the ILT without political or theological hesitation, most reviewers (with the notable exception of an intermittently brutal piece in the *Irish Times*) heaped lavish praise on it, declaring Martyn's mediocrity the future of Irish theatre.[28] Almost certainly more than to the play's artistic quality, such nearly unbridled enthusiasm—especially when compared to deeply negative reviews of a repeat production in London later that year—speaks to the eagerness with which most of the Dublin papers attempted to support the ILT.[29] At the same time, the Dublin reviews of both plays also show politically disparate segments of the ILT's prospective audience each in their own way explicitly qualifying that support as specifically for a 'helpful' theatre.

A letter from P.J. Dwyer in *The Express* elaborates on the nature of this enthusiasm for the ILT by turning *The Countess Cathleen*'s famous tag-line against Yeats to underline the primacy of the national movement over any theatrical one, and certainly over Yeats' own career:

25 This phrase is from an article headed 'Irish Literary Theatre,' *Irish Times* (9 May), Holloway 36.　26 *Daily Nation* (10 May), Holloway 48.　27 George Watson, *Irish Identity and the Literary Revival: Synge, Yeats, Joyce and O'Casey*, 2nd ed. (Washington, D.C.: Catholic University of America Press, 1994) 67.　28 Even the *Daily Nation*, as if to prove its claims of support for a national theatre after its attack on *The Countess Cathleen*, produced a decidedly favourable notice (Holloway 51-2). Abandoning all reserve, the *Irish Daily Independent* characteristically found it 'impossible to speak in moderation of Mr Edward Martyn's drama "The Heather Field"' (Holloway 59). For the *Irish Times* review of 10 May, see Holloway 53.　29 Reviews of the 6 June London performances of *The Heather Field* were unfavourable at best and contemptuous at worst. The *Daily Telegraph* dismissed it as 'a drama of drainage' which could 'have no

Mr Yeats must not count for too much the applause which hailed his play, for it was rather the new Celtic movement that the majority of the audience greeted so rapturously. They clapped 'the motive, not the deed.' In their, no doubt, praiseworthy efforts to uphold the Irish Literary Theatre, many drowned alike their national pride, their religious scruples, and their profound disgust.[30]

Like so many critics of the ILT, Dwyer expected that the theatre movement would serve the national one in a measurably useful way, an expectation that he and others ultimately concluded the ILT had both taken advantage of and failed to meet. The frustration behind this dissent confirms both the fragility of the theatrical enterprise and a sense that much of its audience badly wanted the ILT to succeed, even if they wished anyone but Yeats had been behind it.[31] Out of such a conflicted bundle of impulses, the forces around the ILT emerge as at once tenuous and powerful.

The events and discourses examined here have an importance beyond their immediate context: by building on preexisting tensions within the broader literary and national movements, they established a loose framework that continues to affect the terms in which we discuss the history of Irish theatre. For much of the intervening century, literary history has tended to follow Yeats in ascribing theatrical controversies to an enduring conflict between Philistine audiences, looking for ennobling images of virtuous Irishry, and Heroic writers, offering something more probingly Artistic.[32] Like most legends, this contains some originary truth, but these conflicts ultimately arise out of more than any simple hierarchy of Artist and Audience, regardless of which element is momentarily on top. In the immediate context, the ILT's own publicity helped limit modern Irish theatre to being interpreted from the outset as largely about itself, as almost meta-theatrically about, as one reporter put it at the time, what 'a really representative Irish drama' should look like.[159] By first encouraging an expectation of a theatre in the nation's service and then, faced with confusion and opposition, attempting to pull back from what they had so 'assiduously advertised', the ILT virtually ensured its own entanglement, as well as that of its successors, in this rhetorical web.

chance of popular success.' More bluntly, *The Times* thought 'it says a great deal for the acting that *The Heather Field* is endurable on the stage at all,' while *The Standard* simply called it 'very dull and gloomy' (Hogan and Kilroy 48). **30** (16 May) Holloway 98-9. **31** The editors of Yeats' letters suggest that 'this controversy … in fact crystallized, rather than created, doubts that had long gnawed at his Irish Catholic readers, but which they had for the most part stifled' (*CLii* 673). **32** See, for example, Hogan and Kilroy's explanation of this season's controversy (30-1). **33** *Irish Daily Independent*, 15 May, Holloway 93.

Note from the Rathmines Underground, or, The Spiders and the Bees

DAVID COTTER, TRINITY COLLEGE, DUBLIN

The population of the building in which I live, in Rathmines, comprises of Kenyan and Algerian refugees, a Hindu, an Egyptian/Italian borderline phenomenon, and me, another borderline phenomenon. All of us, except the Chinese, enjoy smoking hashish perhaps once a fortnight, and some Friday nights we gather in the flat of the Egyptian/Italian, who has brought home enough for all. We smoke the peace pipe, just as the peace pipe was smoked across cluttered coffee tables throughout the island, before political people took over.

These dialogues have provided me with an opportunity to try and understand how Muslims can believe in such bad things. My curiosity impelled our smoky symposia, and we have come to a few conclusions. All religions do or should stand on what is basically one premise: you should try to be a good person, by acting charitably, and considering the positions of others around you; you should attempt to nurture in yourself an energetic brotherly love, and maintain your strength so that you can put out your hand for others, and oppose the power of those who are without charity. We have concluded that the rest—the fasts, the feasts, the dates, the names—is dross.

The words that gather around this core, and cause differences, are usually bad, though in a perfect world they should be appreciated for their folksy charm. The problem, however, is that they can cause us to forget the heart of the matter, and make Religion into a number of religions, that are supported in the way that football teams are supported. This, we all agree—even the communist Buddhists, who are difficult to draw out on anything—is bad religion.

Friday night is rent night, and we are sometimes interrupted by the appearance of the landlord's agent. He dresses like a businessman, and he is busy with his mobile phone. We smirk at one another behind his back. His appearance raises a number of questions, such as: who is Irish, what is Irish, and whether or not these are useful questions to ask. Mathew Arnold and Yeats might guide us in answering the first two of these questions, with their Celtic and Saxon types. We may also find aid in a number of other stereotypes. There are drunken Irish and fighting Irish, and there are the Irish of a tear and a smile always fighting for a place in the eye. Sometimes, when things are rough, when it has rained for a week, for instance, I annoy foreign friends by singing gaily that when Irish eyes are smiling the whole world is smiling too.

I cannot find the landlord, or his agent, in any of the more established definitions of Irishness. In fact, according to some of the criteria laid down by these authorities, Arabs are more Celtic in spirit than this lifelong inhabitant of

Rathmines, this collector of rent. Before we ask him to leave our land, however, we should be careful in our establishment and our use of tags such as 'Irish'. The Cyclops chapter of *Ulysses* illustrates the idiocies to which the paranoiac need to identify the self with an aggregate may lead. Bloom defines a nation as 'the same people living in the same place', and Ned replies 'I'm a nation for I'm living in the same place for the past five years.'[1]

If identity is dependent upon rootedness in a place, as Heaney also suggests, the quality of Irishness is stripped from centuries of diaspora, and Irishness is an exclusive club in yet another way. Undoubtedly, an impulse to exclude American voices will be expressed somewhere in this book. There is no need, however, for us to feel sorry for them; except, perhaps, as individuals. In their own places they commit the crimes of American and Canadian Studies, and they, too, will offer a leg up first to their own.

A definition of Irishness that is dependent upon rootedness in a place might call Joyce's Irishness into question. Of course, he always wrote about Dublin, but he wrote from exile. There is, however, a definition of Irishness which includes exile as one of its criteria; that says exile, like the tear and the smile, is especially ours. We all know that the place is falling down with wild geese that are gone.

Such definitions are always spurious, in servitude to context. Bloom's Jewish-ness and his Irishness are both defined by exile. This is because Joyce considered the Irish to be like the Jews and, for him anyway, an important similarity was a heritage of exile. On at least one occasion Joyce considered the Irish to be gentle people. The worst thing we can do with such a statement is read it as an expression of Joyce's convictions, and attempt to make something of it. Instead, we should consider it as a throwaway sentiment, one of those involuntary imbecilities of which all our lives are composed, and which, in Joyce, are gathered in such density as to constitute a proof of our incertitude. Everybody knows that all Irish people are not gentle, and no doubt Joyce was aware of this too. All Jews are not gentle either. Joyce drew an Irish Cyclops who, although he is gentler than the Saxons in Circe, could not adequately be described as gentle.

We should keep in mind that Irishness, like any idea, is always a model, and never a reality. It is too bad that we have to waste our lives emulating models. We might say that there is this one group: the Irish. Or we might say that Irishness is dependent upon membership in one of two cultures. We might be more open yet, and include also both immigrants and emigrants. Or maybe, as we stray further afield, we might consider Irishness to consist of thousands or millions of particles that drift through our minds, making places, like Blake's America, Europe and Asia; tribes that migrate across bodies without organs. Perhaps Irish is a useful term, because it allows the mind to focus, as might an image on a card in the Tarot deck, and because it gives schizophrenics people to be.

1 James Joyce, *Ulysses* (London: Penguin, 1986) 272.

I will now offer an example of the way in which the category of Irish Studies might be detrimental to a reading of Joyce. Say we felt that sexual masochism was somehow at the crux of Ulysses, and we wanted to understand this masochism in Joyce. It would be useful for us to establish a connection between Stephen, Joyce and Bloom. If we tried to do so, however, someone might object that the death of Rudy, and Bloom's Jewishness, are enough to account for his masochism.

To accept such an explanation, however, is to be tricked by a simple smokescreen that Joyce has lain, in order to keep the unsubtle reader out of his work. In 'Circe', Stephen's and Bloom's faces become one with Shakespeare's, and they are all three crowned by the horns of the cuckold. Cuckoldry is central to Joyce's masochism, and to the theory of artistic creation that Stephen expounds in *Ulysses*. It is in this theory, also, that Joyce suggests that we might seek the artist, and his motivations for creating, in his work, but that we should not assume the obvious in determining the author's autobiographical point of reference; he is as likely to be the old ghost as the prince. In Stephen, and the young protagonists of 'The Sisters', 'Araby' and 'An Encounter', we see the forces and reactions that contribute to sexual masochism: in Gabriel, Richard and Bloom, we see the fruition of this masochism.

Despite what anyone might say, Joyce is a personal writer, and nowhere is this more true than in the searing confessional of 'Circe'. The chapter may explain the psychodynamic potentialities of the book, or it may be a reiteration of history, but this is avoiding the issue. In 'Circe', Joyce is addressing the human condition, and in particular his own. Joyce did not go to the trouble of writing 'Circe' to play off of the masochistic, feminine stereotype of the Jew, or so that he could present an experiment in meta-narrative, or a parody of the Abbey 'style'; he has much more invested. It is the personal commitment, the self-engagement, that drives this chapter out at us.

In *Ulysses*, Joyce became a Jew, among other things, so that he could dissociate his masochism from himself, and from his Irishness. He left tracks, however, because of the exhibitionistic qualities of this perversity. Why this ambiguity, this coy game of showing and hiding? There are a number of explanations for his need to show, the first of these being a need to undermine the identities in which he was incarcerated. He wanted to hide, because of a fear of retaliation from paranoiacs who would resent the insinuation of this paradoxical perversity into the category of Irishness. His masochism was an agency that would disintegrate, through parody, any aggregates of which he partook. Irish studies is one such aggregate. Evidence that Joyce's fear of reprisal may have been well founded is in the continued resistance to the topic of his masochism. If there is interest in this topic, it is in expectation of another sane indictment of the abuses performed by members of the Catholic Church. This is part of it, no doubt, but there is more. What is it that we expect to learn from gathering historical and sociological detail?

Because Joyce's masochism is so similar to the masochism of other people from other cultures, and so alien to the sexualities of many of those brought up in the same circumstances as himself, it seems that Catholicism provides only the trappings that this phenomenon is sometimes made to wear. The phenomenon itself may be considered more substantial, more rooted in the essence of the human condition. This psychic construct is not necessarily Oedipal, but it is the result of a triangulation between authority, and the subject and the object of desire. Catholic ritual, Irishness and Jewishness, are simply run through this desiring machine, as fuel. More essential to the masochistic equation is the potentially universal experience of watching a mother and a brother, for instance, crushed by the Despotism of Fact, so that pity, overweened, turns the brutality of the sexual urges upside down and inside out, and, with flaming sword or paddle, drives these urges, naked and humiliated, out into the desert. More important than the question of the Irish or the Catholic qualities of Joyce's masochism, is the question of why pity should renounce genital penetration with discharge in the womb.

We are likely to lose something if lines of inquiry are determined by help-wanted ads in *The Guardian*, the MLA or *The Times*. Literature should not be portioned out between the various fields of national studies. This causes it to be subordinate to the disciplines of history and sociology. The sociological project of delineating groups always overlooks the margins between these groups, and the people who straddle these groups, failing to be caught by these nets. It is possible that Vision, with a capital V, emerges in such people. It may be the case that the percentage of people undecided in these surveys is not a superfluous figure, but rather the heart of the matter. To learn an identity by studying Irishness is cheap, a cop out; it is from McDonalds. Meaning does not reside in the bog beneath our feet, but in the bogs in our minds. It is cowardice for us to think for a market, though there is only dignity in the desolation to which integrity will lead. Sincerity should become for us the only thing that matters.

I would try to state this less emphatically, but that it seems to me the world is about to fall down around our ears. Our society is not so good that we should sit and muse on how we got here. In fact, the bad manners of our drivers should be enough to convince us to forget everything we know about ourselves, and start again from scratch.

In the wrong hands, Irish studies could become a tool for perpetuating an exclusive hierarchy, and those dangerous certainties that deceive us into thinking we are standing straight and at ease, among stable things. While the study of such a field might be useful for schizophrenics, there is always a danger that paranoiacs will continue to be involved.

Let us keep in mind that all of life is a fight between giant twins. In one corner, there is all that roots us in ourselves. In the other, there is the disintegration of will and identity, and the escape from that bundle of coherences that sits down to breakfast. Now, everything is telling us to forget the body without organs, the timeless moment, the groundless truth of 'there is no truth saving in thine own heart'. But this is not only about an old war in which realism beat romanticism; it is a question of epistemology.

More and more, markets make us value literature for the support it can offer to surveys in which people have ticked the tag that fits them best. This causes us to neglect the senses in which all religions are one, and to ignore that which is the same beneath differences, that which is never superfluous. Our market-driven academies teach nobody to speak the truth and draw the bow.

The suggestions I have made can not be supported by any evidence or proof. Their only aim is to discredit opinion and certainty. I feel confident in urging us all to take heed that we do not let our certainties steal our lives. Because at the bottom of the sea I have seen something like a jellyfish turn itself inside-out repeatedly.

Becoming National: Daniel Corkery and the Reterritorialized Subject

PAUL DELANEY, UNIVERSITY OF KENT AT CANTERBURY

In the closing pages of the literary primer, *A First Book of Irish Literature* (1934), a brief account of the work of Daniel Corkery is provided. According to Aodh de Blacam, its author, this portrait is drawn primarily from Corkery's reputation as 'the exponent of a new national literature'.[1] De Blacam asserts, for instance, that Corkery has 'influenced rising Ireland more considerably than any other modern writer' (casting a silent nod towards the young protégés Frank O'Connor and Seán O'Faoláin, and a blind eye to the inheritance of the Abbey Theatre and James Joyce), and suggests that his influence has been of critical significance in the development of a national art-form.[2] 'Our survey [should] close with his doctrine', de Blacam notes, partially because it 'must notice' the importance of his person.[3]

Corkery's doctrine, as outlined by de Blacam, is familiar enough to most readers of Irish culture. Based upon the critical triumvirate of Nationalism, Religion, and the Land, it has often been depicted as an exclusivist argument which set the limits for cultural expression in the fledgling Free State.[4] Corkery himself has accordingly, traditionally, been remembered as the cultural commissar

1 Aodh de Blacam, *A First Book of Irish Literature: Hiberno—Gaelic—Anglo-Irish; From the Earliest Times to the Present Day* (Dublin: Talbot Press, n.d. [1934]) 226.   2 Ibid. 227.   3 Ibid. 227, 226.   4 See, for example, Terence Brown, *Ireland: A Social and Cultural History, 1922-1985*, 2nd edn. (London: Fontana,

or 'effective laureate' of de Valera's Ireland, and his work has become almost shorthand for an intolerant and provincial mode of defining the indices of national identity.[5] This reduction of Corkery to the level of type has been contested in recent years, most notably by Patrick Maume's critical biography of 1993, where a fuller account of this polemical figure was provided. Subsequent reappraisals of Corkery's significance have largely been effected through a postcolonial lens, with Declan Kiberd, for instance, placing Corkery alongside the Gikuyu critic Ngugi wa Thiong'o, and Conor Carville also drawing upon contemporary postcolonial theories in order to trace the conflicting narratives of 'pedagogy' and 'performance' which are often in evidence in Corkery's work.[6] I propose to read Corkery from within this critical context, and to consider especially whether he might be thought of as an example of a theoretically 'minor' writer.[7] Whilst reading Corkery as minor, however, I also hope to trace some of the ways in which Corkery speaks the rhetoric of majority desire. For Corkery was concerned with the formulation and defence of many of those traits and characteristics which were to dominate cultural life in de Valera's Ireland. In the course of this paper, therefore, I hope to consider whether Corkery might be read as an embodiment of the process whereby the minor becomes major.

In their study *Kafka: Toward a Minor Literature*, Gilles Deleuze and Félix Guattari offered the following formulation for marginal expression. For a literature to be considered 'minor', it must comprise a collective and potentially revolutionary set of writings written by a minority in a major or dominant language.[8] According to Deleuze and Guattari, the conditions which enable such expression are threefold: firstly, minor writing has to attempt a 'deterritorialization' of a formative 'major' language; secondly, it has to be charged with a sense of praxis and political immediacy; and thirdly, it has to rest upon a practice of collective enunciation and communal expression. As a corollary, they also suggested that minor writers should work from within the existing parameters of the literary canon in order to intervene in claims for the social cohesion of the dominant discursive system.

By placing minor literature in opposition to the established canonical tradition, Deleuze and Guattari effectively distinguish between it and the literatures written by minority groups in what might be termed 'minor languages'. For

1985) esp. 63-7; see also R.F. Foster, *Modern Ireland, 1600-1972* (London: Allen Lane, 1988) 167-8n. For a particularly virulent recollection, see George Brandon Saul, *Daniel Corkery* (Lewisburg: Bucknell UP, 1973). 5 David Cairns and Shaun Richards, *Writing Ireland: Colonialism, Nationalism and Culture* (Manchester: Manchester UP, 1988) 124 6 Homi Bhabha has suggested that both narratives simultaneously underlie and undermine the most authoritarian nationalist sentiment, and has juxtaposed a pre-given 'pedagogy' or essence with an awareness of the nation as a 'performative' assemblage of multiple identities and disparate referents See Homi K. Bhabha, *The Location of Culture* (London: Routledge, 1994) 145-6. 7 To this effect, I intend to concentrate upon the development of the terms of Corkery's critical triumvirate, and especially upon his articulation of the terms Nationalism and the Land. 8 See Gilles Deleuze and Félix Guattari, *Kafka: Toward a Minor Literature*, trans. Dana Polan (Minneapolis: University of Minnesota P, 1986), esp. Chapter 3: 'What is a Minor Literature?' 16-27.

whereas the latter form of writing might be thought to be concerned with an affirmation of identity politics, the former mode of discourse can be said to be characterized by an implicit and anxious questioning of the terms of collective identification. That is to say, minor writers can be said to be defined by a dislocation or deterritorialization of their surroundings—something which calls the conditions of their collective identity into question. It is for this reason that Deleuze and Guattari note that 'the problem' of minor literature is primarily 'the problem of immigrants, and especially of their children'; it is also for this reason that they suggest that 'the challenge' of minor literature is to make one become 'a nomad and an immigrant and a gypsy in relation to one's own language'.[9] Given Corkery's ambivalent relationship to the canonical traditions of both Irish and English (Corkery was a lifelong enthusiast of the former language who wrote extensively in the latter, and who served as Professor of English at UCC for sixteen years), it seems tempting to explore his work from within this context. Conor Carville, for instance, has claimed that Corkery's work 'constantly becomes minor through its economy of expatriation', where expatriation is taken to relate to both the historical condition of exile as well as the performative process of re-formulating identity within the nation.[10] In so far as Corkery draws attention to the dislocation of any such identity, his project might well be considered deterritorial in scope, and his narrative read (to use a famous phrase) as 'a quaking sod' of authorial instability.[11] What is more, this instability might be heard to resound through the paradigm which Corkery was to propose for national expression. For his critical triumvirate of Nationalism, Religion and the Land was itself adapted from an earlier anthology of Irish writing, *A Treasury of Irish Poetry in the English Tongue*, which was collected by Stopford A. Brooke (an Anglo-Irish rector) and T.W. Rolleston (a former Trinity College scholar).

Corkery confessed as much in the early pages of *The Hidden Ireland* (1924) when he alluded to Brooke's introduction to the 1900 collection which claimed that nationality, religion, and 'what England calls Rebellion' were the 'distinctive elements' of Irish literature.[12] According to Brooke, the influence of nationality and religion were of particular importance in the post-Parnellite years, as Ireland edged ever closer 'towards a national existence' which was to be shaped by cultural and constitutional forces.[13] This was understood to have occurred at the expense of the spirit of rebellion, with Brooke confident in the assertion that 'political poetry' had given way to a literature which 'on the whole ceased to be

9 Ibid. 19   10 Conor Carville, 'Becoming Minor: Daniel Corkery and the Expatriated Nation', *Irish Studies Review* 6: 2 (August 1998) 146.   11 Daniel Corkery, *The Hidden Ireland: A Study of Gaelic Munster in the Eighteenth Century* (Dublin: M.H. Gill & Son, 1924) 120; see also Daniel Corkery, *Synge and Anglo-Irish Literature* (Cork: Cork UP, and London: Longmans, Green & Co., 1931) 14.   12 See Stopford A. Brooke, 'Introduction' to *A Treasury of Irish Poetry in the English Tongue*, ed. Stopford A. Brooke and T.W. Rolleston (London: Smith, Elder & Co., 1900), esp. xix-xxiv; cf. Corkery, *The Hidden Ireland* ix.   13 Brooke, 'Introduction' x.

aggressive against England'.[14] It is quite significant, therefore, that within a few lines of proffering this third element of national expression (whereby a key aspect of 'native' writing, to paraphrase Corkery, was circuitously defined by 'foreign' criticism, or by 'what England calls Rebellion'), Brooke refined his terms of reference to read rebellion as 'the love of one's own land'.[15] For he was thereby able to avoid the presence of an increasingly exclusivist form of Irish cultural politics, and instead identify a modular conception of literary identity which was governed by an English norm—in terms of both the verse it recognized and the framework within which it was read. Such an identity, however, could be found guilty of 'too much cosmo-politan philosophy' by Irish Irish readers such as D.P. Moran.[16]

As numerous critics have noted, the question of cosmopolitanism was 'one of the most contentious issues in the formative years of the Revival' and the early years of Independence.[17] It was often taken to denote any politics which proposed an inter-nationalist perspective, and which promoted commonality at the expense of difference. Any such politics was suspected of eliding rather than contesting the consequences of the imperial venture. Such a charge was made against the Brooke-Rolleston collaboration by D.P. Moran. In a review of their *Treasury* for *The Leader* in December 1900, Moran characterized their work as a 'muddled' exercise brought on by Brooke and Rolleston's liminal position in Irish society. According to Moran, 'the haze of Trinity' surrounded Brooke and Rolleston, and led them to believe in a past which was shared by native and colonialist alike, a past which preceded the originary moment of intervention.[18] Such beliefs in a cosmopolitan pre-conquest tradition were countered by Moran's ruthless critique of historical amnesia, and his determining 'the price of Trinity [as] exile from the Gael—even the Anglo-Gael'.[19] Rolleston's response, and Moran's further reply, underwrote the parameters of this debate, and both articles were published in the pages of *The Leader* in early 1901. In his response to Moran, Rolleston supported Brooke's earlier proposition, and defended a humanist approach to literature which would prioritize the 'vast fund of material common to all humanity' over insular nationalist concerns.[20] Moran's reply expressed regret that Rolleston should choose to 'juggle words' in Brooke's defence, and insisted that any defence of the cosmopolitan should be predetermined by a resuscitation of the representative nation which typified 'one thing or another, Irish or English'.[21] According to Moran, this focus should be given primacy over the 'mongrel school of thought', which was exemplified by the Brooke-Rolleston col-

14 Ibid. xxxiii.   15 Ibid. xxii.   16 D.P. Moran, 'More Muddle', *The Leader* (22 December 1900), rprt. in *The Field Day Anthology of Irish Writing*, 3 vols., ed. Seamus Deane, Andrew Carpenter and Jonathan Williams (Derry: Field Day, 1991) ii, 971.   17 Luke Gibbons, ed., 'Constructing the Canon: Versions of National Identity', in *Field Day Anthology*, ed. Deane et al., ii, 952.   18 Moran, 'More Muddle' 971.   19 Ibid. Moran attempted to prove this rule by acknowledging the exceptional figure of Douglas Hyde.   20 T.W. Rolleston, 'The Brooke-Rolleston Anthology', *The Leader* (5 January 1901), rprt. in *Field Day Anthology*, ed. Deane et al., ii, 973.   21 D.P. Moran, 'Our Reply', *The Leader* (5 January 1901), rprt. in *Field Day Anthology*, ed. Deane et al. ii, 974.

lection, if 'we want to go back to the Gael, [to] the matrix of the Irish nation', for such a recovery was presumed to be never otherwise recoverable 'via mongrel-land'.[22]

Given the vehemence of Moran's critique, it is perhaps surprising to note that Corkery should have adapted Brooke and Rolleston's model to define his principles for national expression. Moreover, such surprise is perhaps exacerbated when one considers that within a few months of the Rolleston-Moran debate, Corkery was himself writing for Moran's paper and attending classes of the Gaelic League.[23] Indeed, his attempts to rework the Brooke-Rolleston 'mould' appear all the more remarkable when one recalls Corkery's attacks on the cosmopolitan, and his condemnation of 'the desire to be assessed and spoken well of by another people'.[24] For Corkery's criticism of an internationalist approach to literature was founded upon an awareness of the need to develop independent critical values, and to establish a critical reading public in the decolonizing state; to achieve this, he re-worked certain aspects of Moran's earlier argument. In his response to Brooke's preface, for instance, Moran had stated that 'one must judge a book from the point of view of the audience it makes a bid for', and had accordingly dismissed Brooke and Rolleston for 'mak[ing] a bid for an English audience' instead of concentrating upon the interests of their native Irish readership.[25] According to Moran this was evidence of the muddle which prescribed the potential for a truly national expression; according to Corkery it exemplified the influence of the Ascendancy, and pointed towards the dangers of imitation and cultural 'topsy-turvydom'.[26] Corkery contrasted this with the behaviour of any 'normal' or non-colonized people, and famously declared that 'the difficulty is not alone a want of native moulds; it is rather the want of a foundation upon which to establish them'.[27] In the process, Corkery described the typical colonialist practice of cultural dislocation, and outlined many of the consequences for the colonized subject. As Corkery noted, its effects were profoundly disorienting, as defining practices and complex value systems were denigrated by imperial favour, and were supplanted by foreign or 'exotic' viewpoints. Corkery adjudged that this legacy of 'flux and uncertainty' had worked against the formulation of a discretely national identity in post-independence Ireland.[28]

From this perspective, Corkery's appropriation of the Brooke-Rolleston model might be read as an example of minor inflection. For there is a sense in which Corkery's rehearsal of Brooke and Rolleston's thesis was dependent upon a certain critical inventiveness, which enabled him to re-fashion their model in accordance with the traditions of Irish cultural nationalism. When Corkery first

22 Ibid. 974, 975.   23 Moran's criticism and Rolleston's reply were published between late December 1900 and early January 1901. Patrick Maume has noted that Corkery's first article for *The Leader* was published later that year, on 14 September, under the pen-name 'Lee'. See Patrick Maume, '*Life that is Exile': Daniel Corkery and the Search for Irish Ireland* (Belfast: Institute of Irish Studies, 1993) 9.   24 Corkery, *Synge and Anglo-Irish Literature* 3.   25 Moran, 'More Muddle' 971.   26 Corkery, *Synge and Anglo-Irish Literature* 39.   27 Ibid. 13, 14.   28 Ibid. 14.

inserted their model into the opening pages of *The Hidden Ireland*, for instance, it was to no more than echo Brooke's earlier account of the three distinctive elements of literary expression ('Nationality, Religion, and "what England calls Rebellion"').[29] However, when Corkery returned to this paradigm in the early pages of *Synge and Anglo-Irish Literature* (1931), it was to re-define these elements in terms of Religion, Irish Nationalism, and the Land. Initially this was attempted without reference to 'the late Rev' Brooke, with the elder scholar only receiving slight mention several pages after his work had already been appropriated.[30] Indeed, when Brooke was finally credited in *Synge*, it was with having defined the already refined paradigm 'of Religion, of Nationality, [and] of the Peasant'.[31] The seldom noted slippage from 'Nationality' to 'Nationalism' might be considered indicative of Corkery's intent to screen the indices of national identity, and to move the argument from resting upon a pedagogical or pre-given state of being to proposing a prescriptive politics for collective belonging. Moreover, the slippage from the circuitously defined state of 'Rebellion' to the material realities of Land ownership might be heard as more than an echo of Brooke's 'love of one's own land'. Rather, it might be understood in relation to the historical shift which underlies Corkery's work, as it was included initially in oppositional anti-colonial papers (much of *The Hidden Ireland* was written before the War of Independence, for instance), only to become the dominant poetics of the Free State. With reference to this slippage, for example, it is worth perhaps remembering that Frantz Fanon singled out desire for the land as 'the most essential value, because the most concrete' ambition of the decolonizing agent.[32] It is also worth recalling the terms of resistance in Joyce's *Portrait of the Artist*, as Stephen explained his desire to enter into exile.[33] Placed within this context, Corkery's adaptation of Brooke's model might be read as a complex response to the changing conditions of Irish politics in the early decades of the twentieth century; it might also be considered an effective instance of minor scholarship, as the dominant structures of canonical expression are rehearsed and revitalized by an act of discursive insurrection. In effect, Corkery can be seen to deterritorialize 'what England calls' the Irish character, and, in the process, to effect a reterritorialization of the national subject.

According to Deleuze and Guattari, the movement towards decolonization initiates or 'accentuates' the process of deterritorialization whilst simultaneously 'invit[ing] all sorts of complex reterritorializations', which can be 'archaic, mythic, or symbolist' in design.[34] This, they suggest, is an implicit 'danger' of decolonizing politics which deterritorialize in order to reterritorialize, and overthrow imperialist discourse

29 Corkery, *The Hidden Ireland* ix.   30 Corkery, *Synge and Anglo-Irish Literature* 22.   31 Ibid.   32 Frantz Fanon, *The Wretched of the Earth*, trans. Constance Farrington (London: Penguin, 1967)   33 Cf. Stephen's insistence that 'I will not serve that in which I no longer believe whether it call itself my home, my fatherland or my church'. James Joyce, *A Portrait of the Artist as a Young Man* (1916; rprt., London: Penguin, 1992) 268.   34 Deleuze and Guattari, *Kafka* 24.

in order to 'remake power and law'.[35] Decolonizing nationalists provide an exemplary instance of this danger, for not only do they define themselves in relation to their desire for reterritorialization, they also aim to repair many of the social and psychological dislocations which were suffered under colonial rule. Moreover, and although their desire has a specific materialist basis (re-ownership of the land), it is nonetheless often expressed in terms which propose a transcendent or essentialist sense of belonging. This desire is often predicated upon the belief in an intrinsic national essence which must be realized in some tangible territorial form—something which has the potential to be both potentially progressive (in so far as it counters imperialist myths of cultural and intellectual inferiority), and readily reactionary (as it re-articulates many of the generic groupings of imperialist discourse).[36]

Deleuze and Guattari explain this desire for reterritorialization by way of 'fatigue' and a 'lack of invention', suggesting that in such instances, minor writers are more concerned with 'the revival of regionalisms' than with formulating alternative modes of self-expression.[37] That is to say, in such settings, those who are marginal or minor pass from a politics of innovation to one of imitation, and subscribe to pre-existent and 'archai[c]' models of communal expression.[38] Implicit within this revival is a general forsaking of the potential of 'becoming minor', with the minor writer (or emergent nationalist) rather being heard to mimic the rhetoric of majority desire, for the act of 'becoming minor' is always necessarily a process (it is always a becoming), and is always at odds with any definitive state of 'national being'.[39] As Abdul JanMohamed and David Lloyd have indicated, '"becoming minor" is not a question of essence ... but a question of position'.[40] The lapse into imitation, then, can be said to betray a literal sense of fatigue, and to promise the revival of certain characteristics and traits which might be deemed modular for national existence. In effect, it permits the establishment of a poetics of official nationalism. As Deleuze has suggested, 'what defines the majority is a model you have to conform to ... A minority on the other hand, has no model, it's a becoming, a process ... When a minority models for itself, it's because it wants to become a majority, and probably has to, to survive or prosper'.[41] It is at the point of fatigue, then, that the minor writer can be seen to simultaneously 'subvert *and* reproduce' the major contents of imperial governance.[42] For it is at the point of reterritorialization, that that the minor writer is empowered with the content to 'remake power and law'

35 Ibid. 86.   36 Cf. David Lloyd, *Nationalism and Minor Literature: James Clarence Mangan and the Emergence of Irish Cultural Nationalism* (Berkeley, Los Angeles and London: University of California P, 1987) x.   37 Deleuze and Guattari, *Kafka*, 24, 33.   38 Ibid. 14, 24.   39 Ibid. 60. I borrow the concept of 'national being' from the title of AE's *The National Being: Some thoughts on an Irish polity* (Dublin and London: Maunsel, 1916).   40 Abdul R. JanMohamed and David Lloyd, 'Introduction: Toward a Theory of Minority Discourse: What Is To Be Done?', in *The Nature and Context of Minority Discourse*, ed. Abdul R. JanMohamed and David Lloyd (New York and Oxford: OUP, 1990) 9.   41 Gilles Deleuze, *Negotiations, 1972-1990*, trans. Martin Joughin (New York: Columbia UP, 1995) 173.   42 Seamus Deane, 'Imperialism/Nationalism', in *Critical Terms for Literary Study*, 2nd edn., ed. Frank Lentricchia and Thomas McLaughlin (Chicago and London: University of Chicago Press, 1995) 356.

in the pages of 'a "great literature" '.[43] It is at this stage that a minor literature is translated into a major discourse.

With this in mind, Corkery's desire to reterritorialize might be read as a supplemental redress to Conor Carville's depiction of Corkery 'becoming minor'. For Corkery was concerned with the recovery of many of those archaisms, regionalisms, and self-invented traditions which Deleuze and Guattari interpret as the signature of the reterritorialized subject. It is perhaps tempting, therefore, to consider O'Faoláin's account of the 'exhaustion' which was suffered by his former mentor as an example of Deleuze and Guattari's account of deterritorial 'fatigue'.[44] Moreover, it is perhaps suggestive to read Seamus Deane's description of the experience of 'monotony', as it relates to criticism on and by Corkery, as an elaboration of Deleuze and Guattari's lament for the minor writer's 'lack of invention'.[45] Corkery's model, then, might be read in terms of imitation rather than simply introversion (as it collapsed into symbolic reterritorializations of the national subject), and his work might be taken as an example of the process whereby an inventive potential becomes swamped by the rhetoric of official nationalism. To this extent, Corkery might rather be remembered as an embodiment of the process whereby the minor becomes major.

An Influential Involvement: Wilde, Yeats and the French Symbolists

NOREEN DOODY, TRINITY COLLEGE, DUBLIN

French symbolist writing made a significant contribution to the creative imagination of both Oscar Wilde and W.B. Yeats. Wilde and Yeats journeyed separately through Symbolist methods, each producing fine poetic and dramatic symbolist work of their own which eventually synthesised in the creative, literary relation Yeats reached with his fellow countryman.

Oscar Wilde's symbolist play, *Salomé*, was staged for the first time in England on 10 and 13 May 1905, and for a second time on 10 and 18 June the following year. Yeats attended both the 1905 and 1906 productions of this play which would have significant implications for his creative work.[1] Indeed, his creative reaction

43 Deleuze and Guattari, *Kafka* 86.   44 Seán O'Faoláin, *Vive Moi!: An Autobiography* (London: Rupert Hart-Davis, 1965) 133. In *Vive Moi!*, for example, O'Faoláin claimed that Corkery's exhaustion was brought on by the political tumult of the early decades of the twentieth century, and 'the dehydrating nature of provincial life' in Cork.   45 Seamus Deane, *Strange Country: Modernity and Nationhood in Irish Writing since 1790* (Oxford: Clarendon, 1997) 157.

NOREEN DOODY
1 The first performance of *Salomé* in London (1905) was given by the New Stage Club at the Bijou

to the performance was immediate. Following the 1905 performance he began a series of radical revisions of his three completed plays: *The Shadowy Waters, On Baile's Strand* and *Deirdre*. Each of these revisions evidence elements and concepts derived from Wilde's *Salomé*. This is especially noticeable in the play, *Deirdre*, which Yeats revised in 1906 and which benefited, therefore, from his having seen both productions of Wilde's play.

Yeats was impressed by the intellectual concepts of *Salomé* and its vital images, among them the dancer and the severed head of the prophet, Iokanaan. Emotionally, Yeats was struck by the sensuality of Wilde's play and the subtle range of emotions registered by Salomé herself. Pragmatically, he admired the construction of the play.[2] Yeats played and experimented with these devices and with the metaphysical and emotional content of Wilde's play converting them, eventually, into key strategies within his own creativity. His use of *Salomé* can be seen in the early plays: *The Shadowy Waters, On Baile's Strand* and *Deirdre* and also in *The Player Queen*. *Salomé* also informs *Four Plays for Dancers*, much of the poetry of the middle period and some of the later period and comes to its fullest outward expression in two late dance plays, *The King of the Great Clock Tower* and *A Full Moon in March*.

Yeats' engagement with *Salomé* goes back some twenty years prior to the performance of Wilde's symbolist play in the Bijou Theatre in 1905 and has as its background Yeats' deep rooted interest in symbolism and French Symbolist writing. In the 1890s, when Wilde was mixing with the chief exponents of the Symbolist Movement in Paris and rivalling their achievements in writing his own symbolist play, Yeats was entering into this new movement and embracing it with all the enthusiasm and excitement of youth.

Symbolism was, as Oscar Wilde put it, 'a new and fascinating disease'.[3] Symbolist art involved the integration of all its constituent elements—movement, colour, lighting, costume, language, music and was somewhat indebted to the idea of total theatre evolved by Richard Wagner, composer and playwright (1813-83). The Symbolists reacted against a materialist culture which was as evident in the nineteenth century theatres of Paris as it was in those of London. The Symbolists aspired to an apprehension of a knowledge beyond the everyday concerns of ordinary life—to reach and show the Infinite through images and to evoke a sense of mystery in juxtaposing finite images with infinite apprehensions. Poet and critic, Arthur Symons defined Symbolism as the expression of 'the unseen by the visible'.[4]

Theatre in Archer Street, Westbourne Grove. *Salomé* was produced at the King's Hall, Covent Garden, London (1906) by the Literary Theatre Society. 2 Letter of 6 May 1906, ed., Ursula Bridge, *W. B. Yeats and T. Sturge Moore: their Correspondence 1901—1913* (London: Routledge and Kegan Paul, 1953) 8-9. 3 Richard Ellmann, 'Discovering Symbolism' *Golden Codgers: Biographic Speculations* (London: OUP, 1973), 105. 4 Arthur Symons, *The Symbolist Movement in Literature* (London: Heinemann, 1899) 4.

Wilde wrote his play, *Salomé*, in French during the winter months of 1891 in Paris. He recalls returning one evening to his lodgings in the Rue des Cappucines from dinner with friends, to whom he had been relating the Biblical story of *Salomé*, and taking up a blank notebook, began to write his play. Wilde continues his colourful account, describing how some hours later he left his writing and went up the street to the Grand Café where he told the leader of the café orchestra, 'I am writing a play about a woman dancing with her bare feet in the blood of a man she has craved for and slain. I want you to play something in harmony with my thoughts.' Wilde was satisfied with the response of the orchestra leader and later told a friend, 'Rigo played such wild and terrible music that those who were there stopped talking and looked at each other with blanched faces. Then I went back and finished *Salomé*.'[5]

Salomé went into rehearsal at the Palace Theatre, London, in 1892, the great French tragedienne, Sarah Bernhardt, in the title role. Towards the end of June the Lord Chamberlain, official licenser of plays, refused to grant a licence to *Salomé* because it contained Biblical material. Despite the angry protestations of Wilde the refusal to allow the play's production remained in place. The matter was the talk of London; the young Yeats and every other artist and writer were aware of it. Articles appeared in journals on both sides of the Channel; Wilde gave interviews in French and English newspapers; he was lampooned in *Punch* for having threatened to take out French citizenship in protest at the treatment of his play.[6] The play was banned on the grounds of its Biblical content but the fact that it was a Symbolist drama may have also influenced the Lord Chamberlain in his assessment of its suitability for English audiences. In 1892, although very little of the actual work of the Symbolist Movement had reached England rumours and stories abounded. The legacy of the Decadence and its association with perverse pleasures clung to the new movement.

Although the Symbolist movement had not found a strong foothold in England there was a keen interest in it among a number of literary people. The Irish writer, George Moore, had written a number of articles on Laforgue, Rimbaud and Verlaine which he collected in his book, *Impressions and Opinions* (1891). Moore would be replaced later by Arthur Symons who became French Symbolism's chief apologist in England. Already in 1889, Symons had published his first piece on the Symbolists—an obituary on the death of Villiers de Lisle Adam for *The Woman's World*, then edited by Oscar Wilde. Symons was a friend of Yeats: both writers were members of *The Rhymers Club*, a society of young poets, many of whose members were ardent supporters of the new Symbolist movement.

Wilde's *Salomé* was published in French in Paris in 1893 to the critical acclaim of the greatest Symbolist writers of the day. Its 'symbolic force', Katharine Worth declares, 'was felt at once in Europe'.[7] Maeterlinck, foremost among the Symbolist

5 Richard Ellmann, *Oscar Wilde* (London: Hamish Hamilton, 1987) 324.   6 Ibid. 352.   7 Katharine Worth, *Oscar Wilde* (London: Macmillan, 1983) 71.

dramatists, recognising the strength of Wilde's play, called it 'mysterious, strange and admirable'; he found it a mesmerising force and claimed to have 'emerged for the third time from this dream whose power I have not yet explained to myself'.[8]

The ultimate source of Wilde's drama was the biblical story of Salomé. The story concentrates on the wife of Herod, Herodias, who in revenge for St. John the Baptist's denunciation of her, has her daughter, Salomé, dance before Herod and secure his promise to behead the prophet. In Wilde's play, Salome, herself, is obsessed with desire for Iokanaan or John the Baptist, and in return for fulfilling Herod's lustful wish and dancing before him, she secures Iokanaan's severed head and consummates her desire in kissing his mouth. Upon which act she is killed at Herod's command. Both Salomé and her mother, Herodias, had been popular images for art since they first appeared in the Bible and they appeared in many works of art in the nineteenth century, including those by Heine, Flaubert, Mallarmé, Laforgue and Arthur Symons.

Stéphane Mallarmé, the French Symbolist poet, on reading Wilde's *Salomé*, accorded him the highest accolade, asserting that of all the images of Salomé, Wilde had 'definitively evoked' her.[9] At the time, Mallarmé himself, was working on a long poem on the Salomé theme, 'Hérodiade'. He never actually finished this epic work but portions of it were published prior to the publication of Wilde's drama and would have encouraged Wilde's creation. Mallarmé's interpretation of the Salomé/Herodias character, however, bears little resemblance to Wilde's complex protagonist. Wilde's *Salomé* is an amalgam of the Bible's innocent daughter and her venal mother, Herodias; she is a character compounded of lethal desire and innocent love. Mallarmé depicts his heroine as cold, chaste and unreflective, while Wilde's Salomé is strong and independent. Wilde asserted that he could not believe in a Salomé 'who is unconscious of what she does'.[10] This treatment of a female character was unusual for the time.

In 1894 the English version of *Salomé* was published and fully illustrated by Aubrey Beardsley's spare, voluptuous black and white drawings. The timing of the publication coincided with the highest moment in Yeats' enthusiasm for the art of symbolism. Yeats had just returned to London from Paris, where he had met the poet, Paul Verlaine, and was filled with exuberance over Villiers de L'Isle Adam's symbolist drama, *Axel*. He was, now, more than ever enthusiastic and sympathetic towards the symbolist method of dramatization. Yeats' mind was in tune with Symbolism—prepared ground in which *Salomé* would eventually flourish. *Axel* had lasted five hours on stage and although Yeats' command of French was poor, he had been enthralled by the performance. His interest was such that before leaving England he had ploughed through the French text of the

8 Richard Ellmann, *Oscar Wilde* 354.   9 Ibid. 354.   10 Christa Satzinger, *The French Influence of Oscar Wilde: Dorian Gray and Salomé* (Salzburg: Salzburg University Studies, 1994), Oscar Wilde to Enrique Gomez Carrillo 196.

play and on his return from France had tried, unsuccessfully, to have it performed.

Yeats was enamoured of its symbolist representations—'the forest castle, the treasure, the lamp that had burned before Solomon'—and its aspiration to transcend the everyday and reach out to some fundamental truth. There was an aura of sacredness about the play. It had totally captivated Yeats' Parisian acquaintances including his host, the magician MacGregor Mathers, while Maud Gonne had accompanied Yeats to the theatre to see the play. Remy de Gourmont, writing at the time, describes the impact which Villiers' play had had on this young generation: 'Villiers de L'Isle Adam has opened the doors of the unknown with a crash, and a generation has gone through them to the Infinite.' Yeats felt this semi-religious power in *Axel*, as though he and his young contemporaries had been initiated into a 'secret Order'. They discussed and examined it in the context of their energetic enquiries into the fundamental questions of life and the nature of being. Yeats recalls—'It was about those things that most occupied my thought and the thought of my friends, for we were perpetually thinking and talking about the value of life.'[11] Although, in later years, Yeats was vaguely embarrassed at the extremity of his youthful feelings for *Axel*, they were heart felt and strongly held in 1894. Yeats was intoxicated by the play and it fixed the place of symbolism forever in his creative imagination.

Wilde's play was in some ways similar to *Axel*. Both plays were sensually erotic and at the same time had the measured movement of ritual. Both achieved the Symbolist aim of an apprehension of the spiritual. The musical element was common to both, although, while *Axel* employed orchestra and choir, *Salomé* coincided more with Mallarmé's Wagnerian aim that word, image and action combine in 'visible music'. Wilde did not, as Verlaine advocated, consider 'la musique avant toute chose',[12] he used it in equal measure with the other elements of his drama, creating a more integrated, balanced composition than Villiers. *Axel* lacked the cohesive force of Wilde's play which achieved, as Katharine Worth believes 'the first triumphant demonstration of the symbolist doctrine of total theatre'.[13]

Salomé successfully presents all of the elements required by symbolist standards. Its major and minor narrative movements suggest a musical composition and this impression is intensified by the recurring leitmotifs, a procedure Wilde followed from Maeterlinck. The colours black, white, silver and red are interlaced through the action and images of *Salomé* are reflected in the moon involving an interplay of lighting, scenery and language. Wilde achieves a notion of the mystical in conveying opposing images of life and death, miracle and mundane,

11 W.B. Yeats, *Preface* to Villiers de l'Isle Adam's *Axel*, transl. by W.P.R. Finberg, 1924, rpt. in M.R. Gaddis, translation of *Axel* (Dublin: Dolmen, 1970) xiii.   12 Arthur Symons, *The Symbolist Movement in Literature* 89, 129.   13 Katharine Worth, *Oscar Wilde* 73.

love and lust, innocence and desire and body and soul. He expresses these concepts through a network of inter-linked images which culminate in the great unifying image of dance. The play succeeds in revealing an intellectual theory and its symbolic metaphysical apprehension and in expressing one, single emotion—the emotion of desire. *Salomé* is a full bodied and passionate play, and because of this had greater appeal for Yeats than many of the French Symbolist works, even those by the foremost of them, Maeterlinck, whom, he felt, tended towards a certain evanescence in his expression of the intangible and insubstantial. The critic, William Archer, writing in the journal, *Black and White* (1893), acknowledges *Salomé's* musical debt to Maeterlinck and compares the work of both dramatists:

> There is far more depth and body in Mr Wilde's work than in Maeterlinck's. His characters are man and woman, not filmy shapes of mists and moonshine. His properties are far more varied, less conventional. His ... palette is infinitely richer. Maeterlinck paints in washes of water colour. Mr Wilde attains the depth and brilliance of oils. *Salomé* has all the qualities of a great historical picture ...[14]

Yeats' view of Maeterlinck was somewhat in line with Archer's appraisal, for he felt his work lacked 'the ceaseless revery about life which we call wisdom'.[15] He found Wilde's play more satisfying and of greater relevance to his idea of the profoundness of art than many of the contemporary symbolist plays. Although, undoubtedly, Wilde's play was variously indebted to some of these. Maeterlinck's *La Princesse Maleine* and Flaubert's *Herodias* and *La Tentation de St Antoine* have been suggested as sources for *Salomé*. There are some similarities but they are incidental; they lack the drama, the concentrated precision and psychological depth of Wilde's play.

Wilde's immediate source of inspiration is said to be Gustave Moreau's series of paintings, in particular, his sensuous rendering of the voluptuous Salomé dancing and the image of her holding the Baptist's head, a look of horror and revulsion on her face. These two pictures do indeed depict both aspects of Wilde's Salomé. Huysmans in *A Rebours* graphically details the image of Moreau's bejewelled Salomé.[16] His erotic depiction captures the sensual appeal of the dancer and its strength as an image. Wilde's ingenuity draws both of these images—the craven and the innocent—into one complex and powerful character. It is this composite mixture and the fundamental wisdom of Wilde's drama which Yeats found so irresistible.

14 William Archer, Review of *Salomé* in *Black and White* (11 March 1893) xiv.   15 Alan Wade, *The Letters of W.B. Yeats* (London: Rupert Hart Davis, 1954) 255.   16 J. K. Huysmans, *Against Nature: a new translation of Á Rebours*. Transl. by Robert Baldick (1959 rpt. London: Penguin, 1973), (*Á Rebours* originally published 1884) 64.

Wilde's protagonist, Salomé, outstrips her rivals in complexity. She is a mixture of desperate longing and determined covetousness. She embodies an advanced concept of proactive female desire and is a vibrant, developing character. This is the type of woman who will fill Yeats' dramatic imagination from the strong willed Deirdre of the 1906 revision and the sexually aware Decima of *The Player Queen* to the austere venality of his later Queen in *A Full Moon in March*.

Wilde goes beyond his precursors. His story of Salomé is grounded in a dynamic and challenging philosophical base and it is this version of *Salomé* which had an enduring and energising effect on Yeats' creative imagination. For while Yeats agreed with Wagner's principal of total theatre, he is dismissive of his notion that a play should appeal primarily to the emotions rather than to the intelligence. He believed that an artist is concerned with all that is profound in life and not in passing trivialities. This is why an artist such as Wilde held his interest while Maeterlinck, for all his style and technique, did not. As J.F. Flannery notes in *Yeats and his Idea of a Theatre* despite their similar aspirations 'Yeats and Wagner were poles apart'. Flannery pinpoints the underlying aim of Yeats' work—'[Yeats] believed that the expression of profound philosophical convictions was of greater importance than simply stirring emotional responses'.[17] He appreciated the cumulative expression of the one emotion in Wilde's play but he was more fatally captivated by the symbolic expression of his philosophical precepts within the climactic scene of the play.

The climax of *Salomé* is reached in the symbolic union of life and death, when Salomé's lips meet those of the dead Iokanaan. That moment reveals the hard core of Wilde's intellect in its symbolist apprehension of transcendence. In this moment Wilde has created a liminal space where life and death meet and he has suspended the known concepts of the temporal and spatial, assembling in this symbolic clearing the most potent forces of existence— sexuality, love, suffering, death, life. This moment has been foreshadowed earlier in the play—'God is in what is evil, even as He is in what is good'.[18] Salomé has lusted for Iokanaan and has had him murdered, in the act of kissing his dead mouth she attains to the mystery of love and gains self realization. Wilde proposes the notion that the spiritual is attained through the carnal and from this fusion the transcendent is realised. At the symbolic moment of cohesion a transcendent knowledge of the complete nature of existence is at least possible and is signified by Salomé's achievement of self-knowledge. These metaphysical concepts of Wilde remained a vibrant, fixed force within Yeats' creative imagination.

During the intervening years between seeing *Axel* and *Salomé*, Yeats' interest in symbolism increased. He shared this interest with his friend, Arthur Symons who

---

17 James Flannery, 'A Dramatist in Search of a Dramatic Form.' *W.B. Yeats and the Idea of a Theatre: the early Abbey Theatre in theory and practice* (New Haven and London: Yale UP, 1976) 108-9.   18 Oscar Wilde, *Salomé* in *Complete Works of Oscar Wilde* (Series: 1948, Collins Classics. Glasgow: Harper Collins, 1994) 594.

between 1895 and 1898 wrote many articles on French writers and eventually collected these pieces in a most influential books of the '90s, *The Symbolist Movement*, (1899). Yeats, familiar with its contents long before its appearance in print, had benefited greatly from Symons' knowledge of European writers.[19] Symons, for his part, draws attention to Yeats' pioneer work in the Symbolist mode in the English language by dedicating his book, *The Symbolist Movement*, to his friend and calling Yeats 'the chief representative of that movement in our country'.[20]

In the same year as Symons published *The Symbolist Movement* (1899), Yeats published his book of poetry, *The Wind Among the Reeds*, much of which was made up of symbolist poetry. Yeats had already published a book of mystical, symbolist stories, *The Secret Rose* (1896), some of which, together with some poems, he had previously contributed to *The Savoy* (1896), an essentially symbolist journal of which Symons was editor. Yeats was absorbed by symbolism and the artistic and philosophical possibilities which it offered. He saw the symbol as the poet's ultimate means of discovery and of empowerment and aimed at constructing a network of personal symbols which he would re-use throughout his work until each symbol acquired the dimensions of convention. Eventually, each symbol would act and interact with one another as though they were deeply encoded words in a new and mystic language system. He hoped that through such a symbolic structure he might access some apprehension of a transcendent knowledge. Yeats, in time, attains his objective and key symbols in his system are those which he first appropriated from *Salomé* in his revisions of *The Shadowy Waters*, *On Baile's Strand* and *Deirdre*—such as the kiss, the gaze and the dance.

These two Irish writers, Oscar Wilde and W.B. Yeats, were inspired by French symbolism and were its foremost exponents in English literature in the 1890's. Wilde's attraction to French symbolism enabled his writing of *Salomé*; Yeats' involvement with French symbolism facilitated his attraction to his countryman's symbolist play, *Salomé*, which would prove to be vitally influential to his own creative work.

'A Terrible Heretic': James Joyce and Catholicism

GARETH JOSEPH DOWNES, ST ANDREWS UNIVERSITY

In this paper I am concerned with exploring the relative absence of any substantial critical appraisal of the powerful, yet ambivalent, position that the Irish Roman Catholic Church occupied, as a material institution, in the social

19 W.B. Yeats, *Autobiographies* (1955; rpt. London: Papermac, 1991) 319, 320.   20 Arthur Symons, 'Prefatory Dedication', *The Symbolist Movement in Literature* v.

formations that have existed in Ireland since the nineteenth century; and the manner in which Irish writers, particularly James Joyce, have discursively engaged with the material and discursive practices of the Irish Church. The absence of a materialist reading of Joyce and Catholicism is a glaring omission in the expanding field of Irish cultural studies. That the Irish Roman Catholic Church has maintained a privileged and influential position within Irish society has never been a matter of any doubt, and it is curious that in recent studies of Irish literature and culture very little account has been given of the Church's hegemony in comparison with the extensive appraisals of the cultural impact of British imperialism and Irish nationalism. For Stephen Daedalus in *Stephen Hero*, 'The Roman not the Sassenach, was … the tyrant of the islanders.'[1] However, it is the unresolved nature of the complex colonial relationship that exists between Britain and Ireland that understandably still commands the greatest critical attention.

I will briefly discuss those recent critical accounts of Joyce which, whether operating within the theoretical paradigms of post-structuralism, deconstruction, French feminism, New Historicism, or postcolonialism, have done so much to construct the current critical consensus that Joyce is a radical and subversive writer whose texts disrupt, destabilize, and reveal the fictive nature of the overly-fixed and seemingly normative discursive and narrative practices of British imperialism, Irish nationalism, and Roman Catholicism. I will also engage in some speculation concerning the relative failure of recent excellent cultural and historicist studies to complement their extensive appraisals of Joyce's engagement with the contemporary discursive and material practices of British imperialism and Irish nationalism, with a similar appraisal of his negotiations with Roman Catholicism. It is still a curiosity that over twenty years since the publication of such ground-breaking studies as Colin MacCabe's work of 1979, *James Joyce and the Revolution of the Word*,[2] critical accounts of Joyce's complex negotiations with the Church of his upbringing and education in his texts, with one or two rare and notable exceptions, are frequently restricted to the relatively pat observation that Joyce reacted vehemently to the discursive and material practices of a reactionary and oppressive Church. And beyond providing an account of the role of the Irish hierarchy in the fall of Parnell, and how the social tensions resulting from that event are dramatised in the famous Christmas dinner episode in *A Portrait*, the position of the Church in Irish society in the post-Parnell period has only warranted a vestigial presence in recent studies.[3] While I believe that the undertaking of a materialist reading of Joyce and Catholicism is both timely and overdue, I would suggest that such an absence is primarily due to the complexities and controversies that have arisen in the attempts to assimilate postcolonial discourse into the critical concerns of Irish cultural studies. A discussion of the Irish Church's hegemony, and its often uneasy and ambivalent relationship with both the

1 James Joyce, *Stephen Hero*, ed. Theodore Spencer (London: Paladin, 1991) 57.   2 Colin MacCabe, *James Joyce and the Revolution of the Word* (London: Macmillan, 1979).

emergent forces of Irish cultural and political nationalism and the dominant forces of the imperial British state, arguably overcomplicates the theoretical paradigms of postcolonialism, and cannot easily be considered in its scrutiny of the binary oppositions at work in the colonial situation.

In *Postnationalist Ireland* Richard Kearney argues that Catholicism, especially after the Famine, did enjoy the profoundly important psychological status of being the formerly proscribed faith of an oppressed people. However, the Irish Church's position as a constituent part of an international ecclesiastical institution that was hierarchically subject to an increasingly ultramontane Vatican, meant that its relationship with the Irish nationalism of the majority of its adherents was frequently equivocal, and on occasion openly hostile. The pivotal role of the Church's position within the Irish social formation meant that it functioned as a highly conservative and pragmatic institution. In the period after the Act of Union the Church was primarily concerned with consolidating its position. It was scrupulous in its protection of the gains it had secured from the British state, specifically in relation to education—by the end of the nineteenth century the Church had won from the state a *de facto* separate Catholic education structure up to university level. And weary of the 'wolves of disbelief',[4] it was vigilant against any profane attempts to widen the secularization of Irish society. Such a position placed the Church in an ambiguous relationship with both the British state and the emergent forces of Irish nationalism. Kearney writes:

> One of the main reasons the Catholic hierarchy was not officially allied to Irish nationalism, during the eighteenth and nineteenth centuries, was because it feared the nationalist-republican ideas being imported into Ireland from the French revolution were anti-Catholic. The fact that these were also anti-British meant, logically, that a tacit alliance of interests bound Maynooth and Westminster together: the Catholic hierarchy actually approved the abolition of the Irish parliament and union with Britain in 1800, while the English government financed the establishment of the Catholic seminary at Maynooth in 1795. After the fall of Parnell and 1916, however, it became clear to the Church that the soul of the Irish nation was up for grabs and that the need for a unifying collective identity for the newly emerging state could best be provided by a form of Catholic nationalism which allowed (in Joyce's words) 'Christ and Caesar go hand in hand'. Indeed, the 1937 Constitution of Dáil Eireann came close, at times to ratifying the equation of Catholic, Gael and Irishman. While this was modified by subsequent amendments, the strong influence of the

3 For an excellent recent account of the role of the Irish hierarchy in Parnell's fall, and Joyce's 'literary Parnellism', see James Fairhall, Chapter 4: 'Growing into History', *James Joyce and the Question of History* (Cambridge: CUP, 1993) 112-60.   4 Joyce, *Stephen Hero* 58.

Catholic Church on matters of state was witnessed as late as the knife edge 1995 referendum on divorce.[5]

Although the consideration of the cultural impact of the Church on Irish society cannot be easily accommodated into the postcolonial paradigms that have come to form such a large proportion of the debates in Irish cultural studies, it is a necessary complication, and one that should be critically engaged with.

If Irish cultural studies is to overcome the allegation Terry Eagleton recently made in *Crazy John and the Bishop*, that the attempt to assimilate postcolonial discourse has contributed to a 'narrowness' of approach within the field (he also bemoans a 'narrowness' of subject), then this very complexity should be embraced and celebrated.[6] While the comparatively recent application of postcolonial theoretical paradigms and models to the study of Irish literature and culture has undoubtedly enlivened debate, and provided a dynamic and divisive context in which historicist studies of Irish writers can take place, there is a risk that those very paradigms can become as overly-fixed and restrictive as the very discursive practices and narrative strategies that they seek to interrogate. I would suggest that an interrogation of the Church's hegemony, and its relation to the hegemonic practices of Irish nationalism and British imperialism, in late-nineteenth and early-twentieth centuries Ireland, would go some way in redressing Eagleton's charge of 'narrowness'.

Although it is hard to imagine a scenario in which Joyce will no longer be a totemic figure in the pantheon of English literary studies, Joycean criticism over the past two decades has been successful in challenging Joyce's canonical status as an apolitical revolutionary prose innovator in a High Modernist context. In *Joyce, Race and Empire*, Vincent J. Cheng has condemned this canonization as an insidious strategic sleight that shifted 'attention away from the manifestly political context and ideological discourse of Joyce's works onto his unarguably potent role and influence in stylistic revolution.'[7] It was a critical redaction that was partly initiated by T. S. Eliot's 1923 review of *Ulysses*, '*Ulysses*, order and myth',[8] and which received consolidation and legitimacy during the post-war period in which the formalistic and unworldly practices of the New and practical criticisms prevailed in the institutions of Anglo-American academia.[9] Indeed, as Declan Kiberd argued in his keynote address to the 16th International James Joyce Symposium in Rome in 1998, for all the huge debt of gratitude that is owed to Richard Ellmann by subsequent generations

5 Richard Kearney, *Postnationalist Ireland: Politics, Culture, Philosophy* (London and New York: Routledge, 1997) 7-8.   6 Terry Eagleton, *Crazy John and the Bishop and Other Essays on Irish Culture* (Cork: University of Cork Press in association with Field Day, 1998) ix.   7 Vincent J. Cheng, *Joyce, Race and Empire* (Cambridge: CUP, 1995) 2.   8 T. S. Eliot, '*Ulysses*, order and myth', *Dial* 75 (November 1923) 480-3.   9 See Eamon Hughes, 'Joyce and Catholicism', *Irish Writer and Religion*, ed. Robert Welch (Gerrards Cross: Colin Smythe, 1992) 117; Vincent J. Cheng, 'Of Canons, Colonies, and Critics: The Ethics and Politics of Postcolonial Joyce Studies', *Re: Joyce: Text: Culture: Politics*, eds. John Brannigan, Geoff Ward, and Julian Wolfreys (London: Macmillan, 1998) 224.

of Joycean and Irish critics for his magisterial biography of Joyce, his reading of his life and work, perhaps more than any other, has contrived to maintain the uneasy consensus that Joyce was an international High Modernist who overcame the debilitating and oppressive circumstances of his upbringing and education in Edwardian Ireland. Trevor L. Williams has noted, in *Reading Joyce Politically*, that materialist and Marxist critics of the same period were also disinclined to view Joyce as a subversive, or political, writer, and *Ulysses* was regarded as no more than the creation of a decadent bourgeois mind.[10] Dominic Manganiello's 1980 study, *Joyce's Politics*, was of considerable significance in challenging the received wisdom that Joyce was an apolitical writer who merely occupied a position of mischievous neutrality.[11] And Seamus Deane's writings on Joyce during the 1980s were extremely influential in provoking research on the specifically Irish context of Joyce's work.[12]

A full account of the significance of the critical interest in Joyce amongst the luminaries of French post-structuralism is beyond the scope of the paper. However, it should be noted that the enthusiastic celebration of Joyce's writings by Jacques Derrida, Jacques Lacan, Hélène Cixous, and Julia Kristeva, in reading Joyce as a proto-deconstructionist writer whose texts frustrate the phallogocentric narrative and discursive strategies of Western high-capitalist social formations, provided a high profile context in which more specifically historicist studies of Joyce could take place. Although the French writer Phillipe Sollers may have brandished a copy of *Finnegans Wake* at the 1975 International James Joyce Symposium in Paris, proclaiming 'Je vous montre une révolution,'[13] without an understanding of the historical conditions of constraint, there can be no real sense of the discursive shock of Joyce's determination to pass beyond the pale of those narrative strategies, whether of Roman Catholicism, British imperialism, or Irish nationalism, which seek to interpellate him as an individual subject.

Over the past decade a number of critics in Ireland, Britain and North America have been instrumental in contextualizing the theoretical assertions made by post-structuralism for Joyce's realization of a radical *écriture*. Again, a full survey of this literature is impossible at this particular juncture, but of the book-length studies that have attempted to scrutinize the assertion that 'Joyce's writings dismantle those traditional ideologies that render us sexed and civil subjects',[14] by a more discriminating, and less theoretically bound, historicism, James Fairhall's *James Joyce and the Question of History*, Emer Nolan's *James Joyce and Nationalism*, and, to a certain extent,

10 See Trevor L. Williams, Chapter 2: 'Joyce from the Left: A Brief History', *Reading Joyce Politically* (Gainesville, Florida: UP of Florida, 1997) 13-55.   11 See Dominic Manganiello, *Joyce's Politics* (London: Routledge and Kegan Paul, 1980).   12 See Seamus Deane, *Celtic Revivals: Essays in Modern Irish Literature* (London: Faber and Faber, 1985); 'Joyce the Irishman', *The Cambridge Companion to James Joyce*, ed. Derek Attridge (Cambridge: CUP, 1990) 31-54.   13 Phillipe Sollers, 'Political Perspectives on Joyce's Work', *Joyce & Paris*, eds. Jacques Aubert and Maria Jolas, vol. 2, 107; cited in Suzette Henke, *James Joyce and the Politics of Desire* (London: Routledge, 1990) 205.   14 Emer Nolan, *James Joyce and Nationalism* (London: Routledge, 1995) xiii.

Vincent J. Cheng's *Joyce, Race and Empire*, all published in the early to mid '90s, have articulated some of the conditions of constraint that Joyce's writings negotiate. Although the focus of their historicist analyses is primarily the nature of British imperialist and Irish nationalist discourse in the Irish social formation prior to partition, Fairhall and Nolan do devote a not insignificant amount of space to the discursive position of the Church, and its often ambivalent relations with the British state, and the emergent forces of Irish nationalism. The necessary strictures of their individual theses dictate that this relationship is only partly considered, and as I suggested earlier, as Nolan and Cheng's studies are, to varying degrees, articulated within the discursive paradigms of postcolonialism, the Irish Church, which can neither be unequivocally identified as an Althusserian Ideological State Apparatus of the British state nor as a legitimating force for the claims of Irish nationalism, is not subjected to similar scrutiny.[15]

In *Joyce and Nationalism*, Nolan argues that although post-structuralist and French feminist readings of Joyce have been indispensable in realizing the politically radical nature of his texts, the historical moment in which that thinking emerged in France complicates its application in other contexts. As she notes, post-structuralism developed as a critique of totalitarian and monolithic systems, and the hegemony enjoyed by the bourgeois high-capitalist social formations of the West, and as such, its analyses of nationalism occurs within the context of the experience and interrogation of European fascism. Nationalism, in this respect, cannot be examined without recourse to the consideration of the formation of notions of essentialist racial and national identity in Romanticism, and the rise of fascism in Europe. Nolan argues that the 'full complexity of nationalism in the political culture of modernity' has not been properly understood, and in her book attempts to read Irish nationalism, and Joyce's relationship with it, in a manner which the more restrictive analyses of nationalism in post-structuralism does not permit.[16] (Nolan does not observe that the rise of fascism in the Irish Free State in the 1930s, in the form of the Eoin O'Duffy's Blue Shirts, was more a result of reactionary Catholic fears of godless Communism than the construction of essentialist notions of Irish identity.) Her awareness of the context in which post-structuralist discourse has been enunciated, and her argument for a more pragmatic and discriminating application of its theoretical paradigms, is instructive. If a post-structuralist analysis of Joyce and Irish nationalism is frustrated by the very conception of nationalism in that discourse, I would suggest that part of the reason for the continued absence of an appraisal of Joyce and contemporary Catholicism is that in contemporary literary and cultural theory there has been very little consideration of the nature and manner of the discursive practices of ecclesiastical institutions in any given social formation, and consequently there has been very few literary studies of a given writer and his or her reaction to such practices.

15 See Louis Althusser, 'Ideology and Ideological State Apparatuses (Notes towards an Investigation)', *Essays on Ideology* (London: Verso, 1984) 1-60.   16 Nolan, *James Joyce and Nationalism* xiii.

In Chapter 5 of *A Portrait of the Artist as a Young Man* Stephen Dedalus is discussing with Cranly his reasons for leaving the Church of his upbringing and education, and for leaving Ireland. Cranly tries to temper the obstinacy of Stephen's reasoning, and says:

> … you need not look upon yourself as driven away if you don not wish to go or as a heretic or an outlaw. There are many good believers who think as you do. Would that surprise you? The church is not the stone building nor even the clergy and their dogmas. It is the whole mass of those born into it.[17]

However, for Joyce, as for Stephen, the Church in Edwardian Dublin was a stone building of the clergy and its dogmas. It was a material institution that was not to be thought away. During the latter part of the nineteenth century the Roman Catholic Church was a formidable social and political force.[18] In the post-Parnell period the dynamism of the Catholic radicalism that had secured Catholic Emancipation, a *de facto* separate Catholic education system, and facilitated the growth of the Church as a powerful material institution, had subsided. The hegemony of the authoritarian Irish Church, which had become increasingly ultramontane in character under the pastorship of Cardinal Paul Cullen, guaranteed the prevalence of a bourgeois Catholic morality that was both repressive and anti-intellectual. The triumph of ultramontanism within the Irish Church was symptomatic of the institutional climate that came to prevail within the Church as a whole under the pontificates of Pius IX, Leo XIII, and Pius X.[19] Contemporary culture was held to be in serious error of the precepts of Mother Church, and the Vatican responded to the pressures of the post-Enlightenment world by cultivating an institutional and philosophical climate of medievalism. With the declaration of papal infallibility in 1870 the Vatican facilitated the creation of a discursive environment within Catholicism that was philosophically and politically deeply conservative, if not reactionary, in nature. And Leo XIII's encyclical *Aeterni Patris* designated a facile scholasticism as the touchstone of Catholic orthodoxy. During the period in which Joyce grew to maturity the *Index of Prohibited Books* was re-established under the guidance of the Holy Office, the successor to the Inquisition, and the Vatican vigorously prosecuted any departure from Catholic orthodoxy with *force majeure*, and such Catholic modernist scholars as the Dubliner George Tyrrell were 'Indexed' and excommunicated as blasphemous and obstinate heretics. I would argue that Joyce's engagement with

17 James Joyce, *A Portrait of the Artist as a Young Man*, ed. Seamus Deane (London: Penguin, 1992) 267.
18 See David W. Miller, *Church, State and Nation in Ireland: 1890–1921* (Dublin: Gill and Macmillan, 1973); Desmond Keenan, *The Catholic Church in Nineteenth-Century Ireland: A Sociological Study* (Dublin: Gill and Macmillan, 1983).   19 See Gabriel Daly, *Transcendence and Immanence: A Study in Catholic Modernism and Integralism* (Oxford: Clarendon, 1980); Lester R. Kurtz, *The Politics of Heresy: The Modernist Crisis in Roman Catholicism* (Berkely and Los Angeles: University of California P, 1986).

Catholicism is of a far greater complexity and of more significance in terms of Joyce's attempt to forge an unfettered Irish consciousness, than his negotiation with the discourse of British imperialism and Irish nationalism; but it cannot be seen at a remove from those other engagements. In *A Portrait* Stephen famously declares to Davin that he will endeavour to fly by the entangling nets of 'nationality, language, religion'.[20] Although recent studies of Joyce's negotiations with the nets of British imperialism and Irish nationalism have made an enormous contribution to the field of Irish studies, there is a pressing need for a study of the entangling nature of that final net, 'religion'.

Delfas, Dorhqk, Nublid, Dalway: The Irish City After Joyce

DESMOND FITZGIBBON, NUI, MAYNOOTH

In a 1924 article in the *Irish Statesman* entitled 'Back to the Provinces', Lennox Robinson calls for greater literary attention to be paid to life outside the capital: 'Everyday a novel is dying in provincial Ireland for need of someone to write it, and it will take the genius of an Eoin MacNeill some centuries hence to recapture, with infinite research, the social life of our generation ... Back to the provinces, must be our cry, back to the country town, to the small shop, the big licensed grocery business, the country doctor, the country priest, the schoolmaster.'[1] While recognizing the aesthetic and socio-historical value of books such as *Ulysses*, George Moore's *Hail and Farewell* and Eimar O'Duffy's *The Wasted Island*, Robinson declares that 'the novel about Dublin has been done to death, we know the formula too well, we know the six distinguished "reel" (*sic*) people who will appear in it, and it no longer amuses us to spot them.' Furthermore, he puts to writers the 'shattering question— "Can you go one better than *Ulysses?*"'[2]

20 Joyce, *A Portrait of the Artist as a Young Man* 220.

DESMOND FITZGIBBON
1 *Irish Statesman* (2 Feb. 1924). Robinson is echoing some of the sentiments expressed by William Boyle in 'Some Types of Irish Character' (*Studies*, 1912: Vol. 1, 221-36). Boyle comments: 'The books of Irish town life are so few and unimportant as scarcely to be noticeable ... What a chance is here for young writers! The funny life of the small towns, the petty conceits and varieties of the twopenny-halfpenny gentry— all countries have the same thing, but ours is somewhat different. When will some writer, some member of this class, arise who is big enough in intelligence to give us this section honestly.' (230) Furthermore, Robinson's call for a literature describing provincial life had been considered by Joyce years earlier—the projected sequel to *Dubliners* was to be called 'Provincials'—but he must have realised that he had already captured the atmosphere of stifling provincialism in the stories of his native city. 2 One feels that this question is also addressed to Joyce himself. *Finnegans Wake*, of course, is much more than an attempt to emulate the portrayal of Dublin he achieved in *Ulysses*.

A reply came the following week (9 February 1924) from one Rosamond Jacob ('F. Winthorp') who describes him(her?)self as 'a passionate reader and secret writer of novels.' Jacob disparages Robinson's views on the redundancy of the novel about Dublin (and by implication, all cities), and also criticizes the arcane methods employed by modernist writers such as Joyce: 'it is a truism to say that thousands of novels could be written about Dublin people, if only their authors could get sufficiently interested in their subjects to lose sight of their own cleverness.' The comments of Robinson and Jacob raise many questions, most notably the status of *Ulysses* as the apotheosis of urban fiction, and the 'sense of belatedness'[3] Joyce may have instilled in those who came after him. This paper will consider these questions, and hopes to show that later Irish exponents of urban fiction have either largely ignored (or deliberately eschewed) the rhetorical strategies employed by Joyce, and have wisely embraced the interventionist rather than the inventive aspect of his legacy. This is largely because, regardless of the content of his last two novels, his very methods seem insuperable.

But this, of course, wasn't always the case. For example, *Dubliners*, despite its formal brilliance, offers us little that had not been done before. Here, the city appears to be highly legible but makes for uncomfortable (and, at times, familiar) reading: its citizens are 'paralysed' and seem almost like the Liffeyside equivalent of characters from Russian fiction. And yet, with the publication of *Ulysses* in 1922, we see that Joyce has produced a very different world, one that is largely benign and notable for its complex dynamism.

It is clear that the path from the 'scrupulous meanness' of *Dubliners* to the near rhapsody of *Ulysses* led through the solipsism of *A Portrait* and *Exiles*. But more importantly, and despite his admission to being ignorant of the plastic arts, Joyce had taken note of the revolution in spatial aesthetics pioneered by Cubist painters like Picasso who overthrew the tyranny of Renaissance perspectivism, and Futurists like Marinetti and Balla who emphasized dynamism and simultaneity in all art forms. Combining this with Freudian psychology, a vague understanding of Einstein's Theory of Relativity and using the resuscitated hyper-associative narrative method of Dujardin, Joyce was able to overturn the subordination of space to time, and replace the nightmare of history with the dream of geography. In other words, he recognized that the city's primary characteristic is its malleability, that its 'concreteness' belies its plasticity.

Such a conception of the urban form called for a radical synthesis of the traditional rhetorical strategies employed by writers to describe place. These include (re)naming, parallelism[4], mutation and layering, all of which are used by Joyce in

3 Harold Bloom's term, as used in *The Anxiety of Influence* (1973).   4 This is one of the more common strategies used by writers. Joyce, of course, compared Dublin to the every other city, and ultimately the universe; Albert Recht in his *Handbook to a Hypothetical City* (1986) sees Belfast as an Asiatic pile populated by a Mongol majority and a Tartar minority; John Hewitt, however, prefers the nineteenth century tag 'the Athens of the North' but acknowledges the limitations of analogy in general in his poem

Ulysses and *Finnegans Wake* as he goes about his alchemical programme of transforming the base substance of the city. Let me clarify what I mean by the base substance of the city. It can be described as such on two levels: firstly as raw subject matter for the artist to manipulate, and secondly (and more important still), as a man-made geography that has been depicted in largely negative terms throughout the ages.[5]

Joyce engages in the 'city versus country' debate more fully in *Finnegans Wake*[6] but I'll restrict my analysis to specific examples of how his spatial aesthetic develops into an openly interventionist spatial politics. The most obvious interventions by Joyce are presented in the contrasting town-planning escapades of Leopold Bloom in *Ulysses*, which can be read as parodic articulations of the municipal reform debates that were so prevalent in Dublin (indeed, throughout the world) in the first decades of the twentieth century. The forums for these debates ranged from innumerable housing conferences to model city exhibitions where two main options were presented for public consideration—that of the communitarian Garden City Movement as advocated by Ebenezer Howard and Patrick Geddes, and the more radical modernist alternative proposed by architects such as Le Corbusier and Adolf Loos. Joyce presents both options in *Ulysses*. For example, in 'Circe', the *fiat* city, the 'Let-it-be' city of Bloomusalem, is a 40,000-room monstrosity, and architecturally may be said to comment on the work of utopian planners such as Le Corbusier, who, incidentally, felt that the method of *Ulysses* related to the principles of his own work. Bloomusalem, itself, is clearly the absurd product of a monumental ego,[7] and parodies the New Jerusalem, which Blake said, should be built in 'England's green and pleasant land.' That Joyce should have Bloom announce the construction of a 'golden city' in Dublin's 'red-light' district is more than a deliberate act of profanity. It brilliantly encapsulates what has been seen as the contradiction at the heart of all cities: namely, and put simply, that they bring out the best and the worst in man.

The second reference to contemporary town-planning debate is in 'Ithaca', where Bloom—individualistic to a fault—rejects the communitarian *Rus in Urbe* solution of the Garden City. In this, he accords with Le Corbusier who, despite an initial dalliance with notions of 'rurban' living, eventually came to think that

'Parallels Never Meet.' He describes how 'allegorising the actions and the actors / finding Peloponnesian parallels' for life in his native province is an absurd and reductive exercise because the actors ultimately 'trip and flounder in their togas', *The Collected Poems of John Hewitt* (Belfast: Blackstaff, 1991) 139.   5 An in-depth treatment of the perennial dispute between the urban and the pastoral environment is beyond the scope of this paper, but suffice to say it all started when someone pointed out that there was no architecture in Eden and that the first city mentioned in the Bible (Enoch) was built by a murderer, namely Cain.   6 For example, the city, as personified in HCE, is described as a 'cumberer of the Lord's Holy Ground' and a 'hoary hairy hoax'. ALP, who represents the natural environment, is described in more positive terms throughout, *Finnegans Wake* (1939; London: Faber, 1975) 70.   7 It is fitting that Tim Harrington, renowned flunkey and thrice lord mayor of Dublin (1901-3), is one of many luminaries who pay homage to Bloom in Nighttown, and witness the construction of the new Bloomusalem. He had chaired a conference on Dublin housing just months before, but nowhere in his report does he suggest building a colossal edifice in the shape of a pork kidney.

there was no point in sending people out into 'fields to scrabble earth around a lot of hypothetical onions.'[8] Instead, Bloom Cottage, Saint Leopold's, Flowerville, will be a 'thatched bungalowshaped 2 storey dwellinghouse of southerly aspect ... Standing in five or six acres of its own ground ... [and] not less than one statute mile from the periphery of the metropolis'.[9]

In *Finnegans Wake*, Joyce continues his engagement with civic reform, satirizing the work of philanthropists and de Valera's government that relied on the success of the Sweepstake lottery to fund its social programme. In chapter fourteen, Jaun addresses Issy, telling her that they should 'circumcivicise all Dublin country ... clean out the hogshole and generally ginger things up'.[10]

The inventive and interventionist aspects of Joyce's spatial politics I have outlined briefly have served variously as a touchstone, whetstone and millstone for later writers. For the remainder of this paper, I wish to consider the extent of Joyce's influence on successive generations of Irish writers who concern themselves with the city-form. The situation is complicated because it is hard to describe Joyce as the leader of any clearly defined school of Irish writing. If one takes Zola's Naturalists, the early Revivalists, the American 'Beats', each had their agenda and discernible curricula for acolytes to follow; but Joyce, if considered as a teacher, would appear to many to use the pedagogic approach of an inspired (and inspiring) madman. Rather than ascribing a school or movement to him, it would be more appropriate to say he encouraged a certain 'tendency', elusive and insufficient as that term may seem.

Furthermore, there is the question of to what extent Dublin serves as a template for subsequent urban fiction. This is not so problematic if one accepts that all cities are fundamentally unique. Dublin is *not* the urban equivalent of Arcadia, to be regarded as a frozen archetype upon which to etch one's story. Rather it is one of many urban patterns passed down to us through history and even being created in our own time. They range from the Celestial City to the original twinned-towns of Sodom and Gomorrah, from imperial Rome to Milton Keynes, from the magical cities of the Tuatha de Danann to the ecclesiastical city of Glendalough, from Babylon to Belfast. All are capable of inspiring the writer's imagination. Each calls for its own treatment. Every writer has his own problem to solve and should, if he is honest, allow Dublin to be factored into the equation *to some degree*, for no other reason than that Joyce made sense of city-life in ways that had never before been imagined, let alone achieved.[11]

---

8 Cited in John Rennie Short, *Imagined Country: Society, Culture and Environment* (London: Routledge, 1991) 88.   9 *Ulysses* (1922; Paris: Annotated Student's Edition, ed. Declan Kiberd, Penguin, 1992) 837-8.   10 *Finnegans Wake* 446-7.   11 The corollary of this suggests that just as Robert McLiam Wilson's Belfast wouldn't exist without Joyce's Dublin, Joyce's Dublin, in turn, wouldn't exist without the Paris of Zola and Baudelaire, and to a lesser extent Dostoevsky's Saint Petersburg. Works of a pastoral nature do not have this co-dependency, this cumulative debt, existing as they do in direct relation to the Arcadian prototype, which admittedly, is the terrestrial version of the primordial landscape of Eden.

If one takes *Ulysses* to be the most rounded embodiment of Joyce's spatial aesthetic, it is clear that the first generation of Free State writers paid little attention to it. Sean O'Faolain, writing in 1947, said that Joyce 'came at a bad time.' (Here O'Faolain is referring to the revolutionary period 1916-23.) He continues by saying that 'By the time Joyce was being widely read by the 1920-50 generation—read, that is, in the full sense of reading and rereading him, mentally digesting him, retailing favourite bits of his works, delighting in his ruthless veracity, his sub-surface humour, his incomparable command of words, his bird-like eye, his unforgettably graphic phrases, we were already set.' Although O'Faolain and Frank O'Connor did write about their native Cork City, their novels are technically very conventional, being more reminiscent of nineteenth-century realist fiction than the high modernism of Joyce.[13]

Another of this post-'22 generation, the Aran Islander, Liam O'Flaherty, might be seen as the most immediate successor to Joyce, but O'Flaherty's Dublin 'thrillers' such as *The Informer* (1925) and *The Puritan* (1932) show no evidence of Joyce's spatial alchemy. The respective approaches of these two writers towards analyzing the urban form could not be more different. Joyce was something of 'a meticulous little filing clerk' (to use Francis Stuart's description), but O'Flaherty refused to sift through the minutiae of city-life. He once wrote: 'It is no use showing me the city in detail and giving me figures and facts. I could see nothing and learn nothing. I learn merely by intuition. I feel essences. I do not see surfaces. I comprehend the whole, in my own manner, for my own purpose, without knowing the composition of the various parts.'[14]

O'Flaherty certainly visited more cities than Joyce, but he basically despised them all, with the possible exception of London. Whereas Joyce could refer to Paris as 'a lamp for lovers in the wood of the world',[15] Paris, for O'Flaherty is a 'shameless brothel, where a human soul was almost as cheap as a beefsteak'.[16] Leningrad is 'a stinking tomb inhabited by feckless idiots.'[17] Boston is 'a sewer' which absorbed 'the dregs of all the cheap intellectual patter of the whole world. [It is] neither American nor European, but a frowsey old hermaphrodite, still wearing its bloomers down to the heel in the manner of the nineteenth century'.[18] Dublin, rather generously, is 'that city of improvident scholars'.[19] It is not surprising that he goes on to say that 'City men are not of my fibre'.[20]

All of the protagonists in O'Flaherty's thrillers are originally from a rural background and feel deracinated in the urban environment. The same could be said

---

12 Sean O'Faolain, *The Irish* (1947; London: Pelican revised ed., 1969) 139-41.   13 O'Faolain's *A Nest of Simple Folk* (1934) and *Bird Alone* (1936); O'Connor's *The Saint and Mary Kate* (1932) and *Dutch Interior* (1940).   14 *I Went to Russia* (London: Jonathan Cape, 1931) 134.   15 Quoted in Ellmann 126, and Gorman 135.   16 *I Went to Russia*, 298.   17 Ibid. 177.   18 Ibid. 309.   19 *Two Years*, 204.   20 Ibid. 247. This might imply an almost Yeatsian deification of the peasant on O'Flaherty's part, but the Irish peasant, according to him was, among other things, 'part of the national debt' (*A Tourist's Guide to Ireland* (1929; Dublin: Wolfhound, 1998) 73.

about the characters in the urban novels of Michael McLaverty. For example, in *Call My Brother Back* (1939), he describes the migration of a family from Rathlin Island to Belfast. We are conscious throughout that they replace one set of problems with another. The O'Neill family exchanges a relatively peaceful subsistence agricultural life for one that offers them poorly paid jobs and embroilment in political upheaval. Neither Colm, the protagonist, nor his brother Alec (who is eventually murdered because of his involvement in the IRA), is ever satisfied with his new life in Belfast. In this and subsequent works, McLaverty comes across as a traditional pastoral moralist who finds little of true value in urban life.

A disenchantment of a different order is evident in Brian Moore's Belfast novels such as *The Lonely Passion of Judith Hearne* (1955) and *The Feast of Lupercal* (1957). Of all the novels I've mentioned so far in this section, they are the most Joycean, but their spatial aesthetic owes more to the paralysed city of *Dubliners* than the liberational qualities of *Ulysses* and *Finnegans Wake*. Mid-twentieth century Belfast for Moore is just as pulverizing as Dublin was for Joyce at the turn of the century.

More recent treatments of Belfast have dealt with the dynamics of the city itself rather than in terms of the urban-pastoral dialectic. In novels such as Robert McLiam Wilson's *Eureka Street* (1996) (and particularly in the poetry and prose of Ciaran Carson), we see, among other things, rhapsodic descriptions of the urban form that are reminiscent of passages from Joyce. But that which is most interesting about this work (and novels such as Eoin McNamee's *Resurrection Man* (1994)), is the extent to which it engages with identitarian discourse, with the city being seen as the setting where dramas of inclusion and exclusion are played out. More than in any other city in Ireland, identifying with place in Belfast is complicated by issues related to territoriality and (self-) segregation. To etherealize the city, to aestheticize space, is difficult when that space is so heavily politicized already. Peace-lines, wall-murals and bunting act as obvious markers of political and cultural difference, but the street names (for example, Balaclava, Kashmir and Odessa etc.) are part a double-edged imperial dinnseanchas[21] which manages to integrate and alienate at the same time, depending on the cultural and political allegiance of the individual interacting with his environment. Stripped of their historical resonance, such place names add exotic, if incongruous, texture to a city's narrative, but properly con-textualized, they act as a source of commemorative pride for some, and inscribed reminders of a colonized status for others.

If one considers how the urban form in Ireland has been appropriated and utilized by colonial forces throughout the ages, it is hardly surprising that Irish writers (especially Northern Irish writers from the minority community) have faced the distinctive challenge of negotiating a familiar, yet duplicitous, land-

---

21 Just as in the Gaelic dinnseanchas tradition, the denominating and distinguishing of places by topographical indicators and attendant narratives constitutes an attempt to establish discursive control over space.

scape. Large sections of the *Wake* can be read as detailed explorations of this very issue, with Joyce's favoured rhetorical strategy being his toponymic and auditory imagination. The transformation of Dublin into Delfas, Dorhqk, Nublid and Dalway (to name but four of the city's many renderings) can be read as a playful musing on the capital's quality as pure vocable, but more pointedly, should be seen as an investigation of its semantic potential.

Which leads me onto my final point: the need to re-define what we mean by the city itself. Since Joyce's time, the general trend throughout most cities in Ireland has been one of mass suburbanization, with the urban core coming to be increasingly dominated by corporate and retail concerns. Amidst all of the cries of outrage at the breaking up of inner-city communities and the despoliation of the countryside by low-density sprawl,[22] one cry, 'the city is dead, long live the city!', has rarely been heard. If, like Dickens, we believe that a city is its people, then the fact that most Irish urbanites are now suburbanites means that we have to broaden our definition of what we mean by a city. But suburbia and its inhabitants have long been denigrated and/or misunderstood.[23] Surely, the significance of the suburbs lies not in their architectural, commercial or cultural aspects, but in the basic reality that the majority of the (once) urban population now lives there. This displacement of the urban population has been mirrored by a displacement of the urban aesthetic to the suburbs, which has had important implications for writers who may have otherwise been burdened with a 'sense of belatedness' by following in the wake of Joyce. One feels that the work of Roddy Doyle, Dermot Bolger and Joseph O'Connor offers convincing proof that Dublin at least is no longer haunted by the spectre of a Jew canvassing for ads, or the dreams of a Chapelizod publican.

22 The interventionist aspect of Joyce's legacy can be seen in the emphatic but often crude civic polemic expressed in the novels and poetry of the 'Finglas Realists'. Novels such as Dermot Bolger's *Night Shift* (1985), *The Woman's Daughter* (1987) and *The Journey Home* (1990), and poetry such as Michael O'Loughlin's *Stalingrad:The Street Dictionary* (1980) can be read as a collective indictment of the detrimental policies of successive governments that have condemned people to live in badly planned and often poorly serviced suburbs. This, of course, is not solely a Dublin phenomenon. The protagonist in Northern writer, Anne Devlin's short story, 'Naming the Names', goes so far as to say that where the bombers left off in Belfast, the planners carried on, with redevelopment being akin to the annihilation of communities. This view—that Belfast is falling down with every new building that goes up—gives a disturbing twist to the catchphrase 'Belfast is Buzzing' which resounds (only somewhat ironically) throughout Glenn Patterson's novel *Fat Lad* (1992).   23 The urban historian, Lewis Mumford, refers to suburbs as being 'anti-city'; Humphrey Carver in *Cities in the Suburbs* (1962) deliberates upon what is often depicted as "darkest suburbia and its lasting symbol, the lawn-mower" (p.18); George and Weedon Grossmith's *Diary of a Nobody* (1892), and novels such as H.G. Wells' *Tono Bungay* (1909) and *The New Machiavelli* (1911) stand out as early examples of fiction which satirizes the suburban dweller and his concerns.

French Spectacles in an Irish Case:*
From 'Lettres sur l'Irlande' to Parnell and His Island

BRENDAN FLEMING, ST CATHERINE'S COLLEGE, OXFORD

George Moore's *Parnell and His Island* began as a series of newspaper articles on Ireland published in *Le Figaro* in 1886.[1] It is one of a significant number of translated French newspaper articles on the Irish Question which appeared during the 1880s.[2] *Parnell and His Island* is significant as the first major engagement with the figure of Parnell, and the phenomenon of Parnellism, by an Irish writer prior to Parnell's death and subsequent mythologization.[3] Through its anxious and ambivalent portrayal of Parnellism, it is a critical exploration of the implications of that movement for Ireland. In particular, those anxieties and ambivalences emerge from the fact that *Parnell and His Island* is one of the most explicit representations of the cultural contradictions of Irish landlordism written from within that system. It is the ruptures at the limits of that representation which constitutes it as an important text in the foundation of Irish modernism.

The text is defined by contradiction: its naturalist representation of contemporary Irish conditions simultaneously seeks to repress and expel those very conditions from its representation. The effect of this repression is to problematize and fragment the naturalist representation. This repression is symbolized in the figure of Parnell. He is strangely absent from this text bearing his name; haunting its margins, he is present through his effects. *Parnell and His Island* is riven by anxiety, written by a Catholic landlord chronicling the imminent extinction of his class. Far from signifying mere aesthetic infelicities or shortcomings, such contradictions reveal a crucial moment in the history of the figurative and political representation of Ireland.

For Malcolm Brown, the dissonances created by these divergent perspectives produce a 'schizophrenic' text.[4] He asserts that it contains, 'the most original language ever penned by an unreconstructed landlord on the agrarian question.'[5] He argues that Moore's writings on Ireland, 'in the 1880's showed him to be, in short,

* The title of this article is adapted from G. De Molinari, *French Spectacles in an Irish Case: Letters on the State of Ireland*, trans. L. Colthurst (Dublin: Hodges Figgis; London: William Ridgway, 1880); this essay was presented in paper form to the George Moore Society in 1999.   1 George Moore, 'Lettres sur l'Irlande,' *Le Figaro*, 31 July, 7, 14, 21, 28 August, and 4 September 1886. These were then published, with additional material, as *Terre d'Irlande*, trans. M.F. Rabbe (Paris: Charpentier, 1887). This appeared, with some emendations, as *Parnell and His Island* (London: Swan Sonnenschein, Lowrey, 1887). For full details see Edwin Gilcher, *A Bibliography of George Moore* (Illinois: Northern Illinois UP, 1970).   2 See, Baron E. De Mandat-Grancey, *Paddy at Home*, trans. A.P. Morton (London: Chapman and Hall, 1887); H. Saint Thomas, *Paddy's Dream and John Bull's Nightmare: Notes on Ireland*, trans. Emile Hatzfeld (London: George Vickers, [1886]).   3 For a detailed assessment of such representations, see John Kelly, 'Parnell in Irish Literature', *Parnell in Perspective*. ed. D. George Boyce and Alan O'Day (London: Routledge, 1991) 242-83.   4 Malcolm Brown, *George Moore: A Reconsideration* (Seattle: U of Washington P, 1955) 26.   5 Ibid. 19.

confronted by a hopeless intellectual and emotional impasse. This fact he recognized, and, with his characteristic bland shamelessness, he called his readers' attention to his confusion.'[6]

I contend that such a reading is only partially accurate. The text's 'failure', its 'schizophrenic' quality, is symptomatic of the failure of the naturalist project to represent and contain 'Ireland' within its aesthetic framework. One crucial source of these contradictions is the way in which the text's deterministic naturalism is subverted by the inherent lability and errancy of the translation process.

The translation of *Parnell and His Island* from original French articles inaugurates a strategy of representation that was to become crucial for Moore's critique of the Revival. There, the evolution of the English versions of the stories in *An T-Úr Gort* into *The Untilled Field* similarly exaggerates the recursive strategy by initiating a spiral of translations which are then re-translated.[7] This process de-stabilizes each version's autonomy and reverses conventional notions of hierarchy in the translation process. No longer does the original text have priority over its translation, as the strategy used by Moore subverts any notion of origin. The reappearance of the 'text' through a series of recursive translations, each of which subverts the former, is analogous to Moore's continual self-invention. The text's errancy and homelessness eloquently underline its author's provisional sense of identity. Moore's complicated construction of *The Untilled Field* overdetermines this translational procedure and foregrounds its own hybridity. Through the translation of *The Untilled Field*, Moore implicitly presents a critique which problematizes Revivalist assumptions concerning authorship, translation, and originality. The seeds of this strategy are to be found in *Parnell and His Island*.

Incensed at the censorship of *A Drama in Muslin*, Moore decided on a radical response: he would, in future, publish solely in French. He announced:

> In the face of such opposition it would be useless for me to continue as an English writer. Happily there is no reason why I should; I am nearly as well known in France as in England; I have an admirable translator, as a glance at the series of articles I began last Saturday in the *Figaro* will show ... I will publish my next book in French.[8]

For Moore, to be published in French was not just a pragmatic response to English literary censorship: it also signified the degree to which the problematics and possibilities of literary and cultural translation were vital to his wider critique of personal and national identities. In *Parnell and His Island*, the lability inherent in the translation process are implicitly placed in tension with the deterministic assumptions of naturalism.

6 Ibid. 19.   7 For a detailed discussion of the genesis of *The Untilled Field* see, John Cronin, 'George Moore: The Untilled Field,' *The Irish Short Story*, ed. Patrick Rafroidi and Terence Brown (Lille: Université de Lille, 1979) 113-25.   8 George Moore, letter, *The Times* (12 August 1886) 10.

In 1879, while Moore was endeavouring to pursue a career as a painter in Paris, he received a letter from Joe Blake, the agent of his estate in Mayo, announcing that the tenants were refusing to pay rent. Moore had to abandon his Parisian apprenticeship and return to Ireland. This summons had a profound effect on Moore's subsequent relationship with Ireland. The shadow of that letter from Mayo to Paris hangs over Moore's 'Lettres sur l'Irlande', written as it were in reply, from Paris to Mayo.

Parnell and His Island comprises a series of naturalistic portraits of contemporary Irish life narrated by an absentee landlord who is clearly a version of Moore himself. Moore's dissection of Irish society deploys the disposition of the clinician and the language of physiology. The naturalist strategies of clinical dissection, the nomination of cultural phenomena as pathological, and the author as scientific observer are crucial components of *Parnell and His Island*.

An unsigned review in the *Daily Telegraph* described *Terre d'Irlande* thus:

> [*Terre d'Irlande* places] before French readers the most typical and characteristic aspects of a primitive country and a barbarous people ... [The author] has not only drawn his types with graphic power, but he has rendered them in the realistic manner adopted by painters who depict on canvas whatever comes within the range of their eyes, from a chimney pot to the shoulders of a duchess. He has studied Flaubert and Zola to advantage, and the result is that French readers will now have the Irishman set before them with all his worst qualities depicted in a manner that recalls the hand which drew Emma Bovary, or the dissecting-room method of the popular novelist who sketched the career of the depraved Nana.[9]

Unsurprisingly, Moore's letters in *Le Figaro* drew a hostile response within Ireland. The *Freeman's Journal* characterized them as a series of 'extravagant caricatures'.[10]

Parnell and His Island records a journey from Dublin to Mayo, from urban to rural space, from East to West. The West becomes, for Moore's narrator, a nightmarish evocation of the annihilation of the landlord class, a confrontation with death. These crises are nominated as peripheral experiences, both geographically and psychically. In *Parnell and His Island*, the West is the site of a dystopia. This subversion of an idealized West anticipates Joyce's critique in 'The Dead.' Both problematize the Revivalist topos of the redemptive Western periphery and represent it as a deathly hinterland.

Parnell and His Island opens with the narrator surveying Dublin from a hill at Dalkey. He describes the panorama below:

9 'Paris Day by Day,' *Daily Telegraph* (14 February 1887) 5.

> From where I stand I look down upon the sea as on a cup of blue water; it lies two hundred feet below me like a great smooth mirror; it lies beneath the blue sky as calm, as mysteriously still, as an enchanted glass in which we may read the secrets of the future ... In the exquisite clarity of the day every detail is visible.[11]

A key naturalist strategy in the figuration of Ireland is revealed here: the narrator is empowered as an omniscient observer. Nothing is to be hidden from his penetrating gaze. In an image that will become crucial to the naturalist dynamic in the text, the bay is presented as a mirror enabling perfect reflection of the present condition of Ireland and prediction of the country's future. It represents a model of the naturalist text, which has the apparent potential to provide unmediated access to the realities of the Irish experience. *Parnell and His Island* promises to be just such a perfect reflection of Ireland. Having the veracity and authenticity of a mirror, it aspires to unproblematic, unmediated, and transparent reflection of the literal and figurative landscape of Ireland. For the narrator, the exquisite clarity of the perspective finds a parallel in the economic relations of the country. Thus the naturalist exposition in *Parnell and His Island* is to be the means of revealing the exploitative and brutal economic relations pervading Irish society. The extent to which such clarity is simultaneously inaugurated and repressed is a crucial structural dynamic of the text. As the narrator's gaze traverses the scene below he focuses on one particular scene: that between an impoverished landlord and his financially dependent daughter. The narrator remarks:

> Finally he [the landlord] draws from his pocket a roll of bank-notes black and greasy, notes with worn-out edges, notes cut in two and stuck together, notes which smell of the cabin, notes that are rancid of the sweat of the fields, notes which have been spat upon at fairs for good luck, notes which are an epitome of the sufferings of the peasant in the west of Ireland ... I read in all this, as in an epitaph upon a tomb, the history of a vanished civilization.[12]

These disfigured and riven banknotes are a material sign of the history of contemporary Ireland. As such they are indicative of the status the narrator wishes to attribute to his text. They serve as a material emblem of Moore's text, and this emphatic materiality confirms the naturalist authenticity of Moore's representation. A blurring occurs between the idea of the notes as metaphor for the book and that of their being symbolic of the transaction between landlord and tenant. They signify a metaphoric imbrication between Moore's roles as author and as landlord.[13] The narrator proceeds to detail the degree to which the landlord class exploits the tenantry. He declares:

10 *Freeman's Journal* (21 August 1886) 4-5. 11 Moore, *Parnell and His Island* 1. 12 Ibid. 9. 13 See Adrian Frazier, *George Moore, 1852-1933* (New Haven and London: Yale UP, 2000) 67-94, and Wayne Hall,

For in Ireland there is nothing but the land ... there is no way in Ireland of getting money except through the peasant ... I am an Irish landlord, I have done this, I do this, and I shall continue to do this, for it is as impossible for me as for the rest of my class to do otherwise; but that doesn't prevent me from recognising the fact that it is a worn-out system, no longer possible in the nineteenth century, and one whose end is nigh.[14]

This declaration highlights the ambivalence of the position of the narrator, and by implication, that of Moore. The reliance of the landlord/novelist on those banknotes is morally suspect. The invocation of a deterministic inevitability to the collapse of landlordism demonstrates the ways in which naturalist assumptions are mobilized to disavow responsibility for social injustice.[15]

The point at which the naturalist representation is most severely thrown into crisis is in the portrait 'A Castle of Yesterday'. It is composed of a series of liminal positions and experiences which are both geographical and psychological. As such they comprise a blurring between outer and inner worlds. The location for this sequence of traumatic borderline experiences occurs at dawn in a *ruin* on an *island* in the *West* of Ireland. The twilight of dawn becomes a deathly shadowland. Significantly, the corresponding portrait in *Terre d'Irlande* is titled 'Un chateau mort'.[16]

While sheltering in a ruin the narrator experiences the final crucial transition, the retreat from the anguished present of land agitation into a more consoling past, 'I climb towards the strange stairway, as if I would pass backwards out of this fitful and febrile age, to one bigger and healthier and simpler.'[17] However, this retreat into the past to seek consolation outside of history is rendered impossible. He continues, 'The stair descends to an embrasure in the wall, and the moonlight is streaming through ... I cannot pass this ghostly ray of moonlight.'[18] The encounter with the ghostly and ghastly moonlight deepens the narrator's horror. It becomes a harbinger of death:

That moon ray is not so chill as I, and this bloodless agony is more terrible than mortal death. Death that is darkness were sweet, but this cold white spirit of death dreadful to behold; this icy death of wandering white is a terrible death to be taken in.[19]

This terrifying encounter becomes a metaphor for the threat posed by 'Captain Moonlight' to landlordism. Thus this deathly moonlight can be read as an image of the specific threat posed by Parnell and his supporters. The narrator's terror is

Shadowy Heroes: Irish Literature of the 1890s (Syracuse: Syracuse UP, 1980) 84.   **14** Moore, *Parnell and His Island* 6-7.   **15** Terry Eagleton, *Heathcliff and the Great Hunger: Studies in Irish Culture* (London: Verso, 1995) 216.   **16** George Moore, *Terre d'Irlande*, trans. M.F. Rabbe (Paris: Charpentier, 1887) 193-217.   **17** Moore, *Parnell and His Island* 165-6.   **18** Ibid. 167.   **19** Ibid. 167-8.

quite clearly indicative of the fear experienced by the landlord class. The attempt to seek escape into a nostalgia for a time preceding the land agitation is undone by the omnipresent moonlight. The contemporary threat it symbolizes prevents self-sufficient nostalgia and renders the narrator and his class a mere shadow of his, and their, former selves. Through this ghostly and terrifying encounter with his symbolic annihilation the narrator describes himself as, 'like a spirit escaping through a shadow-land'.[20] The ghostly encounter completely ruptures the naturalist surface of the whole text. It is a moment out of time, disrupting the linearity of naturalist temporality. On the narrator's return to his companion, and symbolic return to time of the narrative, the narrator describes his experience as *unheimlich*: 'The place is still ghostly and strange in the grey dawn, but it is natural and homely compared with the minutes of torture I have suffered up in those ancient walls, wet and smooth with age.'[21]

The *unheimlich* experience among the ruins is both a vision of the past and a prophecy of the future for the landlord class. This section exemplifies the way in which the text relentlessly seeks to contain and obscure the Parnellite threat through its parallel use of naturalist figuration and construction of an idealized time and space outside of history. An 'intolerable' dimension to Irish history disrupts the naturalist figuration. Symbolically, the nightmarish events of this section occur mostly on, or around, a stormy lake. Its turbulence shatters the enchanted calm and stillness the narrator imposed on Dublin Bay at the opening of the text. There, the water's mirror-like qualities symbolized the text's ability to reflect Irish experience. This is now no longer feasible. The mirror has become cracked and fragmented.

The narrative authority of the naturalist narrator/landlord in *Parnell and His Island* becomes deeply problematic as it undergoes a process of fragmentation. He encounters 'M—' who is initially believed to be a Frenchman, but reveals himself as a landlord recently recalled from an artistic career in Paris. His return in a French guise becomes an image of the translation and return of the text itself. The translation of *Parnell and His Island* from 'Lettres sur l'Irlande' becomes analogous to Moore's own indeterminate exilic status. The multiplication of such alternative selves undermines and fragments the autonomy and authority of the omniscient narrator. For Elizabeth Grubgeld:

> *Parnell* reads most significantly as Moore's first autobiography, obligated by the nature of its method to discourage the identification of author with narrator: an autobiography that, by distortion, caricature, and rejection of all it depicts, defines its author by delineating that which he is not, particularly that manifestation of an earlier self, the Irish poet 'Landlord M—.'[22]

20 Ibid. 168.   21 Ibid. 169.   22 Elizabeth Grubgeld, *George Moore and the Autogenous Self: The Autobiography and Fiction* (Syracuse: Syracuse UP, 1994) 21.

This splitting is indicative of the deeper crisis which pervades the naturalism of *Parnell and His Island*. I contend that its formal fragmentation and problematic narrative authority destabilize the text's mimetic claims, so making it an important early work in establishing an Irish modernist aesthetic.

To counter this disruption and fragmentation of the naturalist narration and representation, Moore seeks to contain the threat by aestheticizing it. In the 'Conclusion' to *Parnell and His Island* the narrator explicates his method:

> The scenes in the pages of this book point to no moral—at least no moral that I am conscious of; they were not selected to plead any cause ... they were chosen because they seemed to me typical and picturesque aspects of a primitive country and barbarous people. Unconcerned with this or that opinion, my desire was to produce a series of pictures to touch the fancy of the reader as a Japanese ivory or fan, combinations of hue and colour calculated to awake in him fictitious feelings of pity, pitiful curiosity and nostalgia for the unknown ... Picturesque comfort or picturesque misery *l'un vaut l'autre* in art, and I sought the picturesque independent of landlords and Land Leaguers; whether one picture is cognate in political feeling with the one that preceded it I care not a jot; indeed I would wish each to be evocative of dissimilar impressions, and the whole to produce the blurred and uncertain effect of nature herself. Where the facts seemed to contradict, I let them contradict.[23]

The image of perfect unmediated reflection with which the text began has now been transformed into this assertion of the text's 'blurred and uncertain effect'. The narrator attempts to maintain the integrity of his method by attributing these distortions to nature itself, to an 'unrepresentable' quality in the Irish experience. A review of *Terre d'Irlande* in the *Westminster Review* noted this as the chief characteristic of the book, '[Moore] presents facts or fictions as typical, which are not so; and gives everything warped and thrown out of position, as in a cheap looking-glass.'[24]

Initially *Parnell and His Island* seems to provide a 'true' and 'realistic' reflection of Ireland. Its naturalist representations can be read as part of a strategy to contain the threat represented by Parnell. When this breaks through and throws the whole text into crisis by 'distorting' the reflection, the narrator retreats from his earlier ambition and accords his text the status of an aestheticized and de-politicized object, a Japanese ivory. The image of the text in those torn banknotes has become formally isolated as a decadent image. According to David Baguley such a strategy is a structural feature of naturalist poetics. He writes:

23 Moore, *Parnell and His Island* 233-5.   24 *Westminster Review*, June 1887: 374.

Naturalist aestheticism presents the obverse of the natural process, fixing and transmuting a world in decay. The subject of naturalist fiction becomes an aesthetic object, material for the writer's palette, a procedure totally unpalatable for the politically conscious critic. Lives become still lives.[25]

Parnell and His Island marks a critical moment in Moore's writings. It represents the articulation of the transition from scientific naturalism to a decadent aesthetic. The spectacular disjunctions which arise from the negotiation of this transition through translation make it an important work in the evolution of Irish modernism.

Holograms of Cityscapes in Eavan Boland's Object Lessons

ANA ROSA GARCÍA GARCÍA, UNIVERSITY OF BURGOS

This paper humbly sets out to display Eavan Boland's semantic variability attached to the word 'place' in her collection of essays entitled *Object Lessons*. It does so in view of Jacques Derrida's proposition that any search for an essential, absolute stable meaning must be considered metaphysical, as there is no transcendental signified that is meaningful in itself and is exclusive to its signifier. The best way to begin with this display of multiplicity of meanings is Boland's own definition of the term 'place': 'What we call place is really only that detail of it which we understand to be ourselves.'[1] Herein Boland is not only deconstructing the traditional association of the word 'place' with a unitary physical space, (or taking for granted that 'place' is metaphysical as well as physical), but is also adopting a subjective, multidimensional approach to the concept itself, using a scarcely conventional way of understanding and knowing places. This may need further explanation. By the idea of 'metaphysical reality' I refer to the deep connection between the physical place and its symbolic representations in the signifier. By the idea of subjective approach I mean all the personal preconceptions and experiences, conscious and unconscious relations, included *a priori* in the way a person can relate him or herself to a specific place.

The volume *Object Lessons* was never conceived as a collection of objective critical analyses of theoretical topics on poetry. On the contrary, from the very beginning it was conceived as a hybrid text of literary criticism and prose memoir.

25 David Baguley, *Naturalist Fiction: The Entropic Vision* (Cambridge: UP, 1990) 197.

ANA ROSA GARCÍA GARCÍA
1 Eavan Boland, *Object Lessons* (London: Vintage, 1995) 155.

Boland uses the technique of intertwining several aspects of poetic theory and criticism with the examples taken from her ordinary life and from memories of the past, as both Seamus Heaney[2] and John Montague[3] amongst others had previously done in Ireland. This choice of genre hybridity is not casual. Autobiography offers a freedom denied to more orthodox critical discourse. Critics, fatigued by constant queries about the legitimacy of their respective positions, are tempted to hoist an autobiographical shield in order to develop their analyses without the pressure of academic censorship. Boland, attempting to dive deep into poetic theory, adopts this device in *Object Lessons*. Autobiography acts as a 'refuge' from certain attacks, clearly sheltering those who use it from all but the most personal criteria. This shelter or asylum for personal creativity is the first sense of 'place', out of a multiplicity of signifieds in this signifier we will find in this book: a metaphysical 'space' for literary freedom from norm.

The second meaning of place we observe not only in this book but also in all of Boland's poetic production, is the subtextual connection between the private and the public spheres. According to Patrick O'Sullivan, autobiography is: 'the repository of a transcendent inwardness, the index of civil society's impermeability to political society. It falls to art and autobiography to shelter, in Marx's phrase, "man in his sensuous, individual, immediate existence". The two forms fork in their reputation of the saturation of private by public.'[4] I believe that, in this respect, critical auto-biography has been, and still is a masked extension of theoretical struggle on another plane. I mean by this that it resituates the battle to its own advantage asserting the primacy of the civil over the political, the reflective over the active, 'the road inwards to art over the road outwards to action', as O'Sullivan calls it.

Boland adopts the motto 'the personal is political', so much vindicated by the second-wave feminists, allowing her to move continuously from the exploratory and theoretical to the practical and personal.[5] Indeed, Boland recognizes as much when she asserts that 'merely by the fact of going upstairs in a winter dusk, merely by starting to write a poem at a window that looked out on the Dublin hills, I was entering a place of force. Just by trying to record the life I lived in the poem I wrote, I had become a political poet.'[6] This is the second signified of the word 'place' in her work: life can be a place waiting to be reflected in the poem. The life of an ordinary woman in an ordinary suburb has its own 'place' as a real subject for a poem.

During the last centuries in the literary tradition there is a metaphorical separation between the categories of experience and expression which are poetic and all the rest that is considered ordinary and therefore inadmissible within the

2 Seamus Heaney, *Preoccupations. Selected Prose 1968-1978* (London: Faber & Faber, 1980).   3 John Montague, *The Rough Field* (Mountrath, Portlaoise: Dolmen, 1972).   4 Patrick O'Sullivan, 'Courting the Interior: Contemporary Literary Criticism and the Autobiographical Impulse', *Irish Review* 13 (Winter 1992/93) 1-13.   5 See Robyn R. Warhol, and Daniel Price Herndl, eds. *Feminisms. An Anthology of Literary Theory and Criticism* (Basingstoke: Macmillan, 1997)   6 Boland, op.cit. 183.

poem, a distance between the poetic and the human. This empty space between those two realities is the one Boland aims to bridge: the space between the ordinary world of a Dublin suburb and the literary world of poetic inspiration and criticism. She is actually making up a common place where the public and the private meet. As she imports the private world into the public realm by her subversive writing, the space between private and public shrinks. The world she inhabits, the place she belongs to, is transformed into a public subject matter.

Up to here we have seen discussed different signifieds of the word 'place': *place* as a metaliterary space where the canonical and the personal meet in a hybrid genre; *place* as a bridge where the ordinary and the poetic meet; and *place* as a common area where the public and the private meet. From now on, we will see the deconstruction of the term 'place' in relation to poetry in Irish literature and Boland's work.

For Ronald Schuchard, in his introduction to Heaney's *The Place of Writing*, 'the aura of place imposes itself on one poet's imagination; another poet imposes his singular vision on a plural place; places become havens or heavens; they drive the poet into spiritual or physical exile, they provide poetry with its nourishment and distraction; they liberate imagination and darken consciousness'.[7] This statement shows the manifold relations between the place and the poet we generally recognize in the canon. Namely, the place as the subject, the object or the means for inspiration, as the reflection of one's subjectivity, as the representation of a symbolic meaning, the cause of mind-absence and spiritual abstraction, and the origin of the liberation of imagination and the darkening of consciousness.

'Place' can therefore be the representation of many signifieds. Some concepts related to place used in Irish literature are displacement, dislocation, strangeness, exile and bilocation. The concept of place described above by Schuchard is frequently represented by Irish male authors—though not as characteristic of all of them—as an *outer* space, usually a landscape, an external, geographical place; when it usually refers to a cityscape, it is mostly public areas of it what is described, like streets, parks and squares. Women poets, on the other hand, frequently circumscribe another kind of place: the predominance of internal spaces in rooms and houses links them to one another.[8] On the most obvious level, this is supposed to be the world many women in Ireland inhabit, and they often identify with it more than with the 'public' world of their male colleagues, as we can see in many nineteenth and twentieth-century poems written in Ireland.[9]

---

7 Seamus Heaney. *The Place of Writing* (Atlanta: Scholars Press, 1989) 4. 8 This opinion has been expressed in Patricia Boyle Haberstroth's *Women Creating Women. Contemporary Women Poets* (Dublin: Attic, 1996). 9 For an example of this, see A.A. Kelly, *Pillars of the House. An Anthology of Verse by Irish Women from 1690 to the Present* (Dublin: Wolfhound, 1988). On the other hand, a representative anthology of the exclusion of women poets in the Irish literary tradition is Seamus Deane, et al. eds., *The Field Day Anthology of Irish Writing*. 3 vols. (Derry: Field Day, 1990).

However, we might see this use of imagery of the house and its interiors not as a difference between public and personal, or between place and self, but as a difference in how men and women poets identify self in terms of different 'places'. As more women are published in Ireland, another kind of history and geography surfaces, which validates their image of place as equally important as the more 'public' landscape Irish male poets often write about. Therefore, women poets—and Eavan Boland is no exception—describe this *inner* place they are supposed to inhabit and belong to. 'Belonging' to the place you describe is manifold. It is generally accepted that you can belong to a place physically, emotionally, spiritually, culturally and symbolically.

I think that you belong physically to a place by birthright and by dwelling there; it becomes your place of origin. You belong emotionally to a place when your deepest thoughts, feelings and emotions are experienced there, when this place echoes some previous experience or feeling: it is your place of life, it is a place of the mind. You belong spiritually to a place when you project your image in there, you recognize yourself reflected in it, although you might be physically somewhere else: it is a place of essence. Belonging culturally to a place occurs when you have shared its past and/or its language and it has become your nation, when this place adds something to your way of being and living in the world: it is a place of tradition, a place of identity. Finally, you belong to a place symbolically when you recreate it and represent it, yourself being part of its definition: it is a place of image, a place of representation and recognition.

It is obvious that, physically, Boland belongs to Dublin, both seen as her place of birth and the place she has lived in most of her life. In *Object Lessons,* we are overwhelmed by physical descriptions of the city 'public' areas, and by the descriptions of her different houses. However, the most fascinating point in her writings is the wide array of metaphorical phrase names to refer to Dublin. She coins a wide list of signifiers for the same signified: 'the literary city', 'the last European city', 'the last literary smallholding', 'a city of images and anachronisms', a 'place of resentment and beauty and conflict', 'a sprawling town spreading swiftly into a rapacious city', 'a place which had something of the theater of a city and all the intimacy of a town', to quote but a few. It is as if the word 'Dublin' itself cannot signify its own complex meaning for Boland. As we said at the beginning of this article, it seems that there is no transcendental signified that is meaningful in itself for Boland. The term 'Dublin' has no absolute stable meaning.

In *Object Lessons*, inner places are described physically in relation to electrical machines, like the kettle, washing machine, oven and others. On the other hand, in her poems we are flooded by descriptions of flower gardens, the Dublin hills and meteorological effects to express outer spaces. Emotionally, Boland seems to belong to the suburb of Dundrum, in Dublin. Dundrum becomes the place where she identifies her emotional belongingness to a place. There it is the 'visionary place' of her creative writing. There she expresses an 'inner landscape' of love. It becomes a 'place of the mind', a place of life and development.

I believe that you belong spiritually to a place when you consider yourself inhabiting it, no matter whether you are physically there or not, if you adopt it as your 'place of essence' as opposed as your place of existence. This place, according to Eavan Boland, happens 'at the very borders of myth and history': 'and here, on the edge of dream, is a place in which I locate myself as a poet: not exactly the suburb, not entirely the hill coloured with blue shrubs, but somewhere composed of both'.[10] Here she accounts for the silences of voices of women from the past that have been erased from canonical history and official literature. We cannot deny that, culturally, Boland belongs to Ireland, regardless of her exile in London and New York as a child and teenager. Her first approach to the concept of nationhood was through Tom Moore's songs in the exile:

> For me, as for many another exiles, Ireland was my nation long before it was once again my country. That nation, then and later was a session of images: of defeats and sacrifices, of individual defiances happening offstage. The songs enhanced the images; the images reinforced the songs. To me they were the soundings of the place I had lost: drowned treasure.[11]

In *Object Lessons*, her country is represented by two opposing visions of the cityscape of Dublin. The first vision is the city of history, with powerful images of hanging men, burning barricades, the Pale and the Great Hunger. The second vision is the Dublin of contemporary times in which Gaelic and English languages are fused in street signs, and the harbour is the gate to Europe and America. Ireland means emigration, famine roads, eviction, her great-grandfather's workhouse, the Dublin Hospital where her grandmother died of childbirth, religion suppurating in everyday life, and so on. Boland wants to write her country's past, its fears, its superstitions and memories approaching it from personal experience.

Finally, to belong symbolically to a place happens when you recreate it and make it yourself. For Boland, this place is The Poem, where she can 'follow my body with my mind and take myself to a place where they could heal in language: in new poems, in radical explorations'.[12] However, being inside the poem means more than being a metaphorical representation in it. Outside the poem, the poet is indeed free, does indeed have choices. Once he or she is inside it, these choices are altered and limited. In a real and immediate sense, when she does enter upon this 'old territory that is the poem', the woman poet is in that 'poignant place' where the subject cannot forget her previous existence as object of the poem. This 'poignant place' is for Eavan Boland 'a magnetic field where the created returns as a creator'.[13]

10 Boland, op.cit. 172.   11 Ibid. 129.   12 Ibid. 110.   13 Ibid. 217.

To summarize, through this paper we have scrutinized the different representations of places and spaces found in Eavan Boland's prose memoir *Object Lessons*. Firstly, we saw the literary space where the canonical and the personal criticism met in the hybrid genre of critical autobiography. Secondly, we discovered place as a bridge between the ordinary and the poetic as inspirational motifs for a poem; and the hologram of the common area where the public and the private meet. Then we evolved to the literary and metaphysical relation between the poet and the place, and how a place is the origin of varied reactions to it; as well as the relation between male poets to outer spaces and female poets to inner spaces. Finally, we have analyzed the concept of belonging to a place in its reflection in Eavan Boland's work: a physical relation with Dublin city; and emotional relation with the suburb of Dundrum; a spiritual relation with her place as a poet; a cultural association with Ireland; and a symbolical fusion with the poem itself as a place where she develops as creator.

Actually, we have not exhausted all the possible holograms of the word 'place' in her work, but I hope we have accomplished the task of showing the multiplicity of meanings this concept is given, in an attempt to show the process of deconstructing the uniform relation between signifier and signified, between the word 'place' and its usual relation to 'physical limited space'. The object of deconstructing the word is to examine the process of production, the materials and their arrangement in the work. The aim is to break the unidimensional reading, breaking free of the constraints imposed by its own realist form. Composed of contraries, the word is no longer restricted to a single, harmonious and authoritative reading. Instead, it becomes plural, open to re-reading, no longer an object for passive consumption but an object of work by the reader to produce meaning.

Imagining Memory: Ulysses *and* A Journal of the Plague Year, *or the Novel of the Inventory*

DIANA PÉREZ GARCÍA, UNIVERSITY COLLEGE, DUBLIN

The English writer Charles Lamb likened the experience of reading Defoe's fiction to 'reading evidence in a court of justice'.[1] In the light of this aphorism readers of Defoe will recall the immense body of factual detail, the long and exhaustive enumerations that distinguish his writings. Perhaps no other fictional work of his exemplifies better this tendency to catalogue than *A Journal of the Plague Year*, a novel swamped by fact and ciphers, researched by his author with

---

1 Cit. Ian Watt, *The Rise of the Novel* (London: Hogarth, 1987) 34.

painstaking dedication in an attempt at distilling his narrative out of hard fact. The proliferation of historical and physical data in his works has no doubt contributed to establish Defoe's reputation as one of the first English writers 'to have visualized the whole of his narrative as though it occurred in an actual physical environment'.[2] That is, if we are to follow Watt's analysis in *The Rise of the Novel*, it has lifted his fictional works above the scornful evaluation of his educated contemporaries to place him at the beginning of the realist tradition. However, it might be valuable to consider carefully what is understood by Watt as realism: central to his argument is the idea of the emergence of a literate urban middle class for which writers like Defoe would have catered with fictions that they could find relevant to their interests and aspirations. Thus, Defoe would have consciously constructed stories that resembled reality in order to satisfy this emergent body of readers. However, Defoe's own ideas on how to reconcile truth and its narrative counterpart would indicate that he considered this attempt at verisimilitude somehow problematic. 'To relate real stories with innumerable Omissions and Additions,' writes Defoe, 'I mean, stories which have a real Existence in Fact, but which by the barbarous way of relating, become as romantick and false, as if they had no real Original.'[3]

From the above statement it can be inferred that Defoe's understanding of how to present 'truth' in writing is far more sophisticated than it would appear to the novice reader of his works. It is the mediation between author and material that preoccupies him, as he comes to the realization that the difficulties the writer faces in his attempt at providing the substance of truth are 'endemic to the activity of reporting'.[4] That is to say, Defoe was intent on making his narratives seemingly verifiable, rather than on making them resemble the truth, the latter being clearly the intention behind realism as we understand it.

At this point we might want to consider the reasons behind Defoe's preoccupation with the narrative representation of objective truth. The critic Michael McKeon contends that rather than being immersed in the self-assured triumphalism of an emerging middle class that Watt proposes in his analysis, a dissenting writer like Defoe was intent on reconciling spiritual truth as envisioned by Calvinism with capitalist material gain, as well as being engaged in the new trend for empiricism sponsored by the Baconian revolution. The rift that we find at the centre of Defoe's writings, the one that partially earned him the reputation of being a careless writer, would then be rooted in the unstable nature of early eighteenth-century social categories and epistemological methodology. As such, Defoe emerges as an exemplary representative of this intellectual crisis.

We can now regard the massive body of factual evidence in *A Journal of the Plague Year* from a different perspective, and consider how Defoe tries to bridge the gap between the historical event that frames his narrative and its fictionaliza-

---

2 Ibid. 26.   3 Michael McKeon, *The Origins of the English Novel. 1600-1740* (Baltimore: Johns Hopkins UP, 1991) 113.   4 Ibid. 120.

tion.⁵ With this intention it might be useful to reconsider Lamb's aphorism: Defoe, the thoughtful mediator between his material and his narratives, would have considered how to present and structure this 'evidence', how to freeze his data for the contrastive perusal of his readership. The medium that enables him to turn his narrative into a seemingly verifiable account is none other than print. As McKeon suggests, 'print stabilized culture itself and the past in particular as a realm of experience henceforth susceptible to objective study'.⁶

The repercussions of the typographical revolution on Defoe's attempts at organizing his materials help to explain the anecdotal manner, episodic construction, and unstable organization of a narrative like *A Journal of the Plague Year*, as well as offering new insights into the hostile evaluation that Defoe's narratives were to receive from practitioners of the fully established realist novel in the nineteenth century. Thus Henry James' negative appreciation of Defoe's writings as having 'no authority, no persuasive or convincing force' can be better understood in the context of a novelistic practice, to which James belongs, that does not have to contend with unstable social and epistemological categories.⁷

'We must reflect,' wrote Virginia Woolf about modernism, 'that where so much strength is spent on finding a way of telling the truth, the truth itself is bound to reach us in rather an exhausted and chaotic condition.'⁸ Her reflection can be understood in the context of a twentieth-century 'crisis of truth'. It might be useful here to recall the modernist dissatisfaction with the realist novelists' efforts at 'holding a mirror up to nature' in the construction of their narratives. This dissatisfaction was rooted in a suspicion that the claims to realistic representation held by their predecessors were tainted with the self-assurance of a strong commanding authorial voice, one that offers a univocal transcription of reality, a reality that the modernist perceived as complex and multivocal.

Woolf was indeed partly responsible for contributing to restore Defoe's reputation after two centuries of neglect, devoting an entire chapter of *The Common Reader* to Defoe. She was not alone in her appreciation. In the academic year 1911-12, Joyce delivered two lectures at Trieste University, under the title 'Realism and Idealism in English Literature (Daniel Defoe-William Blake)'. Joyce's lecture sheds new light on both Defoe's and his own work, and for this reason I think that it is worth considering its content in some detail.

Although Joyce's analysis does not escape certain common place or negative evaluations of Defoe's narratives, as when he refers to Defoe's 'matter of fact realism'⁹, or lists a few of his deficiencies, stating that his fictional works 'fall short in love plot, psychological analysis, and the studied balance of character'.¹⁰

5 I am referring here to the Great London Plague of 1665.   6 McKeon, 43.   7 Henry James, *Henry James: A Life in Letters*, ed. Philip Horne (London, Penguin, 1999) 500.   8 Virginia Woolf, 'Mr Bennet and Mrs Brown', *A Modernist Reader*, ed. Peter Faulkner (London: Batsford, 1986) 127.   9 James Joyce, *Daniel Defoe*, ed. and trans. Joseph Prescott (Buffalo: University of New York at Buffalo, 1964) 12.   10 Ibid. 15.

It is when he tackles particular works by Defoe that we can sense an affinity between Defoe's productions and his own. Thus in referring to *The Storm*, he praises Defoe's compositional methods by asserting that: 'in the end the object of the chronicler has been achieved. By dint of repetitions, contradictions, details, figures, noises, the storm has come alive, the ruin is visible.'[11]

Far from assuming that Defoe's inventorying is the result of neglect, or equating it with a primitive understanding of composition, Joyce is appreciative of its narrative achievements. Moreover, as Joseph Prescott has pointed out, the way in which Joyce 'emphasises Defoe's gift for vivifying narrative by the massive accumulation of factual data' suggests his own similar gifts as a writer.[12] Indeed, Joyce's readers could not fail to recognize most of the devices listed above as central to the composition of *Ulysses*. Equally interesting is Joyce's assertion that 'beneath the rude exterior of Defoe's characters' the reader 'will find an instinct and a prophecy'.[13] It is the symbolist in Joyce who is at work here, and this 'prophetic' quality he explores further when he states that 'English feminism and English imperialism already lurk in these souls,' thus shrewdly anticipating much modern criticism devoted to *Moll Flanders* and *Robinson Crusoe*.[14]

This conclusion is hardly surprising when we consider that Joyce starts his lecture neatly tying the arrival of William of Orange in British shores with a celebration of English identity: a celebration, he remarks, mirrored in Defoe's fiction. In this sense his praise of Defoe as the first English writer 'to infuse into the creatures of his pen a truly national spirit,' which in Joyce's analysis is juxtaposed to Defoe's pioneering in devising 'for himself an artistic form without precedent,'[15] might recall in the reader the Quaker librarian's innocent assertion in *Ulysses* that 'Our national epic has yet to be written.'[16] Rather than considering Joyce's laudatory comments on Defoe's innovations as a salutation on the birth of the novel, it might be more profitable to interpret them in relation to Joyce's own concerns: the dignification of human experience at its most banal, the inclusion of the myriad aspects of reality that conform such an experience, his desire to articulate an Irish 'conscience' as yet 'uncreated', and the realization that in his quest for this particular truths he would have to mould a narrative form capable of encapsulating them.

In the light of the above, Joyce's appraisal of the narrative in *A Journal of the Plague Year* as possessing 'something masterly ... and orchestral about it' is a good indicator of Defoe's method of composition as integrating a multitude of elements counterpointed to produce an overall effect.[17] Thus, H.F., Defoe's anonymous protagonist, performs the role of conductor of this peculiar orchestra. It is important to note that Defoe has chosen the journal form as a model for his narrative. Not only, I believe, because this particular narrative mode was favored by the Protestant practice of religious introspection, and would have come

11 Ibid. 16.   12 Joseph Prescott, introduction, *Daniel Defoe* 3.   13 Joyce, *Daniel Defoe* 23.   14 Ibid. 23.
15 Ibid. 7.   16 Joyce, *Ulysses*, ed. Declan Kiberd (London: Penguin, 1992) 246.   17 Joyce, *Daniel Defoe* 17.

naturally to Defoe as a dissenter, but also because a journal is by its very nature a written account. The very fact that Defoe has chosen to title his forged account 'A' Journal, as opposed to 'The' Journal, is an indication of his awareness of the narrative's status as a document amongst many possible others. All this helps to explain H.F.'s anxiety to report incidents as faithfully as possible, with the acute awareness of the chronicler who knows all too well that he is producing a document left open for the reader to verify.

We know, thanks to Frank Budgen, of Joyce's 'magpie method' in gathering materials for his narratives. Richard Ellmann has told us of Joyce's painstaking efforts at documenting his fictions by way of arduous research. There is a sense, then, in which *Ulysses*, like *A Journal of the Plague Year*, is demanding to be verified by its readers. The difference between Defoe and Joyce being, of course, that the first naively believes in his own forgery, while the second is all too aware of the artificial nature of all documents. It is this awareness of the possibilities of print that allows Joyce to arrange his text in a discontinuous manner, offering snippets of information that acquire their real significance by way of retrospective re-assemblage. The readers of *A Journal of the Plague Year* will recognize in this method their own efforts at putting together the mortality bills, rules and regulations, religious and pseudo-scientific explanations, oral, and written accounts that populate H.F.'s thoughtful narration.

Both novels stand then as forged documents that recall attention to their form, to the fact that they are cultural artifacts. This might be the reason behind some of the difficulties that the reader accustomed to nineteenth-century novels has to face when approaching either of these narratives. If the nineteenth-century novelists, as Hugh Kenner points out, took for granted 'a printed book whose pages are numbered ... as simply the envelope for their wares,' both Joyce and Defoe self-consciously exploit the printed book, taxing their readers with a responsibility that would have been felt as quite inappropriate by the canonical realist writer.

Both Joyce's and Defoe's inventorying reflect their characters' desire to fix the uncertainty of their social medium. As H.F. sees the boundaries of normality blurred by the spectre of the plague, he has every reason to fear for the survival of his community. The anonymity of this kind and practical individual further stresses the fact that Defoe's emphasis is in defining what constitutes the make up of a healthily functioning society. A definition that his contemporaries might have found equally necessary. It is by means of parading through the streets of Dublin the very ordinariness of Bloom, whose qualities of tolerance and civic-mindedness stand up to those of H.F., that Joyce tests the health of Irish society. The results are quite drab, as Bloom becomes the object of the muted or plainly outraged misunderstanding of his fellow citizens.

The distrust with which Bloom is perceived by most of the characters in the book is at the core of that social uncertainty that lurks behind *Ulysses'* structure.

In *A Journal of the Plague Year*, H.F.'s perambulations around London offer the desolate spectacle of a society that has realized that contagion starts with trust: the grass growing on the cobblestones, the masses of people walking in the middle of the streets to avoid passing infected houses, and the red crosses marking the doors of the diseased are all muted symbols of the desecration of public interaction. If in *Ulysses* this desecration is far less dramatic, it is by no means less important. A library, a newspaper, several pubs, a hospital are the sites for the exchange of its characters' cultural and political beliefs, a museum serves as a hiding place, a brothel as the site for the reunion of kindred spirits. With the exception of drinking in pubs, none of the public spaces included in *Ulysses* are used by its characters according to their original function. Political spaces are conspicuous by their absence, and it is telling that the most significant reference to the judiciary in the novel is set in the context of the cruel prank played upon the paranoid Mr. Breen.[18]

Both London and Dublin, as limited geographical entities, are extensively inventoried in *A Journal of the Plague Year* and *Ulysses*. Joyce prided himself in the fact that *Ulysses*, should the occasion arise, could be used as a blueprint for the reconstruction of Dublin. In Defoe's retrospective narrative there are references to the big fire, witnessed by him as a young child, that was to change the face of London the year following the plague. In this sense, the city, which can be documented in maps and directories, becomes the overarching body of evidence in both books. A changing and unstable space that is constantly being surveyed and catalogued, just as the readers of these two books can verify H.F.'s and Bloom's itineraries through London and Dublin with the aid of a map.

It is telling that Bloom's thoughts often stray towards practical improvements of the city's infrastructure, as when in conversation with fellow mourners in 'Hades' he suggests the establishment of a tramline to improve the transportation of cattle, as well as a Dublin replica of Milan's funeral tram services.[19] H.F.'s practical mind has carefully weighted the effects of the plague on London's commercial trade, and in this he echoes Defoe's reforming character, frequently engaged in the design of social and political improvements. In the light of the advent of free trade and the industrial revolution, we have come to relate this type of practical and material preoccupation with bourgeois values. At the time of the publication of *A Journal of the Plague Year*, however, Britain was far from being the fully industrialized free trading empire that we associate with Dickens' narratives, whilst turn of the century Ireland was by and large a rural society whose commercial interests were subordinated to those of its powerful neighbour.[20] Thus, H.F.'s and Bloom's engagement with the material world has to be understood as a reflection of their anxiety to secure it. Their practical concerns are those of a proto-bourgeoisie, uncertain as they are of the make up of their social and economic milieu.

18 In 'Lestrygonians'.   19 Joyce, *Ulysses* 122-3.   20 See Diana Spearman, *The Novel and Society* (London: Routledge, 1966).

In the light of the above we can view H.F.'s desire to reconcile his material interests with a sense of divine intervention as an excuse for not fleeing the epidemic, as a manifestation of the early eighteenth-century process of capitalist secularization. Thus the instability in the narration of *A Journal of the Plague Year* can also be understood in terms of the shifting boundaries between material and spiritual truths. In this respect, Bloom, whose love for the technical and material side of life goes largely unshared by others, would seem to be ahead of the rest of the characters in *Ulysses* precisely as a result of this engagement with the material world and the possibilities open for its improvement. It is because he already has an uncomplicated sense of community, violently misunderstood by the Citizen in 'Cyclops', that he can take the leap from the paralyzing ideals of nationhood sponsored by his adversaries to a practical conception of society.

Ulysses begins by stating the desires of two young men to provide Ireland with a renewed source of spirituality, devotes most of its pages to narrate the seemingly banal adventures of its pragmatic protagonist, and finishes with the anticlimactic reunion of the spiritually minded Stephen and the materially concerned Bloom. *A Journal of the Plague Year* opens with the announcement of an imminent crisis, explores the effects of such a crisis in detail, to close at the point of heralding a return to normality, thus perhaps expressing its author's anxiety to both solve and present the problems raised by his narrative. In the process of representing the instability of their respective societies, Joyce and Defoe have signaled the transitory nature of all documents; a transience that is brilliantly reflected in Joyce's parody of Defoe's style, as well as his own, in 'Oxen of the Sun'. In the end the manic inventory performed by their narrators has the ironic effect of exposing the impossibility of completely fixing the uncertainties that lurk behind these novels. Defoe had started by trying to itemize those elements that were to be put together with sobering control by later practitioners of the novel. Two hundred years later Joyce followed in his steps by dismantling their efforts with baffling precision.

Patrick Kavanagh's Poetics of the Peasant

ALAN A. GILLIS, THE QUEEN'S UNIVERSITY OF BELFAST

As is well known, *The Great Hunger* attempted to vandalize Ireland's self-image. What might be called the ideology of ruralism provided a circuitry of images and ideas through which the collective Irish imagination conceived itself to be essentially Romantic. Roy Foster writes that de Valera's 'vision of Ireland … was of small agricultural units, each self-sufficiently supporting a frugal family; industrious, Gaelicist and anti-materialist. His ideal, like the popular literary versions, was built on the basis of a fundamentally dignified and ancient peasant way of life'.[1] Yet by the late 1930s, what Sean O'Faolain called a 'wholesale flight from the fields' was underway.[2] A Commission on Emigration later acknowledged a 'psychological and economic malaise' borne from the 'relative loneliness, dullness and generally unattractive nature of life in many parts of rural Ireland'.[3] And in this emerging context, ruralism was seen to be shrouding Ireland's modernization and poverty. Writers like O'Faolain and Kavanagh thus viewed it with increasing contempt. In *The Great Hunger*, the deteriorating effects of economic change in the country are manifested with the palpability of disease.

The poem parodies ruralism's amorphous structure of ideals:

> The peasant has no worries;
> In his little lyrical fields
> He ploughs and sows;
> He eats fresh food,
> He loves fresh women,
> He is his own master
> As it was in the Beginning
> The simpleness of peasant life.
> The birds that sing for him are eternal choirs,
> Everywhere he walks there are flowers.
> His heart is pure,
> His mind is clear,
> He can talk to God as Moses and Isaiah talked –
> The peasant who is only one remove from the beasts he drives.[4]

If we disregard Kavanagh's irony for a moment, it is clear that ruralism provides a utopian alternative to modernity. By exploding these lyrical fields, Kavanagh fragments the ideal of an organic society integrated with nature, upon which Irish Ireland was founded.

At the core of this ideal is ruralism's great chain of being, in which each entity obtains autonomy within a broader, naturalized amalgamation. Kavanagh's scene is synecdochially structured: the lyrical fields stand for the world; the birds, beasts and flowers stand for the entirety of nature; and the peasant stands for humanity, deriving meaning through an intrinsic relationship with the totality. At the same time, the birds, beasts, flowers and fields stand for aspects of each other and of man and God (and vice versa).[5] Taking offence at this, Kavanagh represents the peasant as an alienated and overworked wreck. His poem insists that Maguire,

---

1 Roy Foster, *Modern Ireland 1600-1972* (London: Penguin, 1989) 538. 2 Sean O'Faoláin, 'Silent Ireland', *The Bell*, 6:5 (August 1943) 464. 3 Terence Brown, *Ireland: A Social and Cultural History 1922-1985* (London: Fontana, 1985) 184-5. 4 Patrick Kavanagh, *Selected Poems*, ed. Antoinette Quinn (London: Penguin, 1996) 40. 5 Hayden White describes synecdoche as a trope that posits 'an *intrinsic* relationship

the man-of-the-earth bereft of the complexities of modernity, is at root no closer to nature than an office clerk. And yet, the poem's power is partially derived through its relationship with pastoral utopianism. It is highly conscious of its own fragmentation, a fallen world in thrall to the promise of synecdochic integration. For example, the first line, 'Clay is the word and clay is the flesh', by the very nature of its mimicry, denotes a secular world conscious of Christ's absence.[6] The line initiates a momentum of desire. The homology of each hemistich, 'Clay is the word' / 'clay is the flesh', draws them together; the caesural 'and' is almost like a pivot upon which they could be folded into one another, yet it simultaneously divides them in parallel isolation. And this gesture of intimated but withheld union is paradigmatic, not just of Christianity, but of many Romantic poetic modes, such as Yeats' early apocalyptic symbolism.

If we disregard the line's poetic structure, however, the message is that word and flesh *do* combine in clay, just as they do in Christ. In other words, the apocalypse has already happened. The opening nihilism of the poem suggests that clay denotes a vacuum of meaning, that this is an apocalypse of non-significance. But clay is more equivocal than this. Elsewhere we are told that 'Unless the clay is in the mouth the singer's singing is useless'.[7] When hardened, clay normally connotes stasis and death. But when wet it is malleable, and clay is inextricably bound up with the imagery of creation. The substitution of clay for Christ, then, is only superficially negative. But it does get rid of immaterialism. The poem's rejection of Christ signifies that the confrontation between word and flesh, or consciousness and the world, is to be mediated directly. The church is said, in a clumsy phrase, to lift 'Prophecy out of the clayey hours', and makes Maguire rush 'beyond the thing / To the unreal'.[8] This is part of his tragedy and why the church must be condemned. Against such abstraction, language, if it became clay-like, would retain body, substance, and relevance to the brute materiality of nature. Concomitantly, if clay became language-like, it would be anthropomorphized and malleable to human subjects. Thus clay-language would be a mid-point between consciousness and nature, and a culture bound by such language would be the antithesis of

> ... that metaphysical land
> Where flesh was a thought more spiritual than music
> Among the stars—out of the reach of the peasant's hand.[9]

This frisson between senses, in the opening line, engenders a dialectic that runs throughout the poem. Maguire is alienated primarily because of his consuming

of shared *qualities*'. Thus, a synecdoche combines elements 'in the manner of an *integration* within a whole that is *qualitatively* different from the sum of the parts'. Synecdoche 'suggests a relationship among the parts ... which is qualitative in nature and in which all of the parts participate'. *Metahistory: The Historical Imagination in Nineteenth-Century Europe* (London: Johns Hopkins UP) 35-6. 6 *Selected Poems* 18. 7 Ibid. 41. 8 Ibid. 25. 9 Ibid. 29.

labour, his need to impose order on an otherwise unproductive nature, so that he and his family can eat. It is this predicament which shatters any vestige of pastoral idealism. Yet one image in the poem tells us

> These men know God the father in a tree:
> The Holy Spirit is the rising sap,
> And Christ will be the green leaves that will come
> At Easter from the sealed and guarded tomb.[10]

Here, the feminine earth is a locus of death, a tomb, transfigured into a womb through propagation with the phallic tree. Both feminine matter and masculine energy are necessary for life. This image stands as a kind of master-image, a magnet pulling Maguire's desire. Conventionally, within Romanticism, the task of impregnating fallen nature with divinity is passed over to man. And in this sense, Maguire's plight is that of the failed Romantic artist. The poem sends him on a quest for synecdochic integration, and his perpetually thwarted desire for this is mostly figured through his interminable sexual yearning.

The other side of the dialectic, though, works against this Romantic propulsion. In one passage, we are told

>   … Maguire learns
> As the horses turn slowly round the which is which
> Of love and fear and things half born to mind.
> He stands between the plough-handles and he sees
> At the end of a long furrow his name signed
> Among the poets, prostitute's. With all miseries
> He is one. Here with the unfortunate
> Who for half moments of paradise
> Pay out good days and wait and wait
> For sunlight-woven cloaks.[11]

Maguire's signature, his identity, is bound up with that of the poet and prostitute, word and flesh. The 'sunlight-woven cloaks' echo Yeats' embroidered cloths of heaven, linking the passage to his symbolist poetics.[12] But the prolonged wait for these cloaks proves that the symbolist world is entirely proleptic. The satiation of desire is always expected in this world, but, like Godot, never quite turns up. Maguire senses that his name (word) will be inscribed in the soil (flesh), yet this is posited as a telos, something that will happen at 'the end of a long furrow' (when he is dead). In the meantime, something half-sensed or barely intuited is

---

10 Ibid. 23. 11 Ibid. 24. 12 'Had I the heaven's embroidered cloths / Enwrought with golden and silver light', W.B. Yeats, *Collected Poems* (London: Picador, 1990) 81.

to recompense. Kavanagh thus implicitly critiques such symbolism as an opiate for the masses, a blockade against knowledge and agency, a poetic attuned to masturbation rather than consummation.

Against this, the poem claims that 'God is in the bits and pieces of Every-day'.[13] A poetic based on the positive connotations of clay seems is offered as an alternative to synecdochic Romanticism. Within this alternative, to focus on clay or corporeal matter is to focus on the here and now. And much of *The Great Hunger* is, accordingly, metonymic. More than this, the world of clay, as opposed to the world of Christ, enables things to stand for, within bounds, whatever the perceiver makes of them. Therefore, metonymic apprehension is spliced with metaphor to allow a verisimilar depiction of contiguous reality illuminated by the depth created by imaginative association. In this mode, Maguire is sometimes released from pining for total meaning, and is allowed to get on with simply being in the world. And yet the absence of a sense of total order, the destabilization of meaning, always shadows this aspect of the poem with doubt, with an intimation of its own limitations.

Thus the poem spins recurrent loops of non-resolution. Apocalyptic tropes are dismissed in places, but the synecdochic urge towards integration remains constant. Likewise, a metonymic-metaphorical apprehension is sometimes embraced, but then is dismissed elsewhere. Every articulation and gesture is made within the wider context of alternative perspectives. The poem is therefore panoptic and ironic. It is put together by a process of juxtaposition that is surprisingly reminiscent of Pound, or at least of other long poems that develop the tenets of Imagism. *The Great Hunger* is built of perpetual shifts in focus and tone. At the same time, however, the poem utilises a narrator who supposedly guides the images. Vivid imagery is often accompanied with a rhetorical heavy-handedness which comes from over-zealous prompts for readers to connect image and narrative. This develops a gap between narrative message (one of monotony, waste and tragedy), and aesthetic experience (one of variety, energy and polysemy). And this tension between the poem's ironic sophistication and its overbearing fatalism is tangible throughout.

The narrative voice plays off the deeper, ironic structures of the poem. For example, after a passage that condemns the church for stemming instinct, we are told: 'For the strangled impulse there is no redemption'.[14] The assurance and attractiveness of the thought suggests this is the poem's, or Kavanagh's, true point of view. But this sentiment is surely questioned when consideration turns to 'Schoolgirls of thirteen', who 'Would see no political intrigue in an old man's friendship'—an idea that is only discarded because

> ... there was danger of talk
> And jails are narrower than the five-sod ridge
> And colder than the black hills facing Armagh in February.[15]

13 Kavanagh, *Selected Poems* 28.   14 Ibid. 25.   15 Ibid. 35.

In ways such as this, the narration swamps the reader in a tide of irresolution, reducing us to the level of Maguire. As Kavanagh castigates his society's image of the peasant, he replaces it with a kaleidoscope of perspectives upon an enigma.

Like Maguire, the reader is trapped by an irony that is ultimately negative: avenues of possibility almost inevitably turn out to be cul de sacs, forcing a return to the one-way passage towards futility. The ironic gamesmanship and play with modes of representation, the vivid creation of a metonymic-metaphorical verisimilitude, the polysemic experience encountered in much of the imagery: all of this works dialectically against, but cannot stem the tide of, the poem's superimposition of a tragic narrative.

But ironically, as the poem progresses towards its apocalypse, it articulates with evermore clarity an argument against apocalypticism. Just before the final section, we are explicitly told there were 'No mad hooves galloping in the sky'.[16] And even at the poem's powerful climax, the apocalypse is reached in the context of yet more unanswered questions:

> Maybe he will be born again, a bird of an angel's conceit
> To sing the gospel of life …
> Will that be? will that be?
> Or is the earth right that laughs: haw haw
> And does not believe
> In an unearthly law.

Interestingly, this last question lacks a question mark, most likely to deflect attention away from the indecision, in order to garner momentum for the conclusion:

> … No hope. No. No lust.
> The hungry fiend
> Screams the apocalypse of clay
> In every corner of this land.[17]

But the apocalypse can only be read in the context of the two unanswerable questions: Is there a God? Is there a natural order?

The ending has powerful connotations. One could read into it the revelation of a God who is angry at the absence of faith, or the revelation of a nature that has not been understood and thus appears vengeful. But such connotations are predicated upon a teleological dynamic that is contrary to the poem's assertion that Maguire's life entails 'No crash, / No drama'.[18] The apocalyptic ending in fact works against the poem's dominant sense of irresolution, providing an emotive punch to counteract it with.

16 Ibid. 42.   17 Ibid. 44.   18 Ibid. 41.

We began, however, with ruralism, whose great chain of being perpetuates the illusion that Ireland is a self-enclosed entity cut off from modernist change and international forces. The synecdochic propensity to relate the lyrical fields with the whole of Ireland engenders a sense of the nation effused with idealism. It should now be clear that, underneath its surface attack, *The Great Hunger* remains dialectically structured by the trope that forms the basis of such ruralism. Arguably, it is of continuing aesthetic importance because of its immersion in the thought structures that it condemns. Indeed, Kavanagh's paradoxical complex of poetic modes, the tensions within the poem's tropic structure, provide an interesting point of intersection with the cultural-historical perspectives through which it might be contextualized.

By maintaining an apocalyptic structure, the poem recognizes the emotional pull of romantic nationalism, the apparent symbolic abyss of any alternative. The alternative that *is* postulated, a kind of metonymic apprehension of the world, content to forgo the stability of static integration with a fixed cosmic order, might be compared to the mode of historical thought articulated by Sean O'Faolain. O'Faolain is posited, in *The Field Day Anthology of Irish Writing*, as one of Ireland's first historical 'revisionists', whose rejection of Romantic-historical thought came in tandem with a view of Ireland as modern and European. Undoubtedly, O'Faolain's (and others') categorical rejection of Romanticism provided Kavanagh with a positive aesthetic alternative: pragmatic Realism. The distinction between O'Faolain's pragmatic realism and Irish Ireland's Romanticism provide a backdrop to the contradictions of Kavanagh's poem.[19] Yet *The Great Hunger* also indicates how the two shadow each other.

Terence Brown argues how prototypical revisionists such as O'Faolain predicated their vision, like de Valera, on a conception of Ireland's autonomy:

> There was a sense … in which the writers and the politicians were not in fundamental disagreement. They may have differed on the historical basis of contemporary Irish society and disagreed profoundly in their conscious assessment of the quality of Irish life, but they shared a faith that the Irish future would depend on … a commitment to the essential worth of Irish experience.[20]

Kavanagh's poem likewise shows a commitment to the country in the midst of its assault. In a sense, his rural scene is as enclosed as the lyrical fields he would explode. In the 1930s (as before and after), the Irish countryside was incontrovertibly politicized: rightwing Fine Gael activists and leftwing Republican

19 O'Faolain, along with Frank O'Connor and Liam O'Flaherty, had a direct influence on Kavanagh's writing in the period leading up to and throughout the writing of 'The Great Hunger'. See Antoinette Quinn's *Patrick Kavanagh: Born Again Romantic* (Dublin: Gill and Macmillan, 1991).   20 Brown, *Ireland: A Social and Cultural History* 159.

initiatives both found root support amongst farmers. But Kavanagh's poem is utterly bereft of such politics and recent history. The one reference to WWII emphasises the community's isolation from it.

One of the dominant motifs in the poem involves boundaries and their transgression. Images of hedges and walls proliferate, symbolizing boundaries between the self and alterity. It is implied that Maguire must break through them if he is to transform his alienated mode of existence. And his failure to do so reflects the poem's own imprisonment within an apocalyptic narrative structure, the debilitating retention of the desire for synechdochic enclosure.

Kavanagh's use of a predetermined tragic narrative or enclosed form, which his poem energetically reacts against, is a means of critique using the emotive force of negation. He inverts idealistic Romanticism to such an extent that its retention becomes quite obscene. Nevertheless, although *The Great Hunger* critiques the non-transgression of boundaries of the self, Kavanagh would later base his poetic on the necessity of a perpetual and fraught dialectic between self and alterity.[21] Without some form of boundaries or sense of self, there can be nothing: the utopia of hybridity is as empty as the utopia of self-sufficient homogeneity.

In many ways, Kavanagh's hedges are a thorn in the side of Irish historical thought, because questions of autonomy and openness continually prove to be a site of incessant contradiction for modes of historical interpretation. For example, Terry Eagleton writes of the Famine as a kind of abyss in historical thought that scatters the sense of the nation and history throughout space and time.[22] Yet the Famine simultaneously becomes a symbol of unity: the experience of disaster strengthening the communal sense of self. In a similar manner, O'Faolain's historiography opens the door to Europe and international forces, yet this ultimately serves to strengthen the sense of nation by altering its foundations so that it can survive the epistemic shift to Modernity.

To an extent, then, *The Great Hunger* reveals the limitations of the historiographical models available to Irish studies. We have noted that Ireland was experiencing deep-structural economic change during the time of the poem. And whilst the 'base' is in transition, Marxists say, any paradigmatic form through which civilization chooses to conceive of itself will be unstable and founded on contradiction. Maguire's poverty remains constant, but the poem deflects attention away from this towards explorations of aesthetic and interpretative models, all of which are futile. Seamus Deane has conceived of Irish historiography as

21 Kavanagh's poem 'Innocence' contains the lines 'They said / That I was bounded by the whitethorn hedges / Of the little farm and did not know the world'. But it ends 'I cannot die / Unless I walk outside these whitethorn hedges'. *Selected Poems* 101. 22 'Part of the horror of the Famine is its atavistic nature—the mind-shaking fact that an event with all the premodern character of a medieval pestilence happened in Ireland with frightening recentness. This deathly origin then shatters space as well as time, unmaking the nation and scattering Irish history across the globe'. *Heathcliff and the Great Hunger: Studies in Irish Culture* (London: Verso, 1995) 14.

dualistic: the only possible alternatives for historical thought lie with either apocalypse or boredom.[23] Kavanagh, describing Maguire, points out 'The hysteria and the boredom of the enclosed nun of his thought', which makes plain, contra Deane, the felt need for a prescription against these emotions.[24] A formulation such as Deane's is synecdochially closed off, occluding the possibility of a historical perspective predicated on the analysis of global economic trans-formation, or on a consideration of class inequality within Ireland.

Then again, Marxism's internationalism is predicated on a conception of the ineluctable interrelationship of historical objects and forces. If one node along an interconnected chain is altered, the qualitative nature of the whole is transformed. As a mode of historical thought, therefore, Marxism is based on the trope of synechdoche as much as nationalism is. Just as revisionism attacks Romanticism but retains the boundaries of nationhood, so internationalist perspectives lead to yet another synechdochic formulation, to the extent that most are predicated on explanatory models that explain diachronic change within synchronic contexts.

This perpetual movement away from synechdoche that somehow leads back to it again reflects the dynamics that structure *The Great Hunger*. It might be that the insistent recurrence of synechdoche points to the fallacy of criticising it, or, by extension, the concept of organicism. The trope or concept is of relative value, depen-dent on its particular usage. Although Kavanagh attacks the hypocrisy of Romantic-ism in relation to contemporary destitution, it is the synechdochic propensity to understand things as interconnected within a provisional whole that brings contradiction to light in the first place. Perhaps more importantly, it is the idea of patterned interconnectivity that provides the impetus to resolve those contradictions. Organicism, whilst exponentially unfashionable at the moment, is one half of most formulations of dialectical change. Kavanagh could not critique rural destitution without an awareness of something better. The challenge that *The Great Hunger* lays down for Irish critics is to decide what their 'something better' might be.

A. E., the Irish Civil War, and the Dialogical Text

JAMES HEANEY, TRINITY COLLEGE, DUBLIN

The idea of popular sovereignty advanced by nationalist ideology is often been expressed as a kind of selfhood. In *Nationalism: Five Roads to Modernity*, Liah Greenfield observes that modern nationalism has tended 'to assume the character

23 *Strange Country: Modernity and Nationhood in Irish Writing since 1790* (Oxford: Clarendon, 1987). 24 Kavanagh, *Selected Poems* 31.

of a collective individual possessed of a single will'.[1] The idea of a 'national self' can, in fact, be traced to Rousseau's original theoretical framework for the transfer of power from the king to the nation. Richard Kearney points out that Rousseau agreed with advocates of absolutist sovereignty that 'the transmutation of multiplicity into unity could only be effected by the "irrevocable submission of every individual to a single, unitary person"'; 'an individual' he identified as 'the collective personification of citizens as a whole', the famous 'general will'.[2]

Civil war brings the idea of the nation as a 'collective individual possessed of a single will' to crisis point. On the one hand, for republicans, this type of conflict suggests that the nation no longer possesses the indivisible collective interest which is supposed to instantiate its unity. Alternatively, for those who conceive of their national identity in terms of a racial or religious essence, the nation becomes an evermore sectarian concept during internecine conflict. Manuel Azaña, President of the Spanish Republic during the 1936-39 conflict in Spain, remarked that in the context of civil war such individuals view the nation as being 'purified by tremendous amputations'.[3]

A.E. (pseudonym of George William Russell 1867-1935, economist, theosophist, writer and organizer for Horace Plunkett's Co-operative movement) was not a sectarian nationalist. However, throughout his political writings, he did frequently resort to the concept of selfhood in order to represent the unity of Irish nation.[4] Furthermore, his most important civil war work, *The Interpreters* (1922), illustrates that he continued to do so during the 1922-3 period in Irish affairs.[5] I want to consider the implications of this for the concept of nationhood that emerges from this text.

The Interpreters takes the form of a dialogue between a number of intellectual, military and political figures who express contrasting opinions on the subjects of nationalism and violent revolution. This discussion is set during an insurrection in which a volunteer-army is attempting to assert the rights of a small nation against a mighty empire dominating it. Most of the work takes place in a prison-cell where four captured leaders of the revolt have been taken by the imperial forces. These rebels, we learn, are to be executed the following morning. Hence, despite A.E.'s statement in his preface that *The Interpreters* 'has been laid in a future century so that ideals over which there is conflict to-day might be discussed divested of passion and apart from transient circumstance',[6] the work itself clearly recalls the recently concluded Anglo-Irish conflict and, more particularly, the occasion of the 1916 Easter Revolt in Dublin.

1 Liah Greenfield, *Nationalism: Five Roads to Modernity* (Cambridge: Harvard UP, 1992) 11.   2 Richard Kearney, *Postnationalist Ireland* (London: Routledge, 1997) 21.   3 Manuel Azaña, 'La velada en Benicarló' in Juan Marichal ed., *Manuel Azaña—Obras Completas III* (Madrid: Ediciones Giner, 1990) 451. (The translation is my own.)   4 For many examples of this see A.E., *The National Being: Some Thoughts on an Irish Polity by A.E.* (Dublin: Irish Academic, 1982).   5 A.E., 'The Interpreters', in Nandini Iyer and Raghavan Iyer eds., *The Descent of the Gods: Comprising the Mystical Writings of George Russell (A.E.)* (Gerards Cross: Colin Smythe, 1988) 243-321.   6 Ibid. 245.

In addition to the above parallels, the text's main characters represent an uneasy mix between A.E.'s own personality and a number of individuals who were either directly or indirectly involved in the events of Easter 1916. The character of Lavelle is perhaps the most obvious in this regard: a poet and idealist, this rebel-leader blends A.E.'s mysticism with the militancy of Padraic Pearse. Culain, 'the man by whose influence the workers of the nation had been brought to take part in the revolt',[7] combines A.E.'s socialism with that of James Connolly, or possibly Jim Larkin. The two remaining revolutionaries among the main characters, Leroy and Rian, are less easily identified. The former is a highly sceptical writer-come-anarchist who rejects all ideologies which threaten the free expression of the individual (including Lavelle's nationalism and Culain's socialism). Rian, an architect, is the least ideologically-armed of the revolutionary leaders. He tells the others that he joined the revolution because 'I believe I desired passionately to build the palaces and cities of dream here on earth, and I wanted the prophets of beauty like Lavelle to prepare the way in people's souls'.[8]

There are also two non-revolutionaries being held in the prison cell, Brehon and Heyt. Brehon is described as an 'imaginative historian'.[9] Although he has taken no part in the movement, his writings, we learn, have greatly influenced nationalists such as Lavelle, who refers to him as 'the father of us all'.[10] Brehon, most commentators agree, represents the figure of Standish James O'Grady; although as John Wilson Foster points out, this character also 'changes shamelessly from O'Grady into the author'.[11] Finally, there is Heyt, an industrialist and president of the empire's Air Federation, who has been locked in with the revolutionaries by mistake. Patrica McFate suggests that this character 'could represent any industrialist who sided with Britain in the struggle for Irish independence', or might be based on William Martin Murphy, who led the lockout against the Dublin workers in 1913.[12] These are the text's six main characters: four revolutionaries, a historian, and a representative of the power which is being attacked. There are also a number of lesser-ranked revolutionaries in the prison-cell who take little interest in the discussion going on around them.

Notwithstanding the fact that its characters and setting clearly evoke the circumstances of Easter 1916 in Dublin, the Irish civil war is also very relevant to a reading of this work. There are perhaps two main respects in which this is the case. Firstly, the book was initially published in November 1922, while the civil war was still raging in Ireland (and letters by A.E. indicate that the text was unfinished as late as 1922).[13] Secondly, the fact that it is profound disagreement regarding the subject of nationalism which animates the revolutionaries'

---

7 Ibid. 260. 8 Ibid. 263. 9 Ibid. 252. 10 Ibid. 262. 11 John Wilson Foster, '"The Interpreters": A Handbook to A.E. and the Irish Revival', *Ariel: A Review of International English Literature* 11. 3 (July, 1980) 81. 12 Patrica McFate, '*The Interpreters*: A.E.'s Symposium and *Roman à Clef*', *Eiré-Ireland* 11. 3 (1976) 86. 13 See A.E., *Some Passages from the Letters of A.E. to W.B. Yeats* (Dublin: Cuala, 1986) 58.

discussion, rather than unity of purpose, also underlines the importance of the 1922-3 conflict to the reading of the text.

The Interpreters is not an easy read: there is little action in the book—practically the whole story revolves around the prisoners' highly abstract politico-philosophical discussion; characterization is only poorly maintained (A.E. concedes as much in his preface); and the setting rarely moves out of the single prison-cell in which all the protagonists are being held. It is also a difficult work to categorize in terms of genre. In the course of his essay on *The Interpreters*, for example, John Wilson Foster refers to it variously as: 'a symposium' (which is how A.E. himself understood the work); 'something very close to a novel'; 'not really a novel'; 'a *roman à clef*; a 'philosophical autobiography'; and 'a voyage-tale'.[14] For Patrica McFate, the work is a *roman à clef* which contains a symposium; a 'synthesis of philosophical discourse [and] political discussion'.[15] In his biography of the author, Henry Summerfield takes the Joycean line, and refers to it as, simply, 'a book'.[16] My own view is that Robert Bernard Davis and William Irwin Thompson are closest to the mark when they describe the work as being in the tradition of the Platonic dialogue; and this generic feature, I will contend, is fundamental to the representation of national unity in the text.[17]

The Interpreters, then, takes the form of a discussion on the subjects of nationalism and violent revolution. However, it cannot be said to provide a very objective examination of these issues. For example, like their author, all the main characters profess deeply-held spiritual beliefs. Consequently, the work is best described as an internal dialogue; one in which A.E. critiques his own political views (and his spiritualism) from a number of alternative perspectives. To avail of Søren Kierkegaard's phrase, in *The Interpreters*, A.E. is being objective *subjectively* and subjective *objectively*.

In 'Politics and Philosophy' Hannah Arendt suggests that this form of writing gives expression to a particular understanding of selfhood. Speaking with reference to Plato's Socratic dialogues, she points out that for Socrates 'living together with others begins with living together with oneself', a process which involves coming to a recognition, and acceptance, of the plurality contained within the 'I'. Internal dialogue is central in this regard because it is through this activity that the plurality of the self is uncovered: 'only in thought', Arendt comments, 'do I realize the dialogue of the two-in-one who I am.'[18] Hence, although there is no sense in which A.E.'s text can be compared to Plato's works at a philosophical level, Arendt's comments illustrate that, in terms of form, there is an important similarity between them: by presenting his own understanding of political ideologies such as anarchism, nationalism, and totalitarianism, in as

14 Wilson Foster 70; 70; 80; 71; 76; 81.   15 McFate 92.   16 Henry Summerfield, *That Myriad-Minded Man* (Gerards Cross, Bucks.: Colin Smythe, 1975) 212.   17 Robert Bernard Davis, *George William Russell (A.E.)* (London: George Prior, 1977) 83; William Irwin Thompson, *The Imagination of an Insurrection: Dublin, Easter 1916. A Study of an Ideological Movement* (New York: OUP, 1967) 185.   18 Hannah Arendt, 'Politics and Philosophy', *Social Research*, 57.1 (Spring, 1990) 89.

full and sympathetic a manner as possible, *The Interpreters* also 'realizes' the dialogical nature of its author's self.

Furthermore, the dialogical understanding of the 'I' in this work is also relevant to the idea of a national self: in the sense that *The Interpreters* presents a number of intellectual, military and political figures attempting to define the basis of their country's nationhood, the symposium is analogous to a nation's attempts to discover its own general will. There is no consensus arrived at in this regard (the various outlooks 'meet' only in the sense that they come together in dialogue). However, in this work, it *is* the activity of dialogue which represents the unity of the national self, in the same way that it represents the unity of the individual self.

The evidence of dialogue is apparent throughout *The Interpreters*. It arises, for example, in relation to the cultural nationalist perspective, represented by Lavelle. This character remarks that he is fighting the empire in order that his nation will once again exhibit 'that unity of character that existed in the civilizations of Egypt or Attica, where art, architecture, and literature were in such harmony that all that is best seems almost the creation of one myriad-minded artist.'[19] (That this is almost a direct quotation from the author's 1916 work, *The National Being*, underlines the fact that A.E. is using this character to express some of his own closely-held political opinions.) A number of the other nationalist-revolutionaries identify weaknesses with Lavelle's idea of an ancient, and homogenous, national identity. Leroy, for example, the anarchist in the group, raises the problem that diversity within national cultures poses for the A.E./Lavelle theory. Leroy points out that 'individuals in the same country ... work in contrary directions'; how can Lavelle distinguish 'among varieties of national ideals those which have the divine signature from the rest?' he enquires. Lavelle concedes that evidence of diversity poses problems for his theory, and tries to argue that certain individuals like himself, who have 'read the history of our nation' and come to feel 'the continuity of national inspiration', have developed the ability to distinguish 'those inspirations which   come from the national genius from ideas which are personal.' However, the other nationalists are unimpressed by this line of argument, and raise a number of arguments to which Lavelle—or rather, A.E.—is unable to respond. Rian, for example, points out that the very fact that the other nationalists are objecting to Lavelle's theory suggests more diversity exists than the poet is prepared to concede. Leroy's own objections are even more damning, hinting, as they do, at the authoritarian potential of Lavelle's cultural nationalism: 'I do not wish to be a slave to the inner Lavelle', he complains to the poet. 'I do not know why you delight to see everywhere the echo of a single mood. I take joy in ... all free imagination, but you desire to impose your dream on others.'[20]

The character of Heyt, a totalitarian representative of the empire, is also relevant to the discussion of nationalism in the work. This character stands in direct opposition to the aims of the nationalist-revolutionaries. 'What place has

---

19 'The Interpreters' 266.   20 Ibid. 266-8.

nationality in the limitless sky', he remarks, after listening to Lavelle's arguments, 'and yet the little nations, if permitted, would proclaim territorial rights in the aether up to the infinite.' The interesting feature of Heyt's totalitarianism is that it seems to replicate Lavelle's thinking on a larger scale. Whereas Lavelle based his nationalism on the concept of a homogeneous national consciousness, Heyt looks instead to the idea of a cosmic consciousness which encompasses the whole of humanity: 'You cry out against the world state which Nature has made like the lion', he suggests to the nationalists, 'but the will of the world soul is seen in the organisms it endows with power.' 'We attain our fullest life', he claims, 'by becoming ... slaves' to the cosmic will.[21]

It is Leroy who draws attention to the similarity between these outlooks. Addressing his comments to the totalitarian *and* the cultural-nationalist, he observes that 'you [both] justify the moulding of humanity to your will by imperialism in the Heavens. I believe in the intense cultivation of human life and think the cosmic purpose is seen in the will of myself and others to be individual and free.' He then repeats to Heyt his earlier objection, raised in relation to Lavelle's nationalism: 'you would make me the slave of a light I do not see, a law I do not know.' 'How is cosmic consciousness to be recognized', he asks the totalitarian, 'when it can be so variously interpreted?'[22] Therefore, the exchange of views here again reveals the author thinking through the possible totalitarian implications of his own cultural nationalism. Alternatively, if we identify A.E. with the Heyt character here, rather than the nationalist—and critics such as Desmond Fennell have suggested that A.E. did come to believe that a world empire might be inevitable[23]—we can see that the dialogue raises the same problem in relation to this outlook as it does in regard to cultural nationalism: namely, that it fails to take account of the complexity, and diversity, of human existence.

As a theosophist, Brehon undoubtedly expresses many of A.E.'s own opinions. Towards the end of the dialogue, this character attempts to reveal the existence of a single, spiritual source, behind the symposium's conflicting political philosophies, which he refers to as 'Own-Being'. Whichever way we approach this source, he remarks, 'it answers us': 'It entered into Lavelle as a boy upon his mountain, and it was with Culain in his dark streets, and with Heyt in his state laboratories and thought of a demiurgic power, and with Leroy in his passion for freedom.' Once the individual comes to an understanding of 'Own-Being', he says, 'the old life should be over, and they should no longer be concerned in the politics of time, and should leave the life of conflict and passion and fit themselves for the politics of eternity.'[24] A.E.'s remarks in his preface suggest that he believed Brehon's theosophy did provide the dialogue with some degree of closure. If such were indeed the case it would undoubtedly call into question the

21 Ibid. 278.   22 Ibid. 274.   23 See Desmond Fennell, *Heresy: The Battle of Ideas in Modern Ireland* (Belfast: Blackstaff, 1993) 44.   24 'The Interpreters' 305.

dialogical status of the text; however, the other characters do expose serious weaknesses in the theosophical position. Rian, for example, points out that Brehon's spiritualism does nothing to address the political and social injustices in society: 'the philosophy', he complains, 'seems to have a kind of incompleteness when applied to the shaping of human destiny'.[25]

Rudd, one of the lesser-ranked volunteers in the prison cell, makes an even more cutting remark: dismissing Brehon's remarks as mere 'folly', he points out that he was fighting quite simply because he 'hated being bullied in the name of a law he had no share in the making. He hated being instructed how to live in the name of a science which was unintelligible, and most of all he hated being told in the name of God how to think.'[26] The 'symposium' closes shortly after these remarks, without Brehon, or any of the other characters, undermining Rudd's pragmatic nationalism. Therefore, this final exchange of views again underlines the 'integrity' of A.E.'s internal dialogue, in the sense that we see the author's theosophy does not stand outside the terms of the discussion.

The significance of dialogical form of *The Interpreters* is not simply that it enables A.E. to expose weaknesses in the various positions he examines, something which could be accomplished by the most monological of texts. Nor is it that the work presents dialogue as a kind of cure-all for what ails the body-politic, as though political differences could be resolved 'if people would just talk to each other'. As we have seen, differences of opinion are not resolved in *The Interpreters*. The importance of form in this work is simply that it shows dialogue to be a fundamental principle of selfhood. In Mikhail Bakhtin's words, A.E. lays bare 'the dialogic nature of human thinking about truth'.[27] In doing so, he reveals that the self cannot, in good faith, commit itself to *any* political outlook until it has considered the alternatives in as full, and sympathetic, a manner as possible; and that the self must be prepared to continually re-engage with those views. In this way, dialogue is presented as a necessary—though not sufficient—condition of conflict resolution.[28] At the communal level, such a concept of selfhood might be likened to the idea of a deliberative democracy: a form of nationhood which *aims* at consensus through open discussion, but whose unifying principle is understood as its citizens' commitment to an ongoing dialogue—what Ramón Máiz has referred to as 'a never-ending process of democratization'—rather than the attainment of consensus in itself.[29]

A.E.'s willingness to engage in dialogue with his own opinions during the Irish Civil War is not only apparent in *The Interpreters*. Although he came out strongly in favour of the pro-treaty position, his journalism reveals that he

25 Ibid. 308.   26 Ibid. 309.   27 Mikhail Bakhtin, *Problems of Dostoevsky's Poetics*, trans. Caryl Emerson (Manchester: Manchester UP, 1984) 110.   28 In relation to this issue see Ramón Máiz, 'On Deliberation: Rethinking Democracy as Politics Itself', in Ernest Gellner and César Cansino eds., *Liberalism in Modern Times: Essays in honour of José G. Merquior* (Budapest: Central European UP, 1996).   29 Ramón Máiz, 'On Deliberation: Rethinking Democracy as Politics Itself', in Ernest Gellner and César Cansino, eds., *Liberalism in Modern Times*, op. cit., 171.

continued to sympathize with the republican point of view throughout the conflict. In February 1922, for example, he wrote that 'it is difficult to argue without spiritual self-contempt against those who desire complete national liberty ... the extremists, as we know at heart, are right in their desires';[30] sentiments which he repeated in his first post-war editorial for the *Irish Statesman*.[31] *The Interpreters* is simply A.E.'s fullest expression of the provisional nature of human thinking about truth.

Myth/History and Past in the Poetry of Eavan Boland

CHRISTIAN HUCK, UNIVERSITY OF TÜBINGEN

Perceiving herself to be without a specific tradition, Eavan Boland is especially interested in the constructions and presentations of the past. By analysing two of her poems I will present an account of her understanding of the different concepts of myth and history. In 'Imago', for example, Boland is debunking traditional Irish myths.[1] She deconstructs not only one particular myth, but Irish myths as a whole: the 'blackthorn walking stick', the 'old tara brooch', 'bog oak', 'harp', 'wolfhound' etc. That these mythical foundations are mostly nineteenth-century constructions of Irish origins is well known, and the unmaking of myths is a current feature of Anglo-Irish poetry after Yeats. Boland, however, seems to be more interested in the complex ways a myth is made to function than to show the falseness of the mythical story.

In this paper I will examine Boland's attitudes towards the presentation of the past in both myth and history, and the relation of both forms of presentation to the ideal of an unmediated past, that is, to an account of the past not distorted by the medium in which it is presented. The bottom-line of this analysis will be that every form of presentation of the past is a construction and an attempt to *re-*present something that is forever lost. Unfortunately, this insight does not free one from the duty of coming to terms with the burden of an unchangeable past, or, as Boland said in her autobiographical prose work *Object Lessons*: 'Yet in the end, in my need to make a construct of that past, it came down to a simple fact. I had no choice.'[2] I will argue that it is necessary to understand the concept of

---

30 A.E., 'Ireland, Past and Future' in *Sociological Review* 14.2 (Apr. 1922) 13-14. (Later issued as a pamphlet.) See also A.E.'s Sept. 1921 pamphlet, *Ireland and the Empire at the Court of Conscience* (Dublin: Talbot, 1921), which, like the *Interpreters*, take the form of an unresolved political dialogue.   31 A.E., 'A Confession of Faith' in *The Irish Statesman* 1.1. (15 Sept. 1923) 3-5.

CHRISTIAN HUCK
1 Eavan Boland, *The Lost Land* (Manchester: Carcanet, 1998) 18.   2 Eavan Boland, *Object Lessons* (1995;

culture as it was developed in the late eighteenth century to fully grasp the difference Boland makes between myth and history.

In 'Imago' we can see that mythical allusions are presented in the form of grammatical ellipses—sentences without verbs. The poem's speaker realizes how it was possible that these static images were once powerfully alive. She knows now that it was herself who gave significance to these representational forms, she took them for real and thereby supplied life to the inanimate objects. Instead of being the acting subject, the speaker subjected herself to the prefabricated objects.

Now, as a grown-up, she has gained insight into these mechanisms. It was she who made the images work, and she lays open what they are without her supply of meaning: they are just simulacra, the outcome of mass-production, acquiring their meaning only by endless repetition, and not due to any link to an original. The supposed original, which is thought to be the foundation of these appearances, rather is the corollary of its own effect. There is no depth to the surface, no figure behind the masks. The speaker considers these images to be 'anti-art', they merely reproduce old stereotypes and clichés rather than pull back the shroud of wonted perception. If modern art tries to lay open the untransmissability of the past, these images simulate a continuity between past and present. This apparent continuity in turn simulates a necessity for the pain that has been suffered in past times. The images of a mythical Ireland are, to speak in the vocabulary of the poem, 'the walking-stick' to follow the 'way' that was 'traded by history'.

In an earlier poem from 1990 we can witness the consequence of an analysis of the function of mythical images. In "Outside History" the speaker declares, 'I have chosen:/out of myth into history I move to be.'[3] But before I have a closer look at this poem, I will try to tackle some of the pending questions concerning the status of myth and history in this concept. How can it be possible to *choose* between myth and history? Is it wrong to *believe* in myth? What has happened to myth, if it has become merely a 'walking-stick' to trod down the 'way to make pain a souvenir'? What is the advantage of history, if it is a construction all the same? To give some hints at how it might be possible to approach these questions I will try to present a brief outline of the development the terms 'history' and 'myth' have undergone since the Romantic period. (I'm sure it's unnecessary to point out that such a project can only be sketchy and incomplete here.) I will argue that in the late 18th-century the fundamental difference between an observation of the world, on the one hand, and the observation of *how* people observe the world, on the other, was widely experienced for the first time. Because of this new mode of observation the focus of interest shifted from questions about the constitution of the world to questions of *how* people actively constitute their world by observing it, i.e., how they make sense of the world.

London: Vintage, 1996) 34.   3 Eavan Boland, *Collected Poems* (Manchester: Carcanet, 1995) 160.

In 'Imago' we find the exemplary form of such an observation of an observation.[4] The speaker talks about how she, when still a child, thought the images were true presentations of a real past. By comparing the way she conceived the same images once as true presentations and now as hollow forms, she is enabled to acknowledge the different meanings one phenomenon can have when viewed from different perspectives. We can see how this second-order observation is doubling the phenomena under consideration: a thing is not merely this or that, but is what it is due to the way in which we understand it. The thing also has a function, a function it does not own merely through its being, but through the way we think about it. It is well known that both literature and the fine arts in modern times became increasingly fascinated with the observation of people who are themselves observing, and Velazquez famous painting *Las Meninas* is only the most prominent example of this phenomenon.[5] The late eighteenth century witnessed an exponential rise of viewpoints, and romantic poetry became obsessed with the observation of observations —be that one's own or somebody else's.

Following Raymond Williams, one can say that the term 'culture' is an invention of the eighteenth century.[6] Culture from then on is no longer the cultivation *of* something natural, but culture *in opposition* to nature. This distinction, between nature and culture, became prevalent. Regardless whether this development was understood as a rise above the determined life of animals, or whether it was condemned as the irretrievable loss of community, it nonetheless brought into being a split that was not to be amended until today. But the important point is, as the German sociologist Niklas Luhmann stressed, that culture was born with the 'Geburtsfehler der Kontingenz' ('birth-mark of contingency')[7]—it was never 'culture' in the singular, but *cultures* from the beginning. The discovery of a distinctively cultural sphere depended on the expansion of regional and historical comparisons of the ways in which human beings organize their communal living. It is well known that the eighteenth century was fascinated with other cultures (hence the rise of ethnological research), and for the first time in Western History it also mourned being cut off from direct continuity with classical Greece and Rome. It became obvious that every single specimen of culture could not be described as being *necessarily* the way it is (otherwise it would be natural). Therefore one can say that

4 I understand observation as a mode of perception using distinctions, where only one side of the distinction is present at any one time. For discussion of the theory of observation and distinction, see Heinz von Foerster, *Observing Systems*, 2nd ed. (Salinas: Intersystems, 1981).   5 For various examples in the history of art see Susanne Lüdemann, 'Beobachtungsverhältnisse. Zur (Kunst-) Geschichte der Beobachtung zweiter Ordnung', *Widerstände der Systemtheorie. Kulturtheoretische Analysen zum Werk Niklas Luhmanns*, ed. Albrecht Koschorke and Cornelia Vismann (Berlin: Akademie, 1999), 63-75. For poetry see Peter Hühn, 'Watching the Speaker Speak: Self-Observation and Self-Intransparency in Lyric Poetry', *New Definitions of Lyric: Theory, Technology, and Culture*, ed. Mark Jeffreys (New York: Garland 1998) 215-44.   6 See Raymond Williams, *Culture and Society 1780-1950* (London: Chatto and Windus, 1958) 15-17.   7 Niklas Luhmann, *Gesellschaftsstruktur und Semantik*, vol. 4 (Frankfurt a.M.: Suhrkamp, 1990) 48.

every culture is generated from the discovery of an outside, an outside itself comprised of other cultures. There is no culture without culture-contact—a phenomenon that Gregory Bateson describes as *schismogenesis*.[8]

The newly arising interest in mythology in the late eighteenth and early nineteenth century can, I think, be understood as a reaction to this experience of contingency, which itself is a corollary of the multiplication of viewpoints and perspectives. Crudely simplified, one could say that the attempts to reinstall the mythical were attempts to reduce this contingency, to undo the doubling of perspectives, to heal the split between (determining) nature and (freeing) culture. I will now try to give a rough outline of the complicated logic behind this desire for myth.

The possibility to compare one's own culture with other cultures makes obvious that life can be different. This discovery at the same time frees one from supernatural necessities *and* comforting security. The safety of fate gives way to the chances of freedom. The call for new myths or a *Neue Mythologie* then is the search for a form of living that secures the newly gained freedom of individuality and compensates for the experienced loss of community. Now the freedom of individuality would have to become a necessity itself. But to be a necessity it would have to be incomparable, because the possibility of an outside position that compares different forms of living would inevitably produce contingency. The new myth would have to make a culture unique, it would have to be exclusive. But this desire for an exclusive culture reveals a paradox, because an exclusive culture would cease to be one. The very point of the concept of culture was that culture emerges only through culture-contact. So, as long as there is an outside, the mythical existence that is aspired would always remain *one culture among others*. The myth a poet offers a society would not be able to lose the flavour of fictionality as long as there is such a thing as a cultural outside. From the outside position the myth would always appear as an ideology, as *one way* to see the world, and the mythical community would have to deal with this allegation. As I understand the desire for myth that arose around 1800 in Europe, the aspired myth comprises exactly those things that are felt to have been lost through the contingency of cultures: necessity, wholeness, security. But as long as the new myth radiates its intentionality it misses the very point of its desired existence: necessity. The very desire for myth makes it impossible to create one, because the fulfilment of that desire implies a creative making that destroys the necessary giveness of myth. The fulfilment of the desire for myth is interrupted by its own desire, and a new myth cuts itself off from being through its own attempt to be.[9] A myth that is brought into being against this interruption cannot be what it was intended to be.

8 Gregory Bateson, *Steps to an Ecology of Mind* (New York: Ballantine, 1972) 61-72. 9 See Jean-Luc Nancy, *The Inoperative Community*, ed. Peter Connor, trans. Peter Connor et al. (Minneapolis and Oxford: University of Minneapolis, 1991) 45-56.

However, after the obsession with mythology during the romantic period, the interest faded. Rather then to *re-enchant* the world through poetry, the novel became the prevalent literary form of the nineteenth century, and with it the search for authenticity. Culture, as I argued, was born as *cultures*, and was never an exclusive entity. At the same time an equally complicated construction was developed—the nation-state. In a complicated procedure, the association of culture and state gave birth to an utterly new understanding of history, both as object and as record. This new form of history is not about genealogies anymore, about the right of power and its glorification, as Foucault describes it.[10] He has shown how the emergence of counter-genealogies in Europe, which was suddenly crowded with memories and ancestors for whom there existed no genealogies, made evident that the right of birth is a right based on chance and luck. It became clear that the history of the one is not at all the history of another—the history of the winner is not that of the loser. But, and here I differ from Foucault, the emerging space between the genealogies of kings and emergent counter-genealogies was soon to be filled by the history of the nation-state, which was built on culture rather than genealogy. The history of the nation took as an advantage the very contingency with which it was plagued. Although the coming into being of a culture and a nation-state could not be described as a necessity, the *new* history could give a detailed description how it transpired that something so improbable came into being none the less.

It was Hegel who first defined the elementary difference between genealogy and the kind of history that emerged in the nineteenth century. I quote from his *Lectures on the Philosophy of History*: 'Family memorials, patriarchal traditions, have an interest confined to the family and the clan. The uniform course of events which such condition implies, is no subject of serious remembrance ... it is the state which first presents subject-matter that is not only adapted to the prose of History, but involves the production of such history in the progress of its own being.'[11] History from now on is regarded as objective, it is freed from the burden to give meaning to the past— what happened just happened, and the historian should present it *wie es eigentlich gewesen*—'how it really was'—as one of the founders of modern historicism, Leopold Ranke, famously remarked. The nation-state (in ideality) is defined by its success and its future prospects, not by its (non-existent) past. (It is beyond the scope of this paper, but, I think, explainable within its parameters, that the rational history of the nation was notoriously grounded on some foundational myths.) It was then that the task to make the past a meaningful space was excluded from the evolving scientific community of historians, and passed on to (global) philosophers and (local) writers. The distinctive feature by which to discriminate between history and what could not be regarded as history shifted from the distinction between truth and falseness to that of truth and fiction. Facts and fiction were intended to be

10 See Michel Foucault, *Il faut défende la société* (Paris: de Seuil, 1996). 11 G.W.F. Hegel, *The Philosophy of History*, trans. J. Sibree (New York: Dover, 1956) 60.

CHRISTIAN HUCK

neatly divided. It does not matter here how rigid this distinction was and is, how much *récit* there is in *discourse*, how much *discourse* there is in *histoire*, and how much truth there is in fiction.

It does matter, however, that this conception contains its own problems, problems that Nietzsche famously brought to attention when he accused the exclusively factual history of the historian to be *uninhabitable*. This could of course not undo the prevalence of history, but did on the contrary, by intensifying the desire for myth, make it an even more apoetical task to create a myth. Bearing these concepts in mind, I want to come back now, after a long detour, to Eavan Boland's poem 'Outside History', and, especially, to the speaker's decision to move 'out of myth into history'.

Boland describes in her autobiographic *Object Lessons* how she found herself to be completely absent from Irish historiography—both as a women from the official history, and as a female writer from the literary history. For the women poet there is no nightmare such as that from which Stephen Dedalus tried to awake. However, to move into history is in no way a move into paradise, rather it is described as a move into 'a landscape in which you know you are mortal.' To leave myth behind is a loss of the 'place where you found you were human'. Myth was able to make sense of pain and suffering by presenting it as unavoidable, but only, I think, as long as the myth is not recognized as one. The term myth is, as I tried to show, of paradoxical nature. It is a nomination that thrusts aside the very thing it is supposed to designate. Therefore the discourse about myth becomes itself a myth. It pretends to speak about something it cannot get hold of: to speak of myth always means to speak about its absence from the world from which one is speaking. For the speaker in 'Outside History' the possibility to choose between myth and history already means that myth is viewed from the outside, and so the move out of myth happens simultaneously with the acknowledgement of the very possibility to move. We find no time of indecision, of contemplating the pros and cons, in the poem. The decision to move follows directly after the discovery of the possibility to move.

My point is that once the speaker knows she can move, once she is able to compare and consider possibilities, she cannot do otherwise. From the perspective of the speaker the mode of myth can be observed as something that prevents a group of people from acknowledging the suffering in their community. Neither is history (the history of the nation-state as developed in the nineteenth-century), of course, true to the suffering that happened in the past. The official historiography seems to speak for the dead to silence the ghosts of the past. However, here, in the realm of history, the speaker finds the place and the possibility to try to acknowledge the pain, and the suffering, and the dead. The discourse of history makes it possible to show that the suffering was not *necessary*, and one can attempt to do justice to the dead.

But still, this does not change the fact that every presentation of the past is a failed *re*presentation, that it can never make present what is forever gone. It is obvious that, as the speaker says, 'we are too late. We are always too late.' Only when we throw away the 'walking-stick' that kept us on our 'way to make pain a souvenir', might we be able 'to kneel beside them' on 'those roads' and 'whisper in their ear'. Something that an outsider, like the 'stars—iron inklings of an Irish January' in the first stanza, are never able to. And poetry, rather than folktales or scientific accounts of history, may be able to write close to, or even on the border of the unrepresentable, because poetry is constantly questioning its own mode of presentation; it draws attention simultaneously to its constructedness *and* the need to construct, to the deficiency of language *and* the impossibility of not speaking. The speaker tries to come close to the past. And in this attempt she is not alone. It was a single 'I' that had to choose, and still a single 'I' that moved

> to be part of that ordeal
> whose darkness is
>
> only now reaching me from those fields,
> those rivers, those roads clotted as
> firmaments with the dead.[12]

But there are others where she chose to move: 'And we are too late. We are always too late.' Those who experience the loss of community form themselves into community.

Vocationalism, the University and the Poverty of Literary Reviewing

STEPHEN HULL, THE QUEEN'S UNIVERSITY OF BELFAST

It seems to me that the connection between the university discipline of Literary Studies and the sphere of literary journalism—a connection which is often taken for granted—is in fact neither as obvious nor as unproblematic as one might think. What I will be suggesting in this paper, is that once you have taken all of the relevant factors into account, you are effectively left with a choice of adopting one of two mutually exclusive perspectives on how these two spheres of activity relate to and influence each other. The perspectives in question view the linkage

---

12 *Object Lessons* 38.

between these two spheres respectively as being the source of either great mutual benefit or quite profound antagonism, and in the final analysis, the question of which camp you are inclined to locate yourself within is determined by what it is exactly that you believe the discipline of Literary Studies to be about, how you conceptualize its aims and objectives, and indeed how you conceptualize the aims and objectives of a university in general.

Just recently I had occasion to be interviewing someone who works within the field of graduate recruitment here in Belfast as to what they perceived a university education, and more specifically a degree in Literary Studies, to be about. Towards the end of the interview the conversation turned—inevitably enough perhaps, given the occupation of the interviewee—to the matter of what to do with the vast numbers of graduates which the universities are currently producing, a question which, as I hope to show, has particular resonance for graduates of Literary Studies, and indeed for all Humanities graduates. A brief excerpt from the transcript of the interview provides keen insight into the view taken on this matter by the person in question:

> ... with the move towards an American-style system where you have to save for your child's education, people's expectations of what the uni-versities will actually provide their child with are on the up, and if people are coming out at the end of the degree and not a lot of them are getting jobs, and a lot of them going on postgrads, something needs to be looked at. Maybe the numbers going into the degree need to be reduced, and that would be what I would think should happen—why put through two hundred students doing English when Northern Ireland and the UK only needs forty English teachers, fifteen journalists or something?—I'm just trying to think of the careers an English student would go on to. Maybe somewhere the numbers need to be reduced, that's how this program operates, we put people into certain channels because of the potential jobs, and that's how we have over ninety-percent success in employment. We would not let everybody go to personnel because the jobs are not there, so we control it. So maybe if the universities reduced their numbers coming into certain degrees, at the end then more would get employed very fast, instead of having a saturation of the market with people with non-professional degrees.

We don't have to look too hard here to see just exactly how this 'vocationalist' agenda carves up the entire sphere of university activity. Having interviewed quite a number of people both from bodies within universities, as well as those external but nonetheless closely affiliated, the single most recurrent feature of responses to questions about purpose in higher education, is an inability to even conceive of this kind of activity as anything other than a mechanism for preparing an individual for entry into a given career.

If we pursue the line of reasoning dictated by the internal logic of vocationalism, the ideal scenario projected for the university is for each and every discipline to have its own specific, dedicated vocational field or channel, into which the total student output of those disciplines can be seamlessly and automatically secured in gainful employment and blissful career-hood. Here again the interview previously cited is entirely representative of the most commonly held notions about the most apposite vocational applications of Literary Studies; it seems that no matter who you put the question to, it is always the same old categories of 'teaching English' and 'journalism' which are wheeled out as the obvious and proper vocational partners to the discipline in question. This most common of assertions is however not without its problems, the most obvious of which being the plain inaccuracy of supposing that someone in possession of a degree in Literary Studies could simply assume the role of English teacher the day after they graduated. The same goes for journalism *per se*. Granted, having an English degree might be thought beneficial to these vocations, but it seems doubtful that it could ever be considered essential.

We need however to be careful not to rob Literary Studies of its rightful heritage —such as that may be—because although positing an English degree as an absolutely fundamental prerequisite to entering the field of journalism *per se* is a self-evidently naïve move, there is nevertheless one particular division of journalism for which the opposite is arguably the case. This of course is the field of literary journalism. It does seem that, in the case of literary journalism, you could take an English graduate, and there would be sufficient similarity between what they actually did as a student and what they would be required to do as a literary journalist; that you're actually approaching the kind of seamless and apparently apposite transition from university to 'world of work' which we referred to earlier. It is at this point that the idea of a linkage between Literary Studies and literary journalism is taken by some to be the source of great mutual benefit. Given the kind of context within which all of this appears to be occurring, it is probably fair to say that it is those from the Literary Studies camp who will be more eager both to insist upon the very existence of such a linkage and, perhaps more importantly, to emphasise its mutually beneficial character. Having been somewhat blind-sided by the, admittedly effective, manoeuvres of those operating this vocational agenda, there are those from within the discipline who are then inclined to seize upon this linkage as a means almost of justifying their discipline's existence alongside all those subjects for which the question of vocational application has never really posed any kind of problem. It is almost as though by seizing upon it in this way they can say 'look our discipline serves a purpose—just like yours.'

The problem in all of this however, is that even though it might appear that this linkage is of great benefit to Literary Studies, and that by emphasising it one can somehow ward off the threat which vocationalism exerts upon those disciplines which fail to meet its demands, the reality is that in embracing vocationalism—to any extent—you are in fact playing straight into the hands of those who operate this agenda. If you concede, to even the smallest extent, that a given discipline exists primarily to service a given profession or vocational field, before very long you can expect vocational logic to begin making determinations to the effect that it simply does not make sense to offer two hundred places on a given course, if the corresponding vocational field will only have openings for one hundred new employees by the time those students are graduating. This is a brutal enough economy to operate even in the case of disciplines which enjoy a relatively large percentage of openings in their designated vocational channels. However when this same economy is applied to a discipline like Literary Studies it becomes nothing short of murderous. Given that there is a case for saying that literary journalism is really the only vocational field which one could sensibly align with Literary Studies, when you then take into account the brute scarcity of openings within this field, you have given the vocational logicians an excuse to all but shut the whole discipline down. One can only imagine that the annual tally of openings in literary journalism here in Belfast would be unlikely to reach double figures, assuming, that is, that the number would tally at all.

This is not the end of the complications incurred as a result of this dearth of openings either. Because when dealing with literary journalism, there is a real danger that if you fail to keep a sharp focus on the brute economic and free-market deficiencies which are the actual source of its limitations, there is a tendency then to misread this limited status as a kind of exclusivity. As ridiculous as it sounds, it is actually quite easy to slip into a way of thinking about this field of activity whereby you effectively accept the idea that something like literary reviewing tasks the intellect to such an extraordinary degree, that it becomes, unavoidably, the preserve of an elite few. Of course such a notion is pretty much par the course for an institution that still sets a lot of stock by not just a canon of 'great writers', but also a canon of 'great critics'. The question here perhaps being why there is still so much in what the field of literary reviewing projects of itself which is set to alienate, rather than encourage potential activists. In principle we might not be altogether opposed to the idea of an elite, providing this elite were taken to refer to a group of people given license to proceed with a humanly worthwhile task, where the group in question had displayed a clear aptitude for completing that task in as unimpeachable a fashion as possible. These however are criterion which would not seem to apply to the current reviewing elite who, as Edna Longley has recently revealed, cannot yet even be relied upon to apprehend and interrogate something as elementary as the traffic of crude stereotypes.[1]

1 Edna Longley, ' "Between the Saxon Smile and Yankee Yawp": Problems and Contexts of Literary Reviewing in Ireland,' *Grub Street and the Ivory Tower: Literary Journalism and Literary Scholarship from*

From what has been said thus far, it would seem to be inherently problematic for the discipline of Literary Studies to be yoked to the field of literary journalism in the manner previously described. Not least on account of the potentially destructive way in which such a linkage invites people to interpret both the discipline itself and its students, and more specifically, the difficulties that inhere in having the discipline made subordinate to practices which, at present, seem determined to parade themselves in a fashion which only raises doubts about their ultimate worth. The question which all of this is building to, is whether our misgivings about the current state of play within Literary Studies then commit us to a belief that the discipline in question retains some latent potential towards something higher and better, and if so, how are we to justify this belief? In the remainder of this paper I hope to show that there is indeed a higher end which the discipline of Literary Studies tends towards, and it is to Cardinal Newman's *The Idea of a University* that I wish now to turn, in order to provide some schemata in which to ground this assertion.

From the outset Newman's approach is in stark contrast to the 'top-down' vagaries of the vocationalist's interpretative ploys. Newman's interest in the idea of a university springs from a profound interest in and concern for that idea. Consequently, the greatest strength of his contribution to this debate is the powerful terminology which he develops for describing those structures which are absolutely endemic to the university project and the degree to which that terminology remains faithful to the idea in question. This is significant for the concerns of this paper insomuch as we then have to consider the implications of having Literary Studies defined as a 'Branch of Knowledge', and 'Knowledge' itself defined as it is in 'Discourse V: Knowledge Its Own End', which proceeds:

> Let me not be thought to deny the necessity, or decry the benefit, of such attention to what is particular and practical, as belongs to the useful or mechanical arts; life could not go on without them; we owe to the many a debt of gratitude for fulfilling that duty. I only say that Knowledge, in proportion as it tends more and more to be particular, ceases to be Knowledge. It is a question whether Knowledge can in any sense be predicated of the brute creation; without pretending to metaphysical exactness of phraseology, which would be unsuitable to an occasion like this, I say, it seems to me improper to call that passive sensation, or perception of things, which brutes seem to possess by the name of Knowledge. When I speak of Knowledge, I mean something intellectual, something which grasps what it perceives through the senses; something which takes a view of things; which sees more than the senses convey; which reasons upon what it sees, and while it sees; which invests it with an idea. It expresses itself, not in a mere enunciation, but by an enthymeme: it is of the nature of science from the

Fielding to the Internet, eds. Jeremy Treglown and Bridget Bennet (Oxford: Clarendon, 1998) 200-23.

first, and in this consists its dignity. The principle of real dignity in Knowledge, its worth, its desirableness, considered irrespectively of its results, is this germ within it of a scientific or a philosophical process. This is how it comes to be an end in itself; this is why it admits of being called Liberal.[2]

I would suggest that Newman comes as close here as anyone has ever come in putting this matter beyond question, in that if the concept of a university is to retain any meaning at all, then it is this principle of Knowledge which must lie at the very heart of all of its activities, operating as its foremost and prime concern. Such an assertion retains massive implications for practice in Literary Studies, in that for this discipline to fulfil its commitment to the university project and function truly as a Branch of Knowledge, I would suggest, requires that it maintain a very stringent and disciplined awareness of 'literature' and the 'literary' as a means to a greater end—and not an end in itself. It is at this point that the ideological cleavage between the two spheres which we are concerned with here really begins to occur. Because in its present incarnation it is very difficult to see how the field of literary journalism could ever really commit wholesale to the almost anti-materialist philosophical habit which Newman outlines. Whether or not the university is actually committed to such a habit at present is another question entirely, but at least it has it within its remit to do so.

Perhaps the greatest irony in all of this, is that what Newman is describing in this instance is 'the critical' itself, and why else would one engage with an activity like literary reviewing other than because it provides a medium in which to actualize the critical, or to put it another way, a terrain through which it can flow? Our discussion thus far however, has been largely to the effect of casting doubt on the ultimate fitness of literary reviewing as a critical medium. When one takes into account the abuses suffered by literary reviewing at the hands of the publishing industry, where critical rigour seems often to be displaced in favour of some marketing imperative, it is not altogether clear why one would ever identify literary reviewing as an organ from which to wring genuinely critical analysis. The consequences of these prolonged entanglements with the publishing industry are quite profound, in that the instant one finds oneself in a position where the overall and driving emphasis is upon the cultural artefact—the product itself if you like—it is at that point that the very possibility of retaining some operational sense of that entity as being a means to a greater end effectively disappears. Such an assertion needs qualifying however, and one has to be open to the possibility that a person could be working within a field such as literary reviewing or publishing, where you simply would not be doing your job unless you were up to your elbows in the product itself, and yet retain that all important awareness of a greater end. To strike such a balance must however, of necessity, be a

2 John Henry Cardinal Newman, *The Idea of a University* (San Francisco: Rinehart, 1960) 85.

tremendously difficult thing to achieve, and something which is probably only achievable when the activity in question is being carried out on the smallest of scales. The context of industry, be it 'IT industry' or 'culture industry', is such an aggressively pervasive entity, that once you are within that context there simply will not be any room left for philosophy, and that it should be so is doubtless no coincidence either.

In reading Newman, perhaps the most startling thing is that he absolutely recognizes the threat posed by the kind of perspective which I have termed vocationalism. For instance, in 'Discourse VII: Knowledge Viewed in Relation to Professional Skill' he states:

> Now this is what some great men are very slow to allow; they insist that Education should be confined to some particular and narrow end, should issue in some definite work, which can be weighed and measured. They argue as if every thing, as well as every person, had its price; and that where there has been a great outlay, they have a right to expect a return in kind. This they call making Education and Instruction 'useful' and 'Utility' becomes their watchword. With a fundamental principle of this nature, they very naturally go on to ask, what there is to show for the expense of a University; what is the real worth in the market of the article called 'a Liberal Education', on the supposition that it does not teach us definitely how to advance our manufactures, or to improve our lands, or to better our civil economy; or again, if it does not at once make this man a lawyer, that an engineer, and that a surgeon; or at least if it does not lead to discoveries in chemistry, astronomy, geology, magnetism, and science of every kind.[3]

Given that Newman is writing this in the 1850s, it is perhaps curious that by this stage in the proceedings the discipline of Literary Studies, which, along with other Humanities disciplines, clearly has the most to lose as a result of these kind of incursions, has yet to develop any significant awareness of all the subtle ways in which these assimilatory processes can take hold. Today, anyone hoping to carve a future for themselves within the university will be only too aware of just how much of a prerequisite having a list of publications to your name has become to attaining that goal. Within this context, literary reviewing is still widely considered to be an appropriate arena from which students of literary studies can initiate themselves to that publishing process, and this in spite of the fact that, as it stands, this practice could quite plausibly be said to represent a threat to a student attaining that state of 'Knowledge' or philosophical habit which the university must hold out as its prime objective to promote.

3 Ibid. 115-16.

STEPHEN HULL

Current responses to this issue are nothing if not heavily polarized. I take this however as symptomatic of the fact that, to date, engagements between the spheres of Literary Studies and literary journalism have occurred in the absence of any sufficiently informed protocol—consistent with the best interests of both spheres. The resulting tensions then force perspectives to either simply take it for granted that these two spheres always have 'done business' and always will, or alternatively to adhere to the seemingly protectionist line which I have been pursuing in this paper. I do nevertheless hope that I have managed here to convey a sense of how, on some level or other, literary reviewing and its associated field of literary journalism end up unwittingly serving as simply another means by which the university is brought to account on the basis of a vocationalist, market-driven agenda. In so doing, they fulfil this agenda's twin objectives of containment and incorporation quite succinctly, acting as a cipher or critical cul-de-sac to the kind of transformative and insurgent potentialities which cluster around ideas of 'the literary' and ideas of 'university'. Once those energies have been dissipated, these fields then serve as an equally effective means of conscripting whatever is left to the whims of the culture industry. And of course, nowhere is that particular branch of industry quite so rife as it is in Ireland in the present day.

Song, Murmurs and Laughter in Irish Writing: Sound and Socialization as Liminal Occasions in Language, Literature and the Self

ADRIENNE JANUS, STANDFORD UNIVERSITY, CALIFORNIA

The instances of Irish writing I'll focus on here concern themselves above all with voices: with the possibilities of expression, and the limits within which this expression is heard and understood. A quote from Beckett's *Watt* nicely presents some of these possibilities and limits:

> Now these voices, sometimes they sang only, and sometimes they cried only, and sometimes they murmured only, and sometimes they sang and cried and stated, and sometimes they sang and cried and murmured, and sometimes they cried and stated and murmured, and sometimes they sang and cried and stated and murmured, all together, at the same time, as now[1]

1 Samuel Beckett, *Watt* (New York: Grove, 1959) 29.

[115]

I'd like then to discuss Irish writing in terms of voices that sing, murmur, and cry. (For crying, I'll substitute laughter, which for Beckett is equivalent, but preferable.) All of the texts I'll discuss here, to a greater or lesser degree, tend to foreground sound in this way, privileging the non-referential, non-discursive aspects of language: from Sterne's whistling uncle Toby, to Yeats' songs for the psaltery, from the Siren song of Joyce's Ulysses, to the haunted murmurs of Irish Gothic and the almost unintelligible murmurs of Beckett's *Not I*. In so far as these texts attempt to represent or perform in language song, murmurs or laughter, occasions that occur at the liminal points of articulate language, they tend to touch upon the limits of standard genre or form. This type of linguistic liminality, in turn, seems co-ordinate with a disturbance of the limits of the self: the limits traced between the conscious and unconscious, the intellect and sentiment, self-reflexive cognition and perception. In so far as song, murmurs and laughter trouble or breach the limits of the self, they figure as elemental moments in the process of socialization—the development and the end, or death, of subjectivity, the transgression of spatio-temporal limits. In the texts I'll speak about, these linguistically liminal occasions of song, murmurs, and laughter, and the process of socialization they enact, are seen as prior to, and having priority over, fully articulated language and the expression of institutionalized moral codes or cultural values—codes and values that, in the instance of Irish writing, most frequently figured as occasions for contention rather than social accord.

I. SONG AND MUSIC

Literature and philosophy in general (and this is a very big, but, I think, largely correct, generalization) tend to present song and music according to two models, the harmonious or the melodious model. Irish texts in particular, and certainly the ones I'll speak about, tend to criticise or problematise both these models. The first, harmonious model, seems the dominant model for Western thought until the late nineteenth century: it finds its beginnings in Pythagorus' and Plato's 'Harmony of the Spheres', runs through to Leibniz' 'Pre-established Harmony', and leaves the imprint of its structure in Kant's categories and Hegel's 'Spirit'. According to this model, the world is represented or governed by harmonious forms that express the correspondence between the ideal and the real, between a transcendent moral order and its phenomenal counterparts. Speculative reason and logic, furthermore, dominate experience, and intellect reigns over perceptual sensation. The harmonious conception of socialization usually involves a strictly hierarchical, conservative system, one based on universal principles and thus resistant to dissonant elements, undisturbed by anomalies of will or desire. Literature based upon this model would be the realist or historical novel, its omniscient narrator testifying to a one-to-one correspondence between language and reality.

This harmonious model of community and of writing is beautifully criticised by Swift in *Gulliver's Travels*. Here, the unreliable, perhaps mentally disturbed, narrator recounts his adventure to the floating island of Laputa, an island whose domains are governed in accordance with the harmonious, universal principles of music, mathematics and astrology. Not only must physical representations in this world accord with universal forms, such that 'outward garments were adorned with the figures of suns, moons, and stars, interwoven with those of fiddles, flutes, harps, trumpets, guitars, harpsicords, and many more instruments of music.'[2] But, to ensure the harmony of the inner world with the movements of these universal forms, the rulers of Laputa must engage themselves constantly in a bizarrely solipsistic type of reflection: 'Their heads,' notes Gulliver, 'were all reclined either to the right, or to the left; one of their eyes turned inward, and the other directly up to the zenith ... it seems the mind of these people are so taken up with intense speculations, that they neither can speak, or attend to the discourses of others, without being roused by some external taction upon the organs of speech and hearing'.[3] So concerned are the Laputans to maintain and monitor the abstract harmonies of the world, that they testify to a semi-permanent absent-mindedness, as well as to a physical absence from the actual lands over which their flying island rules. Despite this, however, the governing Laputans conceive of themselves as dedicated administrators: they are 'perpetually enquiring into public affairs,' says Gulliver,

> giving their judgement in matters of state; and passionately disputing every inch of party opinion. I have indeed observed the same disposition among most the mathematicians I have known in Europe; although I could never discover the least analogy between the two sciences; unless those people suppose, that because the smallest circle hath as many degrees as the largest, therefore the regulation and management of the world requires no more abilities than the handling and turning of a globe.[4]

This reductio ad absurdum of actual differences to uniform, abstract principles of logic and reason inflicts considerable damage upon the domains over which it rules: the once wealthy and productive Lagado, for example, forced to abandon dissonant practices based on tradition and experience, inevitably goes to wrack and ruin. When the people of Lagado threatened to revolt, the governors on Laputa then brutally punish the potential insurgents by blocking out the sun. It is easy, of course, to read this as an allegory for the governance of Ireland at the time. But Swift here also attacks a whole system of Western thought, one that will not easily be changed simply by changing the individual administrators.

Laurence Sterne also offers a critique of the harmonious model of human socialization and literary representation. In *Tristram Shandy*, the principles

2 Jonathan Swift, *Gulliver's Travels* (Hertford: Wordsworth, 1992) 119.   3 Ibid. 119.   4 Ibid. 123.

associated with harmonious accord, namely, speculative logic and reason, are figured in the character of the father, who, in defence of a theoretical truth, will risk family honour and life. As the father says: 'In Forto Scientiae, there is no such thing as Murder ... 'tis only death, brother.'[5] Death, in other words, is simply an abstract concept, the negation of life, and as such, the father declares, 'common air, in competition with any hypothesis.'[6] The only critique of such modes of thought lies in a realm beyond that of logical reasoning, one where irrational sentiment condones sympathy, and the privileging of particular human attachments over an abstract humanity. This critique, however, is as yet essentially inarticulate—it is the whistling of Tristam's Uncle Toby. 'My uncle Toby,' says Tristram, 'would never offer to answer this by any other kind of argument, than that of whistling half a dozen bars of Lillibulero.'[7] Uncle Toby's whistling here, as inarticulate sound, is by no means ineffective against articulate discourse; the sudden manifestation of physical presence as an aural signal effectively blocks reason and logical argument, silences the interlocutor, and demands a change of subject.

Whistling here functions similarly to the second, melodious model of music and song. Indeed, the critique it offers of the restrictive systemization of harmonious models of society and language emerges as only slightly more articulate than Toby's whistling. On this view, the process of socialization occurs through currents latent in an essentialised human nature, a nature governed not by instrumental reason but by intuition, emotion and sympathy. Language, accordingly, must be formed to express these, and literature forms itself around variations on the lyrical first-person. Rousseau, the most infamous proponent of the melodious model of human language and socialization, envisions an ideal pastoral society established by 'needs born of the heard', needs expressed by what he calls the 'parole chantante' in which 'people speak as much by sonorities and rhythm as by articulations and sounds.'[8] Despite Rousseau's contention that the Irish sounded more like croaking frogs than humans speaking, the Rousseauian ideal resonates with idealised perceptions of the Celt and its bardic tradition, a perception taken up by Matthew Arnold's Celtic imagination, revised by James Stephens, complexified by Yeats and Joyce and problematised by Beckett. Stephens, for example, offers an almost parodic Rousseauian vision, though probably unintentionally, in the closing scene of *The Crock of Gold*. Here, Aengus Og, the god of love, and his bride, unite the people in song and dance: 'hand sought for hand, feet moved companionably as though they loved each other ... And then the loud song arose ... they sang to the lovers of gaeity and peace, long defrauded'.[9] The narrator then goes on the describe what seems to be the Celtic version of the manifestation of the general will: 'they moved freely each in his personal whim, and they moved also with the unity of one being ... through the

5 Laurence Sterne, *The Life and Opinions of Tristram Shandy* (London: Penguin, 1967) 92. 6 Ibid. 92. 7 Ibid. 92. 8 Jean Jacques Rousseau, *Essay on the origin of Languages, and Writings related to Music*, trans. and ed. John T. Scott (Hanover: UP of New England) 276. 9 James Stephens, *The Crock of Gold* 227.

many minds there went also one mind.. so that in a moment the interchangeable and fluid became locked, and organic with a simultaneous understanding, a collective action ... which was freedom.'[10]

The Yeatsian conception of song and music in poetry, and its role in the process of socialization, is only slightly more complex than this, in so far as it attempts to synthesise intellect and emotion. Emotion, however, still takes the dominant place. Thus, Yeats insists that the poetic mind must not give itself over to speculative reason, as do governments or armies, but rather to feeling, which, Yeats says, the poet shapes as 'sounds, colours or forms ... into a musical relation, that their emotion might live in other minds' and thus 'make and unmake mankind'.[11] Indeed, Yeats' faith in the power of the poet to shape emotion into powerful sounds leads him to declare that, 'I am certainly never certain, when I hear of some war, or of some religious excitement ... or anything else that fills the ear of the world, that it has not all happened because of something that a boy piped in Thessaly.'[12] In order to increase the affective responses to shaped sound, in order that he too might be that boy piping in Thessaly, Yeats devises a way of poetic recitation to the accompaniment of a psaltery tuned to the modulations of the speaking voice. This poetic speech should be neither chant nor song, but should reveal the musical qualities inherent in language, should heighten emotional affectiveness without disturbing the sense of words. The purpose of such heightening of the musical qualities of speech is expressly social for Yeats. Like Rousseau, Yeats envisions the formation of an ideal Greek community unified by its art, and fashions himself as an Irish Homer. So Yeats muses,

> I have always longed to hear poems spoken to a harp, as I imagined Homer to have spoken his, for it is not natural to enjoy an art only when one is by oneself. Whenever one finds a fine verse one wants to read it to somebody, and it would be much less trouble and much pleasanter if we could all listen, friend by friend, lover by beloved. Images used to rise up before me, as I am sure they have arisen before nearly everybody else who cares for poetry, of wild-eyed men speaking harmoniously to murmuring wires while audiences in many-coloured robes listened, hushed and excited.[13]

This image of wild-eyed men speaking through music returns in the Siren chapter of Joyce's Ulysses, where the Sirens, as Hélène Cixous notes, are men: men whose power to enchant their victims (the laughing barwomen, in this scene) fails in the realm of discursive speech and visual signals. Rather it is song that reaches the socio-cultural barriers between the singing men and laughing barmaids, and that sets up the possibility of some sort of solidarity based upon

10 Ibid. 227.   11 W.B. Yeats, *Essays and Introductions* (London: Macmillan, 1961) 157-9.   12 Ibid. 158.   13 Ibid. 14.

the shared emotions and memories these singing voices evoke. Indeed, song takes hold of literary language in the narrative, as given by this exemplary line: 'Flood of warm jimjam secretness flowed to flow in music out in desire, dark to lick flow, invading.'[14] As we see here, within this new spatio-temporal framework sustained by song, there is no subject position, simply the flow of verb and noun, action and matter. If the Joycean Siren song heralds death, it is a metaphysical death of the monadic, self-identical subject.

Similarly, for Beckett in *How It Is*, song heralds a breaching of the boundaries of the hermetic self, and thus serves as an elemental moment in the development of intersubjective communication—indeed, as Beckett suggests, in the development of human language as a whole. For Beckett, however, human communication and the necessary process of socialization it enacts is motivated not by positive desire, but by a double lack, or a doubled pain: in the first case, the pain of solitude, and in the second, the pain of opening oneself to, or being intruded upon by, another human subject. This breaking through the enclosure of a hermetic subject is rendered figuratively and physicalised as a lesson based in painful torture, as subject A compels subject B to social interaction.

> Training continued … table of basic stimuli one sing nails in armpit two speak blade in arse three stop thump on skull four louder pestle on kidney five softer index in anus six bravo clap athwart arse seven lousy same as three eight encore same as one or two as may be[15]

As we see here, song, a reaction to painful stimuli, precedes the birth into language, as the necessary element not only for communication, but for the simple recognition of the world and others in it. It is song, furthermore, or the musical elements of speech, that serve to quiet, however poorly, the pain provoked by the original occasion and secondary understanding of speech.

II. MURMURS

The context within which murmurs occur is that of a block of the full appropriation of the past, a block that in turn impedes forward progression. Murmuring, then, occurs in response to this block; it serves as a working through of the past by repetition, a repetition intended to motivate a yet unrealized movement towards future possiblity. Irish writing would seem to have a particularly long association with muttering, even though it is not intentionally performed in literary language until Beckett. The Young Ireland movement, for example, in its

14 James Joyce, *Ulysses* (New York: Vintage, 1934) 274.   15 Samuel Beckett, *How it Is* (New York: Grove, 1959) 69.

struggle for full appropriation of the past, as for full appropriation of an Irish literature in English, turned to ballads, to poetry as popular song. But these, according to Charles Gavan Duffy, emerge first as a type of muttering, not song: 'the soul of the country, stammering in its passionate grief and hatred in a strange tongue, loved still to utter them [the ballads] in its old familiar idioms and cadences. Uttering them, perhaps, with more piercing earnestness, because of the impediment.'[16]

In Irish Gothic, murmuring, as a sort of repetition compulsion, indicates both a fixed concentration on a terrible event, as well as the effort to move beyond the constraints this event has set up. In Maturin's *Melmouth the Wanderer*, for example, the narrator's repetition of the line, 'nailed to a door' not only describes the body of Lord Kilwarden, pierced through by the pikes of assassins during Emmet's rebellion, but also is figuratively transferred to the innocent witness of this murder who, in his shock, 'stood by his window as if nailed to it'.[17]

Repetition here displaces suffering across subjective boundaries, localised in this instance to characters within the frame of the narrative. Another repeated line similarly attempts to break through the constraints of localized suffering, but, in this case, the repetition of the cry that issues from Lord Kilwarden, Ô'ut me out of pain', transcribed by the narrator a second time as, 'put him out of his pain,' addresses itself to no-one in particular and at the same time everyone. This repeated appeal opens out towards the whole society of readers, an appeal to acknowledge communally the terrors of such an event and move on past it. It would be apt at this point to speak of Yeats, and of the role of muttering and murmurs in Purgatory and in the poem 'Man and the Echo', wherein the echoed line serves functionally as a type of muttering. But as Yeatsian mutters are structurally similar to those I've already spoken about, I'll move on to Beckett, whose language does not translate murmurs into articulate speech, but directly performs it. In Beckett's short play *Not I*, for example, muttering, circumscribed in relation to the self, is occasioned by an interior movement backwards over the boundaries dividing the subconscious from the conscious, or back over those defensive boundaries dividing repressed memory of a past self from conscious evaluation by a present self. The task that muttering aims at once to accomplish and postpone, is that of unifying the unconscious and conscious, the past self and present self, under the sign of a self-identical 'I'. The play opens with a voice, 'unintelligible behind curtain', and as the curtain rises, the monologue starts with lines scarcely more intelligible: 'out … into this world … this world … tiny little thing … before its time … in a godfor— … what? … girl? … yes … tiny little girl … into this … out into this … before her time … godforsaken hole called … called … no matter …'[18] The inarticulacy of language allows the

16 Charles Gavan Duffy, 'The Ballad Poetry of Ireland', cited by Seamus Deane, 'Poetry and Song', *The Field Day Anthology of Irish Writing*, ed. Seamus Deane (Derry: Field Day, 1991) 5.   17 Charles Maturin, *Melmouth the Wanderer* (London: OUP) 257.   18 Samuel Beckett, *Collected Short Plays* (New York: Grove, 1984) 216.

speaker to circle closer to the traumatic event that caused division within the psyche, without directly naming the trauma or connecting herself to it, thus without directly reproducing the original trauma. The speaker's objectification of past self as third person, 'girl' or 'she' testifies to an abnormal block between past and present self, one that, if not overcome through the course of continued muttering of which the entire play consists, at least is reduced in strength.

III. LAUGHTER

The preponderance of the comic generally in Irish writing is not simply, as Vivien Mercier proposes in *The Irish Comic Tradition*, due to the conservatism of Gaelic tradition. The recurrent privileging of the comic and the laughter it aims to provoke, I would argue, also stems from the functional capacities of laughter as psychosomatic release and social regulation. Indeed, laughter, as Henri Bergson notes, is a particularly effective method of consolidating community and chastising transgression; it thus promotes socilization without recourse to institutional regulation or the rule of law.[19] On a more existential level, laughter may occasion an irrational affirmation of life: against the Beckettian insistence that there is no reasonable way to go on, laughter opens up a momentary space from which one can go on, as the involuntary physical reaction basic to laughter momentarily blocks the train of thought that produced (or at least cognised) the dilemma in the first place. As Helmuth Plessner notes in his study of laughter: 'Where danger threatens the life, soul, or mind of man, there will emerge laughter, and … the possibility to objectify one's own destruction and thus in some way overcome it … then even if the situation is hopeless, it is nevertheless not serious.'[20] This blocking may also originate from a purely linguistic occasion. As Niklas Luhmann has it, 'consciously metaphorical uses of words and concepts, intended ambiguities, paradoxes, and humorous, joking turns of phrase', word play, in other words, 'are …obstacles … to the reflexive turn of communication. These linguistic forms signal that a reflexive question about why and how has no meaning.'[21]

As word play is the realm of the poet, I'll now turn to Yeats for an example of the blocking self-reflexivity through word-play and laughter. In 'A Dialogue of Self and Soul', for example, we se laughter emerging at the point when the intellect is brought up against the limits of the conceivable, and conscious agency against the limits of its capacity for action, such that neither can conceive of a way to proceed within the existing spatio-temporal framework. This deadlock is directly connected to the limits of language. In the penultimate stanza of the

19 Henri Bergson, *Comedy* (Baltimore: Johns Hopkins) 148.   20 Helmuth Plessner, *Lachen und Weinen* (Bern: Francke, 1950) 189 (my translation).   21 Niklas Luhmann, *Social Systems* (Stanford: Stanford, 1995) 153.

poem, the Soul, the voice of the intellect, says: 'The intellect no longer knows/*Is* from the *Ought*, or *Knower* from the *Known* … / When I think of that my tongue's a stone.'²² This metaphor indicates a block, and the tension occurring as a result of its spills over into the involuntary physical reaction, laughter which momentarily suppresses the intellect and conscious agency, and sets up a framework for a new progression, indicated by the movement of the dialogue from the voice of Soul to the voice of the Self. The self, as it casts out remorse (and intellectual construct), becomes ecstatic and hortatory in its repeated affirmation of life and declares:

> I am content to live it all again
> And yet again …
> When such as I case out remorse
> So great a sweetness flows into the breast
> We must laugh and we must sing
> We are blest in everything

In this break from Soul to Self the physical compulsion to affirm life seems to produce its own resolution when the intellect, on its own, has reached the limits of its capacities.

Laughter can also serve as a regulatory function in the process of socialization, disempowering actual social beings or constructs by moving them past the boundary which incorporates them into a subject position, over into a framework where they become a laughable object. This excluding movement corresponds to a movement that enables the inclusion of otherwise marginalised elements or figures of social life. Or, as Bergson has it, laughter activates and mixes 'the pleasure of an emotional bond shared with the members of a group and simultaneously the threat of being excluded.'²³ In the Siren chapter of Joyce's *Ulysses*, it is the male gaze and male desire that becomes the excluded, laughable object, momentarily blinded by the sound of Miss Douce's and Miss Kennedy's laughter. Here is Miss Kennedy, indicated now in the midst of laughter as Kennygiggles, describing Bloom: 'O greasy eyes! Imagine being married to a man like that!' Miss Douce responds: 'Married to the greasy nose!'²⁴ As their laughter takes the subject position, the language through which it speaks starts to laugh, finally to become absorbed by the laughing sounds. At this point, the women are no longer indicated by names but by the conjoined words bronze/gold, describing their hair as well as the sound of pealing laughter: 'Shrill, with deep laughter … bronzegold goldbronze, shrilldeep, to laughter after laughter. And then laughed more. Greasy I knows.'²⁵ In the conflation bronzegold/goldbronze into one word, the two women are brought together in unity under the

22 W.B. Yeats, *Collected Poems* (New York: Macmillan, 1989).   23 Bergson 150.   24 Joyce 260.   25 Ibid. 260.

sound of laughter, Similarly, the sound of the women's laughter transfigures the male gaze: from greasy eye nose to Greasy I knows: the women have become a singular subject 'I', referenced to the plural verb 'Knows', as they are joined in a plurality of knowledge.

It is easy to see here how this chapter inspired Hélène Cixous' 'The Laugh of the Medusa'. This foundational text of French feminism, a call to arms for women writers and for a women's writing, derives its impetus from the powerful, ecstatic, yet knowledgeable laughter of Joyce's women. This explicit attempt to found a type of literature upon laughter parallels the implicit grounding of the Irish writing I've been speaking about upon laughter, murmurs, and song. Represented or performed in these texts at the limits of fully articulated language: song, murmurs, and laughter occur below or beyond the expression of moral codes or cultural values, and often at the limits of self-reflexivity, at the limits of the production and appropriation of meaning. Yet, I would argue, these liminal occasions nevertheless open up a space, even create a new frame orientation, for the reformulation of those things at whose limits they are produced: language, literature and society.

Reproblematizing the Irish Text*

AARON KELLY, THE QUEEN'S UNIVERSITY OF BELFAST

Why reproblematizing the Irish text? Well, I want to argue that no text is historically unproblematical but that the Irish text is conventionally problematized in terms of its uniqueness, its anomaly or peculiarity—in short, its recidivist disregard for the normative, progressive models of world History. In Marxist terms, I want not only to reformulate and redraft the problematics encoded in the Irish text but also to decipher the normative models of literary production as structures of hegemony and ideological transparency. In doing so, I hope to refract the historical questions raised by the Irish text back upon the hegemonic conventions against which they are judged. That said however, whilst the displacement of Irish writing within the major canonical and critical frameworks of literature, and in particular English literature, is therefore to be acknowledged, the problematics of the Irish text are not reducible, I would maintain, to a purely colonial legacy. The national problematics induced by the historical mystifications of the dominant ideologies in Ireland must also be attended to. If, as Seamus Deane contends, Irish writing is subject to a 'long colonial concussion',[1] then surely it is time to waken up. This must be, above all, a historical awakening from this often strategically rather convenient collective dreamsleep. For,

* I would like to thank Colin Graham for his generous and thoughtful guidance with the first draft of this essay.   1 Seamus Deane, *Heroic Styles: The Tradition of an Idea* (Derry: Field Day, 1984) 18.

given Walter Benjamin's postulation that 'every epoch not only dreams the next, but while dreaming impels it towards wakefulness',[2] it is worth considering the imaginative limitations of the willful concussive amnesia producing the Irish literary canon as national *telos*.

In resetting the problematics of the Irish text, and in instigating a historical awakening, I shall turn to Fredric Jameson's formulation of the political unconscious. Jameson's Althusserian grasp of History as an 'absent cause' does not deny the referent of History but rather recognizes that 'it is inaccessible to us except in textual form ... our approach to it and to the Real itself necessarily passes through its prior textualization, its narrativization in the political unconscious'.[3] It insists upon an ideology of form, upon the uncovering of determinate structures of formal antinomy, through its grasp of History not as some reified or passive object or representation but as the experience of necessity that lacerates literary production. Thus, no ideology, however dominant, ingrained or discursively self-enthroned, is coherent enough to survive its own textual figuration. Such a model enables us to examine the problematics of textualizing History without viewing Irish History as problematical in itself. In short, it ensures that an analysis of Irish literature may proceed in terms, not of peculiarity and anomaly, but rather of specificity and intensity.

However, the collapse of such historically sophisticated Marxist frameworks in relation to Irish writing, and the national formation more generally, further contributes to the exigency of addressing the problematics of the Irish text. I shall conduct my analysis with specific reference to the work of Terry Eagleton and the Field Day project. Often Eagleton's work on Ireland is opposed through a hostility to theory *per se*. The challenge facing this essay, and its Marxist approach, is not to reject the work of Eagleton out of hand but rather to reapply and respecify in regard to Ireland—where I would assert his critical engagement breaks down—the interpretative methodologies, which he establishes often so successfully in his other writings. I wish to undercut, therefore, not only the unitary fabric of the national text produced by nationalist canons and their immemorial relation to a colonial metacode, but also the misuse of Ireland as ideological solution to the historical pressures faced by the international Left. I want to affirm Aijaz Ahmad's point, in refuting Fredric Jameson's own reductive work on national allegory, that 'the ideological conditions of a text's production are never singular but always several'.[4] This is not, however, the prelude to some vacuous advocacy of the pluralism celebrated by mainstream Revisionism, or indeed postmodernism, both of which would seek to diffuse conceptually their material implication in the social formations of late and multinational capitalism. This essay is instead intended to affirm dialectically the conflictual antagonisms of the national text.

2 Walter Benjamin. *Charles Baudelaire: A Lyric Poet in an Era of High Capitalism* (London: New Left, 1973) 178.   3 Frederic Jameson, *The Political Unconscious: Narrative as a Socially Symbolic Act* (London: Routledge, 1996) 35.   4 Aijaz Ahmad, *In Theory: Classes, Nations, Literatures* (London: Verso, 1992).

The importance of an Ahmadian sense of ideological multiplicity is indicated by Seamus Deane's reductive notion of what constitutes social unity: 'When a culture is politically homogeneous, like that of Britain, the sectarianism is directed externally rather than internally and is usually xenophobic in character. When, as in Ireland's case, the culture is politically divided, the sectarianism is largely internally directed'.[5] This model of political homogeneity, which is dubious enough even at a rudimentary national level given the devolution of power within Britain, informs Deane's primary justification of the *Field Day Anthology*: 'There *is* a story here, a meta-narrative, which is, we believe, hospitable to all the micro-narratives that, from time to time, have achieved prominence as the official version of the true history, political and literary, of the island's past and present.'[6] This construction of the national demonstrates a capacity to subsume the putatively sectional interests of class or gender for example. Such a model highlights the sense of the national as a code word for the hegemonic subject.

Interestingly, Deane describes the Field Day trajectory as 'like the Abbey in its origin in that it has within it the idea of a culture which has not yet come to be in political terms. It is unlike the Abbey in that it can no longer subscribe to any simple nationalism for the basis of its existence.'[7] This eschewal of 'simple nationalism' adumbrates the attempt to recodify and re-legitimize the canonical nation in the theoretical pamphlets such as those by Jameson, Said and Eagleton, issued by Field Day. As Colin Graham notes, the nation under historically modified conditions stands as the ultimate ethical and cognitive seam for much postcolonial criticism in Ireland, and I would argue, withdraws from the ultimate horizon of History itself.[8] For Francis Mulhern, the obsessive dwelling upon the national question, upon the colonial trauma, as the primary collective identification of Irish people, particularly in the Southern State several generations after independence, is redolent of a 'postcolonial melancholy', which ultimately serves to exonerate and absolve the indigenous propertied classes from culpability in the ordering of both nation states in Ireland.[9] In undercutting the unitary problematic of Field Day's theoretical rewriting of 'simple nationalism', Edward Said's pamphlet on the 'cartographic impulse' in Yeats' poetry notably constructs a homogeneous decolonizing subject, with the aim of affording Yeats the status of 'that of the indisputably great *national* poet who articulates the experiences, the aspirations, and the vision of a people suffering under the domination of an off-shore power'.[10] Where is the attention to class, to religion and most importantly to gender, in terms of this rather sexualized reclamation of the landscape? Indeed, the Field Day Theatre Company's great play of national repos-

5 'Political Writings and Speeches 1900-1988', *The Field Day Anthology of Irish Writing* Vol. III (Derry: Field Day, 1991) 682.   6 Deane, 'General Introduction'. *The Field Day Anthology* xix.   7 Deane, 'What is Field Day?'. Programme Notes for the Field Day Production of *Three Sisters*, 1981.   8 See Colin Graham, '"Liminal Spaces": Post-Colonial Theories and Irish Culture'. *Irish Review*. Autumn/Winter, 1994, 29-43.   9 Francis Mulhern, *The Present Lasts a Long Time: Essays in Cultural Politics* (Cork: Cork UP, 1998) 158.   10 Said, *Yeats and Decolonization* (Derry: Field Day, 1988) 12.

session and renaming, Brian Friel's *Translations*, centres on a rather gendered insecurity about a dumb, feminized Ireland personified by Sarah's character. It could additionally be argued that the play's own most evocative ideological quiescence and formal dumbfounding is the figuration of modernity anxiously gendered in the assertive voice of Maire.

In order to destabilize Ireland as unitary subject with regard to Marxism, I shall contest Eagleton's reading of Maria Edgeworth's *Castle Rackrent* in his *Heathcliff and the Great Hunger*, which accords with the established problematization of the Irish novel in terms of the nightmare of Irish History. For example, in *Great Hatred, Little Room*, James M. Cahalan comments: 'Try as he may, the Irish writer cannot escape that nightmare, that net, that fanaticism in the deep heart's core. The Irish writer has returned over and over again to Irish history, seeing art as a battlefield on which to play out the conflicts contained within that history'.[11] Similarly, Eagleton, in problematizing Edgeworth's *Castle Rackrent*, applies a sacrosanct ideal of art to a degraded Irish society: 'Art demands serenity, stable evolution, classical equipoise; and an island racked by rancorous rhetoric is hardly the appropriate breeding ground for these virtues'.[12] Maria Edgeworth herself appears to confirm the literary difficulties peculiarly produced by Irish social turmoil: 'It is impossible now to draw Ireland as she now is in a book of fiction—realities are too strong, party persuasions are too violent to bear to see, or care to look at, their faces in a looking glass. The people would rather break the glass and curse the fool who held up the mirror to nature—distorted nature, in a fever'.[13] Eagleton seizes upon Edgeworth's looking glass metaphor: 'a unifying mode of representation, which what the mirror signifies, is no longer able to capture a contradictory reality'.[14] This naïve reflective sense of the real is fundamentally undercut by the methodology that Eagleton establishes in his *Criticism and Ideology*, and which broadly parallels Jameson's political unconscious. Through his use of Althusser and the work of Pierre Macherey, Eagleton proposes a mode of formal interpretation which acknowledges that

> the literary text, far from constituting some unified plenitude of meaning, bears inscribed within it the marks of certain determinate absences which twist its various significations into conflict and contradiction. These absences —the not-said of the work—are precisely what bind it to its ideological problematic: ideology is present in the text in the form of its eloquent silences.[15]

11 James M. Cahalan, *Great Hatred, Little Room: The Irish Historical Novel* (Dublin: Gill and Macmillan, 1983) xi.   12 Eagleton, *Heathcliff and the Great Hunger: Studies in Irish Culture* (London: Verso, 1995) 151. 13 From a letter of 1834. Quoted in Seamus Deane, 'Irish National Character 1790-1900'. Tom Dunne, ed. *The Writer as Witness: Literature as Historical Evidence* (Cork: Cork UP, 1987) 105.   14 Eagleton, *Heathcliff* 177.   15 Eagleton, *Criticism and Ideology: A Study in Marxist Literary Theory* (London: Verso, 1976) 89.

Such a complex problematic is here denied the Irish text, which exists as problematical in itself.

Eagleton's coupling of art and stability radically elides the historical context of the production of realism amidst the convulsive social rupture of industrialization and urbanization. Remarkably, given his Marxist grasp of the ideology of form, Eagleton refuses to regard realism as itself an imaginary resolution to social contradictions. Indeed, with regard to the representational metaphor of the looking-glass, Althusser's own formulation of the 'speculary' mirror structure of ideology and its necessary 'misrecognition' enables us to question the dominant mimetic and realist modes against which Eagleton identifies the historical deficiencies of the Irish text.[16] Given this Lacanian focus of the fantasy space of the mirror and its determinate oversights, it could then be formulated that, for the normative/dominant form, the peculiarized fracture of the Irish text designedly forestalls an acknowledgement of the putatively ideal textual subject's own formal *'corps morcelé'*.[17] So Eagleton's correlation of realism and stability in contradistinction to Irish instability aligns itself with the production within normative literary criticism of a distanciated yet comprehensible nightmare (that is, Irish History) in place of a nightmare which cannot consciously be imagined (English History), but which, of course has been impelled into the process of being imagined and resolved in precisely such a formulation. To this end, Maurice Colgan asserts that Thady's claim in Edgeworth's novel to have served the Rackrents for 'two hundred years and upwards'[18] is an untenable attempt to impose an English feudal continuity on a fractured Irish society.[19] Notably, his examples of Irish historical turmoil—Cromwellian confiscations, the Restoration, the Williamite Settlements— are not entirely divorced from English social and political rupture!

I am suggesting that the Irish text problematizes the novel form through its nonhegemonic relation to the latter's representational dominants, which would otherwise achieve ideological transparency for conventional accounts of form. Eagleton maintains that 'there are notably few Irish novels which, in the style of an Eliot, alternate in their pages the perspectives of higher and lower classes'.[20] The formal fracture of *Castle Rackrent* disrupts the superintending narratorial presence regulating conflicting discourses in Eagleton's account of realism and social settlement. Edgeworth's text destabilizes, to use Gramsci's term, the 'transformist' hegemony within the novel form, in which a dominant political subject is able to articulate opposing and subordinate discourses in its own interest.[21] Consequently,

16 Louis Althusser, *Essays on Ideology* (London: Verso, 1993) 54.   17 *'Le corps morcelé'* is the Lacanian 'body-in-pieces', a retroactive fantasy effected by the imaginary unity of the mirror stage, which I am here formulating as the imagined ideological unity of Eagleton's realist text. See Jacques Lacan, *Ecrits: A Selection* (London: Tavistock, 1977) 20.   18 Maria Edgeworth, *Castle Rackrent: An Hibernian Tale Taken from Facts and from the Manners of the Irish Squires before the Year 1782.* (1800) (London: Penguin, 1992) 96. 19 Maurice Colgan, 'The Significant Silences of Thady Quirk'. Cóilín Owens, ed. *Family Chronicles: Maria Edgeworth's Castle Rackrent* (Dublin: Wolfhound, 1987) 59.   20 *Heathcliff* 151.   21 Antonio Gramsci, *Selections from the Prison Notebooks* (London: Lawrence and Wishart, 1996) 57.

the 'transition state'[22] of language in Ireland, the friction between English and Irish, print and orality, discloses sociolectical standardizations and resistances that would conventionally achieve a structural transparency under the naturalization of a unitary national language. The Editor's failure to textualize 'into plain English' the otherness of Thady's voice, which remains 'incapable of translation',[23] problematizes the formal assimilations and sublations that were constitutive of the novel's cultural role in the social and political centralizations and hierarchizations of the eighteenth and nineteenth centuries across Europe, which sought to regulate regions, dialects, classes, genders and nations. Therefore, whilst Declan Kiberd maintains that 'without the concept of a normal society the novel is impossible … but the short story is particularly appropriate to a society in which revolutionary upheavals have shattered the very idea of normality',[24] I would posit that Thady's 'unfinished sentences'[25] permit the following reproposition. There should be a shift in critical emphasis when analyzing Irish fiction from failed novels to radically decentred and nonhegemonic fictions. So rather than being problematical in itself, the Irish novel brings into focus the contradictions of the form; it destabilizes the hegemony of its normative representational structures, not through some unitary problematic but rather a through disjuncture which unravels the conflicts of class, gender, region and so on.

Furthermore, the breakdown in Eagleton's Marxist analysis when confronting the Irish novel foregrounds an uncritical relation to the Irish text, which relates to the position of the British Left more generally. Too often a British Left in crisis has sought recourse to Ireland as the repository of compensatory allegories of community, as the site of a unitary and oppositional popular subject to shore against the fractures of late capitalism. Such wistful utopian investments not only provide little historical or political substance for the contemporary struggles of socialists, women's groups and community projects within both nation states in Ireland; they also assume a further political debilitation when one considers the British Left's catastrophic failure to construct its own national locus for the valiant but often sequestered collectivities who opposed the Thatcherite state, and whose defeat has left a profound historical legacy.

The national question is traditionally a vexed one for Marxism, but any effective emancipatory politics in Ireland must address both nation states as specific, and indeed necessary, constellations of forces upon which to ground its struggle. The challenge for Marxism, then, is to articulate the specificity of these national conjunctures without recapitulating 'the nation' as pre-ordained according to nationalist canons. In a way, nationalism's mapping is a complex fetish, which disavows the social totality that it nonetheless gestures towards. Marxism seeks to uncover the national as a specific constellation of social relations to be revolutionized, whereas

---

22 William Carleton, *Traits and Stories of the Irish Peasantry*, vol. I. (1842-4) (Gerrards Cross: Colin Smythe, 1990) ii.   23 Edgeworth 63.   24 Declan Kiberd, 'Story-Telling: The Gaelic Tradition'. Patrick Rafroidi and Terence Brown, eds. *The Irish Short Story* (Lille: Lille UP, 1979) 15.   25 Edgeworth 61.

as the anxious, utopian imagination of nationalism seeks jointly to mystify and mobilize such conditions. In other words, the national signifier, despite its ideological surface, does not really transcend social conflict but rather seeks to dis- and re-articulate it. Marxism wills re-articulation as ruptural resolution. By seeking to simultaneously hold together and at bay at complex chain of signification, the national signifier may be formulated as *formatively interstitial*: that is, constructed across the axes of class, gender, urbanity and so on. So rather than viewing the conflicts of class, gender or urbanity as interruptive of an organic and transcendental national subject, such axes are actually productive of that dominant subject, the contestatory grounds of its hegemony. Therefore, when Gramsci contends that any emancipatory project must 'nationalise itself in a certain sense',[26] the process entails not the embrace of an organic whole but rather the historical transcription of a national conjuncture onto a global dynamic in an expansive hegemonic trajectory.

With this sense of the conflictive national conjuncture in mind, I shall turn to Eagleton's chapter on inner émigrés in the Irish novel in *Crazy John and the Bishop*, wherein the Irish text is utilized as a unitary subversive model. Although Eagleton covers a broad spectrum of novelists in tracing the problematics of home within Irish writing, he tends to homogenize Irish writers into a unitary national subject of 'outsiders' without due attention to the additional and concrete dispossessions of class or gender.[27] Consequently, the formal dynamics of a text such as Patrick MacGill's *Children of the Dead End* become reducible to the same national subjective condition as the privileged posturing of Francis Stuart's outcasts. Therefore, as with the flawed chapter on the Anglo-Irish novel in *Heathcliff and the Great Hunger* discussed earlier, it is disappointing, but nevertheless symptomatic of the utopian figuration of Ireland by sections of the British Left, that an accomplished Marxist critic such as Eagleton, with his commanding Althusserian grasp of the ideology of the text and its unsaid, should draw such uncritically direct and unitary correlations in Irish fiction between text and nation, text and History.

For at the political and aesthetic core of MacGill's *Children of the Dead End*, there is a profound displacement between class experience and conventional literary form:

> In my story there is no train of events or sequence of incidents leading up to a desired end. When I started writing of my life I knew not how I would end my story: and even yet, seeing that one thing follows another so closely, I hardly know when to lay down my pen and say that the tale is told ... A story of real life, like real life itself, has no beginning, no end. Something happens before and after.[28]

26 Gramsci 241.   27 Eagleton, *Crazy John and the Bishop and Other Essays on Irish Culture* (Cork: Cork UP, 1998) 212-248.   28 Patrick MacGill, *Children of the Dead End* (1914), (London: Caliban, 1985) 111.

MacGill's sense of historical experience, and in particular class experience, contradicting literary form provides an allegory of the displacement of determinate historical problematics within Irish writing, which rupture the unitary atypicality model. Consequently, this essay has sought not only to expose the normative conventions by which the Irish text is judged as structures of hegemony and sociolectical conflict, but also, in turn, to reproblematize the Irish text in accordance with that historical process. In this context, a traumatic historical event, such as the Famine for example, proffers an opportunity not to peculiarize the Irish text but rather to ascertain how the Irish text evidences aporia and disjuncture through which to challenge conventional literary and historical teleologies. The goal, then, is to construct a properly oppositional methodology that may be able to do justice to the historical elisions of class, race, or gender within the discursive modes of specific and globally imbricated sets of social relationships.

In conclusion, therefore, a concrete grasp of the historical embeddedness of the Irish text becomes especially propitious in our own historical moment, wherein myriad reformulations and reifications of Irishness and the national conjuncture strewn across the multinational apparatus offer evermore seductive and ultimately false resolutions to residual and existent historical dilemmas. If, as I have proposed, the national signifier is a complex fetish, then it is fundamentally reworked and resuscitated—rather than superceded—as merely one displaced image amongst an excessive plethora by a disintegrating late capitalist representational economy that proffers the apotheosis of Marx's theory of commodity fetishism.[29] Therein every concrete historical object—the national conjuncture included—becomes a fetishized sign that would disavow the traces of its own production, its absent or missing cause: the multinational apparatus itself. When capital is usefully considered as a representational economy, a stark antinomy emerges at its core that has profound implications for all forms of representation. Although capital is that which ultimately determines a social meaning (i.e. a value) for every object, including nations, within its global reach, it nonetheless has no inherent value or systematization of value. For capital's instability resides in its necessary desire to mask the absent source of its value or social meaning: namely, the totality of forces of production and labour. In terms of literary production, the Irish text, which was formerly denied a historical problematic because of its supposed immemorial trauma, can now under postmodern conditions celebrate the renewed refutation of its History. Postmodernity seeks to transmute the phantasmal site of the Irish text as dehistoricized nightmare into a comparably phantasmal though now desirous and seductive substitute for historical interpretation and transformation. An oppositional methodology must negotiate the dialectic of presence and absence infusing the Irish text's relation to History and the multinational apparatus. It must refute the fetishized national object's desire to fixate

29 See Karl Marx, 'The Fetishism of Commodities' in David McLellan, ed., *Karl Marx: Selected Writings* (Oxford: OUP, 1977) 435-43.

its meaning outside of History by returning its disavowed or missing causal context. I am proposing that Marxism provides a conceptual form for this counterhegemonic method, through which the historical fracture of the text may be located within a repressed totality of determinant materials. Therefore, this essay is not intended as a willing or untroubled attack on Terry Eagleton, whom I consider to be the finest Marxist cultural thinker of his generation, but is rather written out of a profound interest and belief in Eagleton's thought and a commitment that his formal methodology be applied more rigorously to the Irish text and its position within the global totality. To this end, in his review of Colm Tóibín's *The Penguin Book of Irish Fiction*, Eagleton symptomatically deems Patrick MacGill to be, above and beyond all else, 'a tramp'—and not first and foremost a member of the working class, a First World War soldier, an economic migrant displaced not only by colonial oppression but also by the nascent structures of flexible accumulation and multinational capital that today provide the most insidious forms of imperialism confronting humanity.[30] If an awareness of the precise historical conflict of the Irish text is occluded, then it is itself destined to wander on aimlessly as a perpetual vagabond without a historical or social care in the world, its vacuous brogue now lilting with the emptyspeak of late capitalism, its stage Irishness now cloaked in the unraveling patchwork and arrogated marginalia of postmodernity.

The Critic in Pieces: The Theory and Practice of Literary Reviewing

JOHN KENNY, NUI, GALWAY

> Far be it from us to disparage our own craft, whereby we have our living! Only we must note these things: that Reviewing spreads with strange vigour; that such a man as Byron reckons the reviewer and the poet equal; that at the last Leipzig Fair, there was advertised a Review of Reviews. By and by it will be found that all Literature has become one boundless self-devouring Review ...
> Thomas Carlyle, *Edinburgh Review*, 1831.

The primary aim of this essay is simply to assert the importance of reviewing generally and, concomitantly, to encourage a professional self-consciousness in this amorphous area by way, firstly, of a brief survey of the origins and development of the practice and, secondly, by some summary comments on the contemporary

30 Eagleton, 'Skimmer's and Dipper's Guide to Dislocation', *Irish Times Weekend Review*, 20 Nov 1999 10.

situation. I am principally concerned with literary reviewing. While reviewing, at its origins, was introduced in Western culture specifically as a method of communicating the contents of new scholarly publications to other scholars, the practice escalated alongside the expansion of popular literary forms, most notably the novel, and one of the chief complaints of professional reviewers and external commentators alike has been that the imperative of keeping pace with this pandemic genre is responsible for a decline in standards. Certain recommendations for the reviewing of literature can also be applied to the reviewing of scholarly or academic books, but there are also divergent considerations. The exigencies of factuality and accuracy in scholarly publications have in fact encouraged a degree of self-invigilation in reviewers and review organs involved in the area that far surpasses the conscientiousness of those in the literary area. Without wanting to provoke again the 'two cultures' debate, it should be said that while reviews in the humanities are the kind read by the vast majority of people, it is the scientific fields that have more consistently provided a developing theory of reviewing practice.[1]

Extensive empirical work has been done on the historical rise and function of literary journals, magazines and newspapers and some basic trends and attitudes in the reviewing policies and practices of these organs can easily be traced.[2] The variety of book reviewing that emerged in the periodicals of the late seventeenth and early eighteenth centuries had largely professional purposes (the first periodical devoted to the advertisement of new books was the *Journal des Savants*, Paris 1665). Straightforward book notices, summaries and abstracts were provided for scholars in such organs as LaRoche's *Memoirs of Literature* (1710-14), though with a follow-up journal, *New Memoirs of Literature*, synopses of new books began to include some slight evaluative remarks. The enduring assumption, however, was that the proper function of the review was to provide readers with some direct information on the contents of publications rather than with extensive contextualizations or critical opinion of any sort. While occasional commentary, principally by way of biographical information, was offered by the *Literary Magazine* (1756-8) for instance, an editorial asserted that the reviewer's role was 'to give a faithful account of books which come into his hands ... When he affects the air and language of a censor or judge, he invades the undoubted right of the public, which is the only sovereign judge of the reputation of an author, and the merit of his compositions'.[3]

---

1 For a concise overview of developments in reviewing generally, see A.J. Walford's bibliographical essay, 'The Art of Reviewing', in Walford, ed., *Reviews and Reviewing: A Guide* (London: Mansell, 1986) 5-18. Walford's volume is especially useful in that it is divided into specialist areas: Literature and language, history, social sciences, etc.   2 See, for instance, Frank Donoghue, *The Fame Machine: Book Reviewing and Eighteenth-Century Literary Careers* (Stanford: Stanford UP, 1996); Derek Roper, *Reviewing before the Edinburgh, 1788-1802* (London: Methuen, 1978); and Peter F. Morgan, *Literary Critics and Reviewers in Early Nineteenth-Century Britain* (London: Croom Helm, 1983). See also R.P. McCutcheon, 'The Beginning of Book Reviewing in English Periodicals', *Proceedings of the MLA* 37 (Dec. 1922) 691-706.   3 Quoted in Walter Graham, *English Literary Periodicals* (New York: Thomas Nelson & Sons, 1930) 204-5.

New and less determinedly objective editorial policies quickly emerged however, and the influence of reviewers increased with the rise of more argumentative and longer lasting journals like the *Monthly Review* (1749-1845) and the *Critical Review* (1756-90). Also, reviewing issues were complicated by the move of various organs toward the inclusion of reviews of literature as well as of learned publications. While partisanship, though damaging in itself, tended to be quite blatant and thus resistible, a range of other, more discreet predispositions were likely to emerge when the book at hand demanded that a reviewer demonstrate good aesthetic taste rather than simple knowledge or a capacity to summarize. As publishers' output increased rapidly, the basic problem of selection, and the attendant accusations of selectivity, were also bound to arise. The rise of the principal popular form, the novel, was hugely implicated in this (the first journal to consistently review popular literature was the *Compendious Library*, a bi-monthly printed in Dublin, 1751-52). One reviewer for the *Monthly Review* complained eventually in 1788: 'The Reviewer of the modern novel is in the situation of Hercules encountering the HydraæOne head lopped off, two or three immediately spring up in its place'.[4]

Exponential increase in reviewing output compounded the problems review organs already had with encouraging some kind of patterned style and approach amongst their contributors. The general critical consensus is that until the appearance of the *Edinburgh Review* (1802-1929) and the *Quarterly Review* (1809-1967) reviewing had steadily fallen into a poor and scandalized state, with appreciable accusations being made of undue influence from publishers and various interested parties. John O. Hayden, before developing his thesis that the early nineteenth century was the 'heyday of periodical reviewing', asserts simply that 'At the beginning of the nineteenth century the state of periodical reviewing left something to be desired'.[5] With these two organs, and also with *Blackwood's Magazine* (1817-1980), assiduous editorial efforts were made to assert a new professionalism and to distinguish between serious reviews and those written for the increasingly popular and more loosely organised culture and society magazines (between 1802 and 1824 there were more than sixty organs carrying reviews in England). Though 'high' reviews often veered away from the books involved and lapsed into aggressive personal attacks on authors and reviewers from rival journals, a significant innovation was the reformulation of the plain review as a vehicle for longer essays and articles. One period of reviewing practice essentially terminated at this point, replaced by the reviewing experience with which we are largely familiar today. Covering the last two centuries in one of the standard works on the area of literary journalism, John Gross argues that 'it was only at the beginning of the nineteenth century that the review emerged as a really powerful institution, a major social force'.[6]

4 Quoted in J.M.S. Tompkins, *The Popular Novel in England: 1770-1800* (London: Constable, 1932) 15.   5 *The Romantic Reviewers, 1802-1824* (London: Routledge & Kegan Paul, 1969) 1, 7.   6 Gross, *The Rise and*

This was a time of intensified self-awareness in literary criticism. In and around the Romantic period, reviews, particularly those written in the longer form, functioned much in the way that academic criticism does today and they performed vitally in the popularization of Romantic poetry and fiction. Arguing this point, R.G. Cox affirms that that the best work of the early critical journalists showed 'a sense of responsibility, a consciousness of performing a necessary and valuable function, a concern for the maintenance of the highest standards of thought and feeling'. From Cox's perspective in the Thirties, it seemed that this consciousness was 'completely lacking in modern reviewing', and he provides, in contrast, quite a paean to earlier exemplars:

> The Reviews made mistakes, they allowed themselves to be influenced on occasion by political and social feeling, they expressed themselves impolitely and sometimes brutally. On the other hand their prejudices, like those of Johnson, are obvious, and it is easy to make allowance for them: at the same time their offences, which have been greatly exaggerated by a more sentimentally genteel race of critics, are seen on examination to be very small in comparison with their solid merits of seriousness and critical conscientiousness. They never doubted that literature deserved the serious concern of the adult intelligence, and that it was their business to maintain standards of taste which had behind them the consensus of educated opinion. They consistently refused to pretend that excellence was 'common and abundant', and with their extraordinary influence and authority, they played the major part in creating for the writers of their age that informed, intelligent, and critical public without which no literature can survive for very long, and which is so conspicuously lacking to-day.[7]

Cox's nostalgia for the great period of high journalism, as will be emphasised in a moment, is symptomatic of his own time. For the purposes of balance it is more immediately worthwhile to quote Coleridge in a complaint which has significance far beyond that of the creative artist's perennial rejection of negative public criticism:

> But till reviews are conducted on far other principles, and with far other motives; till in the place of arbitrary dictation and petulant sneers, the reviewers support their decisions by reference to fixed canons of criticism, previously established and deduced from the nature of man; reflecting minds will pronounce it arrogance in them thus to announce themselves to men of letters, as the guides of their taste and judgement. To the

Fall of the Man of Letters: English Literary Life since 1800 (1969; Chicago: Elephant, 1991) 12, 11.   7 'The History of Critical Journalism' (1937), *A Selection from Scrutiny*, vol. 2, ed. F.R. Leavis (Cambridge: CUP, 1968) 255, 271. See, also, Cox's essay, 'The Reviews and Magazines', *The Pelican Guide to English Literature, Volume 6: From Dickens to Hardy*, ed. Boris Ford (London: Penguin, 1966) 188-204.

purchaser and mere reader it is, at all events, an injustice. He who tells me that there are *defects* in a new work, tells me nothing which I should not have taken for granted without his information. But he, who points out and elucidates the *beauties* of an original work, does indeed give me interesting information.[8]

Ostensibly negative as this remonstration against the early nineteenth-century reviewer is, its legislative thrust is immensely positive. Coleridge's central position in the development and promotion of modern criticism needs no reiteration; suffice it so deduce from even this single passage a new performative role for the reviewer where deference to 'principles' and 'canons of criticism' will replace earlier laxness. The point is resonant given today's rigid professional categorizations: the reviewer *is* a critic.

Though a complete rethinking of the principles of literary criticism would have to await the twentieth century, the status of reviewing rose steadily in the nineteenth century and, in a complete reversal of the earliest policy of giving the book under review absolute primacy, the phenomenon of the reviewer as personality emerged.[9] While this period is widely regarded as one of 'Heroes and Men of Letters', as John Gross puts it, an increased self-consciousness of their own practices developed amongst reviewers relatively early in the twentieth century and the nineteenth century was perceived to have brought about a gradual decline in standards. The degree to which editorial policies towards the function of reviewing had changed for the worse since the original abtract or synoptic type of review, was indicated by Robert Lynd, literary editor of *The Daily News* from 1913, in his essay 'Book Reviewing' (1920) where he pointed up the depreciation of the quotational review. Some newspapers, he revealed, had actually developed a policy of refusing payment to contributors for space taken up by material directly extracted from the books under consideration.[10]

One of the most thoughtful and vehement pieces on this degeneration is Virginia Woolf's essay 'Reviewing' (1939). Woolf regarded the late nineteenth century in particular as the period of a simultaneous explosion and implosion:

not only did the reviews become shorter and quicker, but they increased immeasurably in number. The result of these three tendencies was of the highest importance. It was catastrophic indeed; between them they have brought about the decline and fall of reviewing ... the value of reviews for all parties has dwindled untilæis it too much to say until it has disappeared? ... reviewing as practised at present has failed in all its objects.

8 *Biographia Literaria or, Biographical Sketches of My Literary Life and Opinions*, ed. James Engell and W. Jackson Bate (1817; Princeton: Princeton UP, 1983) vol. 1, 62.   9 See Gross, 37-110.   10 *The Art of Letters* (London: T. Fisher Unwin, 1920) 228-40.

With an echo of Coleridge's 'fixed canons of criticism' and in testament to Lynd's view that the personality of the reviewer had replaced the imperative of quoting from books, Woolf decided that the review had become 'an expression of individual opinion, given without any attempt to refer to "eternal standards" by a man who is in a hurry; who is pressed for space; who is expected to cater in that little space for many different interests; who is bothered by the knowledge that he is not fulfilling his task; who is doubtful what that task is; and who, finally, is forced to hedge'.[11] Woolf's concern with the practical pressures on even the well-motivated reviewer culminated in her only half-humourous suggestion of a scheme whereby, in analogy with the medical profession, the reviewer would abolish himself and set up as a kind of literary private practitioner. He would meet the writer at first hand at a clinic and amiable, critical, and, above all, confidential relations would be established which would allow the writer to take treatment without any damage to his public reputation.

Cox's belletristic nostalgia, Lynd's disillusionment as an editor and Woolf's desperation as a reviewer, however negatively expressed, are all indicative of a developing awareness in and around their time of the importance of standards in the review pages. As evinced by the significant occasion of the appearance of the *Times Literary Supplement*, first with *The Times* from 1902, then independently from 1914, it was obvious that the reviewer would continue to perform an important function in the circulation of books, at least amongst the educated middle classes. As ideas of the proper operation of literary criticism began to be redefined in the universities, more extended and more careful opinions were expressed on related concerns in the practice of book reviewing, particularly in Britain and America. While important books on the area were published by Frank Swinnerton and Helen E. Haines, legislative studies began to take a more theoretical turn with the appearance of a precisely focused essay by A.B. Baird in the early Fifties.[12]

Thereafter, though often out of the common purview of literary academics, there appeared a number of articles and books aimed at regulating reviewing approaches and styles. While many were concerned with general practice, the evolving classifications of journalistic and academic reviewing were also reflected.[13] Though

---

11 *The Crowded Dance of Modern Life, Selected Essays, Volume Two* (London: Penguin, 1993) 154-6, 157. Woolf's essay is arguably the most important in the history of reviewing. It was intended very much as a broadside and was published separately by the Hogarth Press.   12 See Swinnerton, *Authors and the Book Trade*, 2nd. ed. (London: Gerald Howe, 1933), and *The Reviewing and Criticism of Books* (New York: OUP, 1939); and Helen E. Haines, *Living with Books: The Art of Book Selection*, 2nd. ed. (New York: Columbia UP, 1950). See Baird, 'What We Expect of a Review', *Quarterly Journal of Speech* 37 (1951) 81-6.   13 For general studies, see John Drewry, *Writing Book Reviews* (Boston: The Writer, 1966); Julie A. Virgo, 'The Review Article: Its Characteristics and Problems', *Literary Quarterly* 41:4 (Oct. 1971) 275-91; Sylvia E. Kammerman, ed., *Book Reviewing: A Guide to Writing Book Reviews for Newspapers, Magazines, Radio and Television, by Leading Book Editors, Critics and Reviewers* (Boston: The Writer, 1978). For studies on the academic area, see the journal *Scholarly Publishing*, especially R.S. Wolper, 'A Grass Blade: On Academic Reviewing' [10:4 (July 1979) 325-8]; Bruce D. Macphail, 'Book Reviews and the Scholarly Publisher' [12:1 (Oct. 1980) 53-63]; John Budd, 'Book Reviewing Practices of Journals in the Humanities' [13:4 (July 1982)

university people have played an increasing role in reviewing for literary broadsheets and newspapers over the past couple of decades, academics have not tended to be overly selfconscious of the practice.[14] Currently, the more helpful and conscientious studies issue, perhaps inevitably, from full-time literary editors and journalists. Many of these engage heavily in anecdotal reminiscence but nevertheless provide useful backround information and practical insights into a brand of criticism many areas of which are obscure to outsider practitioners.[15] While such books concentrate on the machinations of individual reviewers and of particular review pages, some variably useful legislative handbooks, guides and primers have also been published by journalists and journalism theorists, and it is these that can perhaps best provide guidance for potential reviewers, both academic and non-academic. The underlying point behind all of these publications is that the short review, the review article, the long review essay, can all, like any other kind of critical writing, be isolated and theorised in a formal or structural fashion.

Along with uniformly providing basic recommendations on such matters as the levels of research, structuration and cogency necessary for a high standard of review-ing, these advisory books tend to provide oppositional emphases on the requisite ideology or function of a good reviewer. One of the more popular handbooks on journalism, MacDougall and Reid's *Interpretative Reporting*, includes a considerable section on reviewing and the authors are quite definite in encouraging adherence to a direct method: 'The greatest service the newspaper that gives space to artistic news can perform for both artists and spectators or auditors', they conclude, 'is to interpret the former to the latter.'[16] The advice is that the judgement of a work should very often be postponed in favour of direct mediation for the reader. On the other hand, Richard Keeble, in a section on 'The Art of Reviewing' in his guidebook for journal-ists, provides a different nuance and argues that a review, along with interpreting or critiquing work, should also be self-contained and distinctly stylised: 'The review must then exist as a piece of writing in its own right. It must entice in the reader through the quality and colour of its prose. It must entertain.'[17]

Deferential as the first view here is to the traditional notion that criticism is absolutely secondary to the primary work at hand, there seems little point in passing over the fact that, in the face of the increasingly insurmountable issue of books, readers resort coequally to the advice of reviewers. From the very beginnings of reviewing practice, review organs have vied with each other for popularity and credibility and no single reviewer can have an edge if all engage in simple inter-

363-71]; and Wolper, 'On Academic Reviewing: Ten Common Errors' [16:3 (Apr. 1985) 269-75].   **14** For one recent exception however, see Ylva Lindholm-Romantschuk, *Scholarly Book Reviewing in the Social Sciences and Humanities* (Westport, CT: Greenwood, 1998).   **15** See, for instance, Karl Miller, *Dark Horses: An Experience of Literary Journalism* (London: Picador, 1998); and Anthony Curtis, *Lit Ed: On Reviewing and Reviewers* (Manchester: Carcanet, 1998).   **16** Curtis D. MacDougall and Robert D. Reid, *Interpretative Reporting*, 9th ed. (New York: Macmillan, 1987) 496.   **17** Richard Keeble, *The Newspaper Handbook* (London: Routledge, 1994) 301.

pretation. Cognisant as the second view is of the necessity for a review to entertain as well as merely interpret if it is to attract readership, there also seems little benefit in allowing the style of a review to distract that readership away from the book at hand. A standard method of the advisory books on reviewing is to provide a listing of prerequisites for the writing of good reviews.[18] Mindful of the various issues glanced over above, I would like to offer a few summary points and recommenda- tions of my own that might tread the middle ground between the views of reviewing as self-effacing mediation and as artful entertainment.

Many reviews continue to be almost indistinguishable from publishers' advertis- ments or press releases, consisting mainly of a long list of superlatives or, as Lynd put it, of 'a thoughtless scattering of acceptable words'. Unqualified praise is naturally deserved by some books, but clichéd praise is only a step away from condescension. There should, in particular, be an interdict on the phrase '*tour de force*'. Indiscriminate praise is perhaps the easiest resort for the busy reviewer but it should be remembered that literary worth is absolutely relative: if everything is good, then nothing is good. The most discreditable variety of approval issues from the friends of an author under review. The danger of this is especially acute in a small literary community like Ireland's where vigilance is all the more difficult for literary editors. A rigid policy line should be held on this however: If a particular writer has engaged in a little backslapping for another, a return favour should never be courted. This happens regularly and is considerably responsible for the inferior status of reviewing as a critical subgenre.

While the matter of 'what is it?' should always be the first addressed by the reviewer, the claim to be able to identify the nature of a work presupposes a capacity to evaluate a work in terms of predecessors of the same ilk. 'How is it?' is a question that should never be avoided even if the answer must be in the negative. Writers of books are as entitled as anyone else to complain away in pri- vate about all and sundry and in particular about adverse reaction to their work in reviews, but, especially if they make complaint in public or in print, it may be worth while asking why reaction to single evaluative readings can often be so vehement. To get the philistinism out of the way first: If the writer fears pri- marily for potential damage to his purse, then he puts his work on a par with any other business and therefore can have no claim to the special treatment generally extended to the creative personality. The marketplace, as all publishers, or at least the conglomerates, are firmly aware, is an unforgiving and competitive arena and no quarter is given these days in the drive for publicity tours and promotions. Until publishers, at the behest of authors or otherwise, replace self-serving

18 One of the more balanced listings of this kind is Brendan Hennessy's in his *Writing Feature Articles: A Practical Guide to Methods and Markets*, 2nd. ed. (Oxford: Focal, 1993). His five prerequisites, in brief, are: the indication of the kind of work under review and what it is about; the provision of informed judgement; provision of evidence for opinions and use of persuasive language; to act as a simple bridge between art practitioner and audience; to set standards while also being readable and entertaining.

unctuous blurbs with advertisments more helpful and less condescending to the contemporary reader then business will remain business; in the meantime, reviewers can be unashamedly overdetermined in the interests of critical balance and can justifiably care little so long as they too are doing business.

The matter is naturally more complicated when a writer above all else fears that his public reputation may be damaged by a negative review. Writers are, traditionally in any case, society's more sensitive creatures and might thus be expected to be considerably damaged by oppositional opinion. Tennyson, famously, had intense reactions to disfavourable reviews and became so distracted by critical hostility that he even at one stage considered emigration. This, I suggest, is an occupational hazard and cannot be helped. If we leave aside for a moment our continued Romantic perception of the writer as a tender individual, a perception that is particularly obstinate in Ireland, it could be supposed that the publication of a creative work is a supreme act of egotistical risk. The ego can only look to itself, and, in a phrase of Chekhov's that John McGahern likes to quote, once a writer has published all he can do with any good grace is to bow. And if he expects, as Coleridge did, that only the 'beauties' of his work be identified, then he may well ask himself if his ego should be on stage in the first place.

There remains the matter of the writer feeling, aside from the incontrovertibility of subjective reviewing assessment, that he is simply being publicly misunderstood in his intentions. Indifference to reviews in a writer can hardly be condemned; but if he does care to respond to a review then the invitation to do so should be a matter of course. The provision of a kind of letters *feuilleton*, as in the popular literary journals, would thus be a welcome addition to those newspapers that engage heavily in reviewing, or at least in 'high' reviewing. If reviewers wrote in the knowledge that the subjects of their quick assessments, or indeed other invigilators, might instantly respond, they would surely be more assiduous in their efforts.

In the context of the rapidly expanding area of academic and scholarly criticism, the review, it might be supposed, can hardly be expected to return to the critical status it once enjoyed. A large section of the reading public however, experiences criticism primarily through review organs and it is a disservice to this readership to assume that critical style and general prose style are minor considerations for the reviewer. Evidence of this assumption is widespread, from reviews of novels that engage almost exclusively in plot summary to reviews of poetry whose primary aim appears to steer as far clear as possible of accessibility of style. If reviewing is to maintain credibility and perform precisely as criticism, then its practitioners should be stylistically conscientious. In effect, the review pages can be the repository of a familiar style displaced and too casually demeaned by the rise of theoretical criticism. While the rigours of university literary studies usually demand a high awareness of modern theoretical developments, an awareness that is often overdetermined in academic publications, the journalistic review is somewhat more amenable to varieties of practical criticism. A medial readership demands a general relaxation of the monotypic, thesis-driven approach in favour of a combinative mode that provides for the equal use of empirical discussion and anecdotal entertainment. Philip Larkin's prescription when introducing his own occasional pieces should be considered lapidary by those intent on any kind of reviewing: 'A good reviewer combines the knowledge of the scholar with the judgement and cogency of the critic and the readability of the journalist.'[19]

Woman and Nation Revisited:
Oscar Wilde's The Nightingale and the Rose

JARLATH KILEEN, UNIVERSITY COLLEGE, DUBLIN

Just after 7:00 p.m. on 21 August 1879 something strange began to happen in a small village in the West of Ireland that was to have a profound impact on the consciousness of the nation and the configuration of Ireland in religious cartography. One of the villagers of Knock, Co. Mayo, was on her way to visit a friend when she spotted a bright light and what she thought were three statues at the gable of the local church. Although surprised they had been left out in the rain, she took little notice of them until she was returning later. On closer inspection, the 'statues' turned out to be apparitions of the Virgin Mary, St Joseph, St John the Evangelist, and the Lamb of God on an altar, floating near the gable wall. The village was duly alerted and over twenty people experienced the vision, although only fourteen were called as witnesses at the official investigation. The villagers did not inform the rest of the world of the momentous event until the next day, but it then became global news. Quickly too a specific interpretation of the vision became widespread among those who gave it any credence.[1]

Marianism and Romanism were synonymous in the English religious imagination. The dichotomy of gender was developed to a high degree in the theology of relation between Protestantism and Catholicism, and with the proliferation of Marian apparitions in the nineteenth century, the Virgin Mary became a point of contact between theology and empire. When *The Times* noted that 'to become a Roman Catholic and to remain a thorough Englishman are—it cannot be disguised—almost incompatible conditions,'[2] it was suggesting a link between

19 *Required Writing: Miscellaneous Pieces 1955-1982* (London: Faber & Faber, 1983) 11.

JARLATH KILEEN
1 For a good account of the apparition, see Catherine Rynne, *Knock 1879-1979* (Dublin: Veritas, 1979).   2 *The Times*, on the conversion of the Marquess of Ripon, 1874.

worship of the Virgin—the most criticised aspect of Catholicism in the English press after 'Papism'—and the 'foreign' condition. This was a sharp division between the 'feminised' religion of Mary and the muscular Christianity of God the Father Almighty. Victor and Edith Turner, tracing the dramatic resurgence of Marian pilgrimages and images in the nineteenth century, argue that while Mary as *Theotokos* (Mother of God) was the most popular representation of the Virgin in the Middle Ages, 'early in the nineteenth century ... the emphasis began to shift towards Mary herself, as an autonomous figure who takes initiatives on behalf of mankind, often intervening in the midst of the economic and political crises characteristic of industrialised mass society'.[3]

The Marian apparitions began to nudge the universal church towards the 'option for the poor' that has been characteristic of the Catholic Church's social policy since Leo XIII wrote the encyclical *Rerum Novarum* in 1891. Sandra L. Zimdars-Swartz points out that the image of the 'victim soul' pervades Marian devotion.[4] Such an image is structured around the idea of the vicarious suffering of Christ and Mary for the sins of the world, and extends to the suffering of individual devotees who see themselves as bearing the pain of the sinful structures and actions of the wider community. Moreover, in places where colonialism has been the most dominant narrative experience, worshippers of Mary see themselves as simultaneously vindicated and violating: vindicated in their resistance to the sins of the colonial power, and violating these structures of coercion and hegemony. In popular imagination, Mary was always on the side of the underdog: she was the paradigm of mercy.[5]

A form of national assimilation began after the Knock apparition. There had been extensive crop failures in Mayo in 1877 and 1878, and in 1879 the first phases in what was retrospectively to be termed the 'Land War' began to take shape. This war was the result of a prolonged period of negotiations between representatives of the dominant strands of colonial resistance: land agitation, physical force aggression, and constitutional strategy, as embodied in the complex relationships between Michael Davitt, John Devoy, and Charles Stewart Parnell. By 1879 it was clear that some form of land organization was necessary. An agricultural depression, provoked by American competition, led to a dramatic decline in crop prices and the value of the principal crops fell by £14 million between 1876 and 1879. F.S.L. Lyons claimed that the extent of the depression was 'unprecedented in scale since 1847 ... [and was] accompanied, especially in the West of Ireland, by actual starvation.'[6] The desperate situation galvanized the main players in the new drama of co-operation and on 16th

3 Victor and Edith Turner, 'Postindustrial Marian Pilgrimages,' in *Mother Worship: Theme and Variation*, edited by James L. Preston (Chapel Hill: U of North Carolina P, 1982) 145.   4 Sandra L. Zimdars-Swartz, *Encountering Mary: From La Salette to Medjugore* (Princeton: Princeton UP, 1992) 246-7.   5 The Virgin of Guadalupe, for example, symbolises the desires of Mexicans for a form of national coherence and has become the 'unofficial, the private flag' of the country: Richard Rodriguez, *Days of Obligation: An Argument with my Mexican Father* (New York: Penguin, 1993) 16.   6 F. S. L. Lyons, *Ireland since the Famine*, (London: Weidenfeld and Nicolson, 1971) 156.

August 1879 the 'new development' articulated its material existence with the formation of the Mayo Land League. This came just five days before the apparition. News of agrarian agitation and the Knock apparition began to emerge from Ireland together, the Blessed Virgin having chosen to appear where the distress was most palpable and the collective repealing of the land system the most intensive. The agitation and the apparition solidified into one movement: the iconography of the Virgin became emblematic of the struggle being wrought by the Land League; the Lady of Knock became Queen of Ireland, the divine representative of *Hibernia*, numinous envoy of the Church against the colonial administration in London.

The Virgin was a peculiarly appropriate figure to merge with the already pro- lific allegorization of Ireland as Woman. From the Middle Ages, a rose or rose-tree has been integral to symbolic representations of Mary. Marina Warner tells us that 'In the rosary, the use of incantatory prayers blended with the medieval symbolism of the rose, until the beads themselves were seen to be chaplets to crown the Queen of Heaven, as garlands for the rose without thorns (*Ecc.*), the Rose of Sharon (*Song of Sol.*), the rose of Jericho.'[7] If the rose had been symbolic of the Virgin since the Middle Ages, 'Rosaleen' or the 'little black rose' had become a standard allegorical representation of Ireland from the middle of the nineteenth century. James Clarence Mangan's 'Dark Rosaleen' was published in *The Nation* on 30 May 1846. He presented it as a free translation of an Irish original which 'purports to be an allegorical address from Hugh [that is, Red Hugh O' Donnell] to Ireland, on the subject of his love and struggles for her, and his resolve to raise her again to the glo- rious position she held as a nation before the irruption of the Saxon and Norman spoilers.'[8] This representation was an echo of similar translations by Samuel Ferguson in the *Dublin University Magazine* in 1834, James Hardiman in the *Irish Minstrelsy* in 1831, and Aubrey de Vere's lyric 'The Little Black Rose':

> The Little Black Rose shall be red at last,
> What made it black but the March wind dry,
> And the tear of the widow that fell on it fast;
> It shall redden the hills when June is nigh.[9]

What the black rose needs to turn red is blood sacrifice. The association of Ireland as rose was grafted on to an existing tradition of an allegorised woman demanding a blood sacrifice to transform her from black hag to blood-red queen. Historically, this can be traced back to the image of the 'sovereignty goddess' in native tradition. The scant documentation that exists suggests that in pre-Christian Ireland this goddess was the centre of an elaborate ritual to validate the local king.

7 Marina Warner, *Alone of All Her Sex: The Myth and the Cult of the Virgin Mary* (New York: Vintage, 1979) 307. 8 Quoted in Diane E Bessai, 'Dark Rosaleen' as Image of Ireland,' *Eire-Ireland* 10: 4 (Winter 1975) 64. 9 Ibid. 81.

She represented the abstract sovereignty the king sought and the physical substance he would rule. Her condition depended on the adequacy of the potential king and was fused with a second tradition that saw her, as *Becuma*, cause the crops to fail until the blood of a young man was mingled with the soil to rejuvenate fertility. This tradition mutated and altered until the nineteenth century, but its essential elements remained: the identification of nation with woman, the necessity of a blood sacrifice to enact a transformation, the natural imagery of winter and spring. The integral Catholicism of this meme was fused with the Knock apparition, and consolidated the notion that this sacrifice was related to a more-than-physical economy of salvation.

This meme has become involved in a debate concerning the ethics of associating abstract 'Woman' with abstract 'Nation': the conflation of the two has been held to be a dangerous intersection, oppressive of real women in real Ireland. The debate reached its most distinctive points in publications of Evan Boland, and Edna Longley's now infamous *From Cathleen to Anorexia*.[10] Elisabeth Butler Cullingford has symptomatically summarized the issues:

> From a structuralist point of view the identification of the land as female reflects the patriarchal opposition between male Culture and female Nature, which defines women as the passive embodiments of matter. Politically, the land is seen as an object to be possessed, or repossessed: to gender it as female is to confirm and reproduce the social arrangements that construct women as material objects, not speaking subjects. When the myth of the goddess is used by men as a political instrument, it is often scribed to an essential female principle rather than the male imagination that has created or manipulated it. Images of women that originated as the projections of male anxieties and aggression are used to validate the need to control or subordinate the female sex.[11]

The real problem with such a set of claims is that as a meta-narrative it is so general, determinative and authoritative in its terminology. It allows for no lacunae or aporia; it fails to conceive of alternative means of configuring the meme. Passionate summaries like Cullingford's are more reactive than analytic and serve little purpose when actually examined for positive content. The charge against texts reducing women to the silent embodiments of matter can hardly stand against the best-known representative of the tradition—*Cathleen ni Houlihan*—where the woman of the title weaves occult linguistic spells around her heroes as her means of national seduction.

10 Eavan Boland, *A Kind of Scar: The Woman Poet in a National Tradition* (Dublin: Attic, 1989); idem., *Object Lessons: The Life of the Woman and the Poet in Our Time* (Manchester: Carcanet, 1995); Edna Longley, *From Cathleen to Anorexia: The Breakdown of Irelands* (Dublin: Attic, 1990). 11 Elisabeth Butler Cullingford, *Gender and History in Yeats' Love Poetry* (Cambridge: CUP, 1993) 56.

What, however, has all this got to do with Oscar Wilde? Wilde has slowly been co-opted onto an 'Irish Studies' program from his tentative inclusion in the *Field Day Anthology*.[12] While studies have tended to see Wilde in terms of a more general tradition in Irish writing (engaging in a type of philosophical ambiguity, a dwelling on both sides of the binary) the details of his engagement with Irish issues have yet to be fully registered. Wilde might seem an unlikely way into this particular controversy, but it may break for a moment the incantatory monotony of critical fetishising of fixed texts as well as suggesting a broader canvas upon which Wilde studies could work. 'The Nightingale and the Rose' was published in 1888 as part of the collection *The Happy Prince and Other Tales*. In the narrative, a student of metaphysics believes himself to be deeply in love with the daughter of his Professor, but the possibility of dancing with her at the Prince's ball depends on his presentation to her of a red rose. A Nightingale in his garden, hearing him discourse on Love, believes that he is the 'true lover,' and determines to provide this rose for him. Unfortunately, the red-rose tree is barren and can only produce a rose if infused with the life-blood of the Nightingale as she sings her most beautiful song. Believing the sacrifice worthwhile the Nightingale presses her breast against a thorn and sings, and during the night the tree produces the most beautiful rose ever seen at the cost of the Nightingale's life. When the Student presents this rose to the Professor's daughter however, she remains unimpressed, having received a better offer of jewels from the Chamberlain's nephew, and she tosses the rose under a passing cart. Dejected, the Student rejects the concept Love and returns to his study of metaphysics.

From our incursion into the contested world of national allegory, we can immediately recognize that the central trope of this story involves the transformation of a barren rose-tree, as the representative of cruel winter, into the life-producing tree of grace. This transformation brought about through the quality of the blood-sacrifice performed by the Nightingale. The pure heart of the Nightingale must be pierced, and the blood drain into the veins of the tree to produce the 'reddest rose in all the world.' Wilde is investing in the typology reproduced by the poets of *The Nation*. Moreover, if we recognize the genre that Wilde is writing in, we will identify the rose, not only with Ireland but also with the Virgin Mary. The fact that critics have not noticed the iconography of the Virgin here is probably due to their unfamiliarity with the genre to which it is linked. Nightingale literature, which reached its zenith in the Middle Ages, enjoyed a renewal in the nineteenth century.[13] From the eleventh century on,

12 Terry Eagleton, *Saint Oscar* (Derry: Field Day, 1989); Declan Kiberd, 'Wilde and Shaw' in *The Field Day Anthology of Irish Writing*, edited by Seamus Deane (Derry: Field Day, 1991); idem., *Inventing Ireland: The Literature of the Modern Nation* (London: Vintage, 1996), 33-50; Richard Pine, *The Thief of Reason: Oscar Wilde and Modern Ireland* (Dublin: Gill and Macmillan, 1998); Davis Coakley, *Oscar Wilde: The Importance of Being Irish* (Dublin: Town House and Country House, 1994); Jerusha McCormack, *Wilde: The Irishman* (New Haven and London: Yale UP, 1998).   13 Jeni Williams, *Interpreting Nightingales: Gender, Class, and Histories* (Sheffield: Sheffield Academic, 1997) 34-74.

there was a new emphasis on the bodily suffering of Christ, and the associations between the theology of the Incarnation and the physical existence of humanity. A gendered passion emerged in poetry of the Nightingale, in which the blood of Christ-Nightingale was matched by the tears of his mother.

Unsurprisingly then, while the imagery of the crucifixion is particularly strong in Wilde's story, as the Nightingale's heart is pierced by thorns, the references to the blood flowing from the Nightingale to the rose is symbolic of the relation between mother and child. Though of course, in appropriately religious terms, this biological function is reversed to demonstrate Mary's spiritual dependence on Christ. As 'Woman' of the Gospels, she is also representative of the entire human race whose collective existence necessitates the constant attention of God and whose ultimate salvation rests on the shedding of Christ's blood. While Mary is universalised in such an economy of salvation, she is also a specific player within the Catholic conception of the redemption. Indeed, to many within the church, she is the *co-redemptrix*, the associate redeemer of humankind through her role as the Mother of God. The position of the rose in the story appropriately constructs a religious geography, a dialectic between the worldly Protestant conception of the Student who constructs a rational metaphysics to understand God, and a sensuous romantic Catholicism which depends on the salvific event of the co-redemption of humanity.

Thus, we can be clear about one thing. More than any other writer dealing with the trope of Woman as Nation, Wilde theologises the imagery. He utilises the triple associations Rose-Virgin-Ireland extremely effectively. The aspirational culmination of Mother Ireland and Mother Church, which received its most effective articulation in the Knock apparition, is realised completely in Wilde's story. The Nightingale is sacrificing herself so that her blood can be the transfusion that her church-country requires to come into bloom though in the midst of the winter of failure. If the typology we have worked out is correct—that the world of the Student is the rational world of Protestantism, while the natural efflorescence occupied by the Nightingale is Catholicism—then the following formulation is possible. The Christ-like sacrifice offered by the Nightingale is so that the full-blooded and beautiful rose, the blossom of Catholic Ireland, can be offered to the Protestant nation, the aloof, haughty Britannia/Professor's daughter, obsessed with the assimilation of wealth rather than the spiritual riches offered by the Nightingale. The sacrifice of the Nightingale becomes, not a literal one, not the actual shedding of blood, but a theological one, a spiritual abandonment of the people, a New religious Departure. While the rest of the country views the apparition at Knock to be the divine blessing on a new political venture, Wilde's story suggests that such an interpretation is misapplied: the silence of the Virgin is understood as a spiritual transcendence rather than a political statement. The call is to an investment in the religious, the symbolic, as opposed to direct political action.

Nationalism, the valorization of the rose-Ireland, here represents a theological force emanating from the symbols of the people. When Edna Longley accuses

Nationalism of sectarianism because of what she calls 'the seamless join between Catholicism and Nationalism,' she effectively misses the kind of point Wilde is making here.[14] Theological nationalism dissolves sectarianism *only if it is* wedded to Catholicism, because only the anti-rationalist universalist bent of Catholic theology can dissipate the sectarian trends of sociological existence. Protestant empiricism serves to force its congregations to fetishize material existence, and yet, in its Puritan streak, simultaneously advocates despising it. Catholicism, especially in the dogmas of Mary, offers a glorified material existence in a totalised personality. And this superlative position of Mary in Catholicism highlights the discrepancies behind Professor Longley's gaff concerning the position of women in Nationalism and Unionism: 'at least Unionism does not appropriate the image of woman or hide its aggressions behind our skirts'.[15] Wilde's imagery suggests that part of the problem with Unionism, as a version of Protestant nationalism, is that it lacks such female appropriation. As Wilde's Christ is a female Nightingale, and Wilde's Virgin a male rose-tree, he is apparently advocating Catholicism as a means to gynandry and androgyny. As Jung was later to praise the declaration of the Assumption in 1950 as hailing Catholicism as the first integrated form of Christianity, Wilde's fusion of genders at the abstract level of theology and nationalism suggests that he had gone beyond God-the-Father long before Mary Daly.

Depending entirely on male appropriation, especially in its scientific obsession with reason, metaphysics and empiricism, the Protestant world of the Student collapses into textual literalness: the last thing he does in the story is return to his study to read. The crude material existence of the Old Adam and Eve, the Student and the Professor's daughter, both children of the knowledge of good and evil, leaves them stranded in the Victorian crisis of faith engendered by the purely patriarchal empirical fanaticism of university faculties and Higher Critical theologies. The sumptuous Catholicism of pre-Tridentine ruritania relies on a glorified material world which finds its enunciation in the New Adam and Eve of the Nightingale and the rose-tree, beyond biological determinism. Such a realization complicates its assimilation of the Woman-as-Nation allegory. Its rose, far off and invioble, is male but has female blood running through its veins; *Cathleen ni Houlihan* is dissolved into an integrated and fulfilled mediatrix. However, totalization is never complete. The Virgin/Rose remains an indeterminate figure, a symbol of mediation between two cultures: male/female, England/Ireland, Protestant/Catholic, mankind/God, Student/Nightingale —caught in the hyphen that Wilde refused to abandon until the end of his life.

---

14 Longely 4.   15 Ibid. 18.

The Journey of the Encounter: The Politics of the National Tale in Sydney Owenson's Wild Irish Girl and Maria Edgeworth's Ennui

FRANCESCA LACAITA, UNIVERSITA DEGLI STUDI DI GENOVA

Maria Edgeworth and Sydney Owenson (from 1812, Lady Morgan) are the initiators in Ireland of that genre in fiction called 'national tale', which came into being in the peripheries of the United Kingdom in the first two decades of the nineteenth century, and out of which the Scottian historical novel would emerge and develop.[1] Its defining characteristics are a 'thick evocation of place' and the addressing of social, cultural, political, and historical questions of nation-building, which in the aftermath of the French Revolution were felt with a new urgency.[2] In Ireland such issues had a particularly problematic significance, as the period after 1789 had been traumatic, marked as it was by sectarian tensions, a major rebellion, brutal repression, and the Act of Union.

The national tale deals with national themes, but its discourse is not 'nationalist' —at least, not in the sense the nineteenth century gave to the word. The genre as a whole seems to locate itself not within the boundaries of a nation, but in the site of a 'hyphenated culture', and, at the same time, to question existing hierarchical relationships between the nations and cultures. As Ina Ferris points out, the national tale 'is a tale that can be written neither by a foreigner nor by a native … its specificity derives from its eluding both categories: standing neither inside nor outside, the national tale occupies the space of their encounter.'[3] And their encounter will become, with Owenson's *The Wild Irish Girl* (1806), a key theme of the national tale. Typically, the early national tale narrates a protagonist's journey from the metropolitan centre into a peripheral territory, and a following encounter with a new landscape, a different way of life and a cultural Other—a displacing, unhinging experience, which challenges received assumptions and finally turns the foreign protagonist 'into the stranger-who-comes-nearer', effecting his or her sentimental education and human maturation.[4] Central to this experience is falling in love with

1 The 'national tale' has been 'discovered' as a genre only recently. Studies dealing with it include Gary Kelly, *English Fiction of the Romantic Period 1789-1830* (London: Longman, 1989) 71-98; Kelly, 'Women Writers and Romantic Nationalism in Britain', in Winnifred M. Bogaards (ed.), *Literature of the Region and the Nation: Proceedings of the* 6th *International Literature of Region and Nation Conference* (New Brunswick: University of New Brunswick in Saint John, 1998), 20-32; Ina Ferris, *The Achievement of Literary Authority: Gender, History, and the Waverley Novels* (Ithaca: Cornell UP, 1991); Ferris, 'Narrating Cultural Encounter: Lady Morgan and the Irish National Tale', *Nineteenth-Century Literature*, 51:3 (Dec 1996), 287-303; Ferris, 'Writing on the Border: the National Tale, Female Writing, and the Public Sphere', in Tilottama Rajan and Julia M. Wright (eds.), *Romanticism, History, and the Possibilities of Genre: Reforming Literature* (Cambridge: CUP, 1998) 86-106; Nicola J. Watson, *Revolution and the Form of the British Novel 1790-1825: Intercepted Letters, Interrupted Seductions* (Oxford: Clarendon, 1994); Katie Trumpener, *Bardic Nationalism: The Romantic Novel and the British Empire* (Princeton: Princeton UP, 1997). 2 Katie Trumpener 131. 3 Ina Ferris, (1996) 292. 4 Ibid. 297.

a native woman or a native man—that is, the experience of the country involves not only a cultural encounter with, but also erotic attraction to the Other.[5] This is recognizably the matter that forms the plot of Owenson's *The Wild Irish Girl*, of Edgeworth's *Ennui* (1809), of Maturin's *The Milesian Chief* (1812), and even of Scott's *Waverley* (1814).

After the 1820s, the reputation of Edgeworth and Owenson as *national* writers has been at best uncertain. Their perspectives were judged to be conditioned by class, gender and cultural limitations, and critics have variously deplored the didacticism and 'big-house' viewpoint of the one, the evasive and sentimental romanticism of the other, and the 'aristocratic' orientation of both. To Owenson has been attributed the 'originative literary stereotyping of a myth of Irishness', based on the Gaelic iconography of national identity.[6] Edgeworth, meanwhile, has been widely regarded as a 'colonist' writer.[7]

Putting the national tale in a historical perspective would, however, show that both its Irish initiators can be considered figures of transition, each in her own way carrying outlooks and concerns of the eighteenth century over into the next. Edgeworth, herself belonging to the Irish Protestant Ascendancy, was heir to the liberal and rationalist thought of the Enlightenment. This brought her to share many progressive ideas of the time and put her out of sympathy with contemporary conservative discourses, centred on religion, tradition, and 'time-hallowed' institutions. Because of her position as a member of a nationally 'hyphenated' class, she was inclined to give national identity a sociocultural foundation, and to construe it as rootedness in place (against absenteeism) and educated spiritual cosmopolitanism (against 'national character', a mark of the uneducated lower classes).[8] As for Owenson, nominally Protestant, but of mixed background, she was heir to the European sensibility of Irish patriotism and antiquarianism of the eighteenth-century. However much she contributed to the creation of the literary tropes of romantic nationalism, her *patriotism* should rather be understood in the eighteenth-century sense of love for one's fellow-people and concern for their welfare, which could go hand in hand with a cosmopolitan outlook and did not involve the desirability of homogeneity on the basis of culture, ethnicity or religion, nor a disavowal of the cultural connections with the rest of the British Isles.[9] Neither Edgeworth nor Owenson thus shared in the ethno-cultural concept of nationhood which prevailed

5 Ian Dennis, *Nationalism and Desire in Early Historical Fiction* (Basingstoke: Macmillan, 1997) 1.   6 Elmer Andrews, 'Aesthetics, Politics, and Identity: Lady Morgan's *The Wild Irish Girl*', *Canadian Journal of Irish Studies*, 12 (1987) 7-19.   7 Among critics who, from different standpoints, point out Edgeworth's 'colonialist' stance are P. F. Sheeran, 'Colonists and Colonized: Some Aspects of Anglo-Irish Literature from Swift to Joyce', *Yearbook of English Studies*, 13 (1983), 97-115; Tom Dunne, *Maria Edgeworth and the Colonial Mind* (Cork: Cork UP, 1984); and Seamus Deane, *Strange Country: Modernity and Nationhood in Irish Writing since 1790* (Oxford: Clarendon, 1997) esp. 28-40.   8 Esther Wohlgemut, 'Maria Edgeworth and the Question of National Identity', *Studies in English Literature 1500-1900*, 39:4 (Autumn 1999), 645-58.   9 See her collection of essays *Patriotic Sketches of Ireland Written in Connaught* (London: Phillips, 1807).

in the British Isles in opposition to the French Revolution, and which placed religion at the heart of collective identity and social ties.[10] Neither was prepared for the nineteenth-century developments towards mass politics and democracy. Although they might have looked at the Irish past with different eyes, both of them believed in modernity and progress as defined by the Enlightenment. It is in this cultural framework, in some respects much different from that of later Irish nationalism, that the wish for Ireland's freedom from English subjection was expressed in their novels.

Early examples of the national tale, Owenson's *The Wild Irish Girl* and Edgeworth's *Ennui*, are made particularly significant by the many similarities between the two narratives, in the light of which *Ennui* seems indeed to have been conceived as a 'reply' to *The Wild Irish Girl*. These two novels can thus be considered the common matrix, from which Edgeworth and Owenson would subsequently take the national tale along different routes. In both of them the focalizer is the traveller from England, narrating in the first person. The protagonists of *The Wild Irish Girl* and of *Ennui* (respectively, Horatio M. and Lord Glenthorn) are both young men of English fashionable society and absentee landlords in Ireland, both have led lives of dissipation and now suffer from ennui. Both have had negative relationships with women which have shaken their social reputation, which can be read as a metaphor for England's relationships with Ireland. Unsurprisingly, both hold strong prejudices against Ireland, which they will visit only in consequence of their failure in metropolitan society. Moving to Ireland will nevertheless be a journey of discovery and self-discovery. In both cases the journey takes the protagonist to the farthest end of the island, the traditional repository of 'authentic' Irishness. Gaelic Ireland is in both tales embodied by a Cathleen Ní Houlihan figure: the 'wild Irish girl' Glorvina in one case, Ellinor, the nurse who turns out to be the hero's mother, in the other. In neither case is the encounter with this figure uneventful, or even painless: it involves a literal loss of balance, a fall, loss of consciousness, and consequent weakness, in which the protagonist is nursed back to health by her.[10] It is in such a state that the defences of the English protagonists oppose the least resistance, and they are most ready to meet and receive the Other. The encounter with Ireland and the falling in love with a female representative of the country may seem to change their attitudes or behaviour, but, in order for the change to be significant, both protagonists must, towards the end of the narratives, face an unexpected and upsetting encounter with a parental figure, who will reveal an uncomfortable truth about their own identity. This revelation is actually a turning-point in the self-awareness of the protagonist, determining his future relationship with Ireland. The nature and the implications of such experiences are however different in each novel.

What most strikes readers of *The Wild Irish Girl* is its hybrid nature, in which the narrative modes of romance coexist with referential discourse (especially

10 Hugh Kearney, 'Contested Ideas of Nationhood 1800-1995', *Irish Review*, 20 (Winter/Spring 1997), 1-22.

eighteenth-century antiquarian discourses) intruding both in dialogues and as paratext. This is in fact functional to the three interrelated moments through which Horatio's regeneration comes about: desire, knowledge, and the acknowledgement of guilt. It is desire, awakened of course by the erotic fascination of the Irish girl and of the 'sublime' landscape, that prompts the English protagonist to cross national and cultural barriers. Loving Glorvina, Horatio is involved with the country to the deepest of his being, at an emotive, sensual, pre-discursive level. His romance, however, is not without political implications, especially considering the language of eighteenth-century sensibility in which it is expressed, and which was by now associated with Revolution. The Irish girl herself is 'wild' in the sense that she is uncorrupted by society and its conventions. Through the virtue of the impulses of the heart, the abandon to youthful eroticism, the very self-expression in lyrical flights and outbursts of passion, the protagonist is loosened from previous social and psychological conditioning, his old ways of thinking are changed, and his one-time sense of national identity is disrupted. Horatio starts to learn the Irish language and, rejecting the dull moralism of English fiction, emphatically declares his preference for the writers of the European sensibility[12]; that is, for a cultural heritage which rooted identity in individual feelings and sensations, fostered a questioning attitude, and was at that time being stigmatized for being 'Jacobin' and therefore 'un-British'.[13]

If Gaelic Ireland—spatially separated from 'Anglo-Ireland', 'romantic', unchanged, timeless—appears enclosed in a Bakhtinian chronotope of 'idyllic time' or 'adventure time', nevertheless, its very ahistoricism allows Horatio a look into the long-forgotten folds of Irish history and native culture.[14] Antiquarian research is evoked to assert the high value and relevance of the latter, challenging the assumption that Ireland was a barbarous, backward country in need of 'civilization'. For all its glamour, however, 'romantic' Ireland is no exotic paradise. Horatio learns the facts of Irish history—of colonization, dispossession and repression; the ghosts of the past (involving his own ancestors) haunt even his romance with Glorvina, and introduce an element of anxiety and antagonism in his relationship with the world of the Irish girl.[15] He will gain his final insight at the end of the narrative, when he finds his father, Lord M., standing at the altar ready to marry Glorvina.

Horatio's rivalry with his father had in fact been ironically foreshadowed at the beginning of the narrative, in similar terms of patriarchal sexuality and father-son

---

11 I. Ferris (1996) 295.   12 Owenson / Morgan, *The Wild Irish Girl* (Oxford: OUP, 1999) 144.   13 I. Ferris, *The Achievement of Literary Authority*, cit., p. 127.   14 Cf. Michail Bachtin, 'Le forme del tempo e del cronotopo nel romanzo', in *Estetica e romanzo* (Torino: Einaudi, 1979) 231-405. Among critics who have pointed out the relationship of *The Wild Irish Girl*'s Gaelic Ireland with Bakhtin's chronotopes are I. Ferris (1991) 130-3, and Joep Leerssen, *Remembrance and Imagination: Patterns in the Historical and Literary Representation of Ireland in the Nineteenth Century* (Cork: Cork UP, 1996), 7.   15 From the beginning, Horatio has to reckon with the legacy of hatred between his family and Glorvina's. He is compelled to assume a false identity in order to gain admittance at her castle, which will further complicate matters towards the end. Early on in his romance, he has a dream of Glorvina as a Gorgon (60). Later, when he begins to suspect he has a rival, he gives vent to his spite by 'relapsing' in his old prejudiced attitudes (173-9).

rivalry, in connection with the tyranny brought about by absentee landlordism.[16] In this light, Horatio's journey into Ireland can also be read as travelling the road his father has before him, and which will ultimately bring him to a confrontation with the figure of his father and with his own past, the reflection of himself in his father, and the realization of his ancestral guilt and of his historical role as oppressor.

Horatio, that is, is not allowed the escapist solution of 'going native', of just abandoning himself to the charms of Ireland and of the wild Irish girl, forgetting about the legacies of the past, his own personal and historical identity. Both father and son have been willing to encounter and know the Other, both have faced hard and disturbing truths about their historical identity, and this is what legitimizes them both to marry Glorvina.[17] Glorvina, too, before finally marrying Horatio, is called on for an act of 'violent forgiveness', when she is faced with marriage into the family that murdered her people.[18] The 'Glorvina solution', as has been called (that is, the marriage of reconciliation between a Protestant and an Irish Catholic as a metaphorical 'solution' to the troubled relationships between England and Ireland) thus implies self-knowledge, the willingness to cross borders, and *love* for *difference*.[19] It is a pluralist, implicitly federative solution, shunning the 'either-or' dichotomy or the 'superior-inferior' hierarchy. Only in this way, as Lord M. writes in the final letter to his son, can 'the names of Inismore and Mæ be inseparably blended, and the distinctions of English and Irish, of protestant and catholic, for ever buried'.[20]

Edgeworth's *Ennui* is, too, a hybrid work, in which a folktale motif like that of the changeling has a pivotal function in the plot, and in which Gaelic Ireland is given uncanny connotations (mainly through Ellinor, 'Mother Ireland' who comes to claim her son) in a prevailing novelistic register. This hybridity, however, appears all the more to emphasize the rejection of traditional modes of life in favour of bourgeois modernity. Ireland is not a land of romance, but a land of trial; 'romantic feudalism', which was associated with Ireland and the Gaelic Irish, is rejected as regressive (there is in fact no noble and ancient Gaelic civilization, but only the world of peasants). Above all, instead of legitimization of English or Anglo-Irish rule through a marriage of reconciliation, legitimization through individual talents, education, legal right, and a 'modern' *Irish* identity is asserted, opposing both 'feudalism' and English domination.

Lord Glenthorn, the protagonist of *Ennui*, has grown up in England in a moral and social *ancien régime*, that is, a world grotesquely marked by dissipation and irresponsibility. 'Englishness' here has clear 'imperial' overtones: there are several references to the dissolute way of life in the decadent days of the Roman empire[21], while the Irish are objects of explicit contempt, or even of physical violence.[22] Glenthorn's near-fatal encounter with Ellinor represents an initiation to previously

16 Owenson / Morgan, 34-7.   17 Ian Dennis, 50-1.   18 Kathryn Kirkpatrick, 'Introduction' to Owenson / Morgan, xviii.   19 Robert Tracy, 'Maria Edgeworth and Lady Morgan: Legality versus Legitimacy', *Nineteenth-Century Fiction*, 40:1 (June 1985) 1-22.   20 Owenson / Morgan, 250.   21 Maria Edgeworth, *Castle Rackrent and Ennui*, (London: Penguin, 1992) 153-4, 156, 168.   22 Ibid. 157-8, 168.

unrecognized human feelings, and of course to Ireland. While nursing him Ellinor talks to him, virtually at a subliminal level, about Ireland, in order to persuade him to settle in his country: 'I was only a lord, as she said, in England, but I could be all as one as a king in Ireland.'[23]

Here appears Ellinor's ambivalent role. She regenerates her son's feelings, but her influence on him is in fact regressive. She evokes a world of folklore and superstition, a Gaelic world stubbornly attached to its medieval tradition, and, most importantly, a feudal world of kingly, virtually absolute power, in which tenants are 'almost vassals'.[24] It was for the sake of such power that she had changed the child at nurse in the first place, a 'gift' which however has hardly brought him happiness and has alienated him from himself and his country. It will also be part of Glenthorn's Irish education to disengage himself from Mother Ireland and her allurement to a romantic 'feudalism' which actually parallels the 'imperial' effeteness of his present way of life.

Glenthorn's education as an Irishman consists first of all in learning to come to terms with a complex reality in which nothing is as it seems and all expectations are somehow subverted. This implies acknowledging the limits set by conditions and overcoming the illusion of omnipotence, in particular, discarding that kind of 'feudal' relationship metaphorically centred on the 'gift' (his unfitting gift of a cottage to Ellinor parallels her own gift to him) in favour of relationships based on right and merit. And it means discovering and proving his own human worth, sense of responsibility and moral independence which his upbringing as an *English* nobleman deplorably denied. In this process, the still-English Lord Glenthorn must be rejected by the female representative of the country, Lady Geraldine, who instead marries a self-made professional man (i.e., what Glenthorn himself will become). This, in turn, foreshadows Glenthorn's own final rejection of title, estate and 'Englishness', and his marriage to Cecilia Delamere.

The turning-point in Glenthorn's education will, however, be caused by his stand on right. For this he alienates the loyalists during the 1798 rebellion, then he also alienates Ellinor who, wrongly believing her son Ody to be involved in a conspiracy, asks Glenthorn just to 'let him off', before any legal prosecution is started against him.[25] 'Mother Ireland' has come again to claim her son. She does not acknowledge the 'rule of law', she is only loyal to natural blood-ties. She has made her son a king, and now she comes back to claim her due, requiring his using an arbitrary power to set her other son free. Incensed at his refusal, she reveals that she is his 'lawful mother' (the adjective is significant)—a fact that he will acknowledge while distancing himself from her by restoring the real Lord Glenthorn (now living as a blacksmith) to his legal rights and becoming Mr Christopher O'Donoghoe, a modern, bourgeois *Irishman* (Ellinor will die soon

23 Ibid. 160.   24 Ibid.   25 Ibid. 270.

after his decision).[26] By working his way back to his former position at the head of Irish society and marrying Cecilia, he legitimizes his right to rule by his own abilities and by the law, while the real Lord Glenthorn proves tragically unable, owing to the influence of an archaic culture and lack of adequate education, to live up to his new position. That the hero at this marriage has to change his name again may well indicate the necessity of a break with previous social and ethnic identities in order to ground the modern Irish one—obviously difficult and elusive.

Both *The Wild Irish Girl* and *Ennui* thus question existing relationships between Britain and Ireland, but the images of the nation appear different in each. What is Ireland? In *The Wild Irish Girl*, Cathleen Ní Houlihan is a young woman who awakens desire in the English visitor, in *Ennui* she is an old woman representing the past and its archaic values. In the first case, the protagonist marries her and meta-phorically founds a new nation, in the second case he detaches himself from her and metaphorically kills her, but he must first acknowledge that he is her son, that he is *Irish*. What is the past? In *The Wild Irish Girl* the hero learns about the greatness of the Gaelic civilization of the past and how his ancestors destroyed it. In *Ennui* the past is identified with 'feudalism', which—whether 'imperial' and English or 'romantic' and Irish—is a liability on personal and social development. What is the future? In *The Wild Irish Girl* it appears to be a type of regenerative plural and multi-cultural identity, in *Ennui* regeneration can only come from bourgeois modernity. In both cases, however, the nation of later Irish nationalism is still far away.

Irish Ireland: Recreating the Gael

BERNIE LEACOCK, UNIVERSITY OF ULSTER AT COLERAINE

Theories of racial identity and race destiny mark the starting point of D.P. Moran's ideological concept, known as Irish Ireland. Moran's opinionated expression of the 'two tribes' theory that the Irish Catholic represented the Gael, or the true national stock of ancient Ireland, strengthened a cultural/religious division which, poisoned the discursive atmosphere of the Revival at a time when to do so seemed particularly un-philanthropic. It was not until the 1920s that a disillusioned Moran revealed that Irish Ireland had been based on the social evolutionist theories of Darwin and Huxley.[1]

26 Ibid. 271.

BERNIE LEACOCK
1 D.P. Moran, 'Current Affairs', *The Leader* (14 April 1923).

Moran's education would most certainly have pre-disposed him to be receptive to the scientific milieu that existed in English Edwardian society. From 1880-82 he attended Castleknock College, Dublin, where the syllabus leaned heavily towards the sciences. Moran then became a journalist in London and furthered his education by attending lectures on economics taught by Sidney Webb and on evolutionary theory, taught by social Darwinist W.S. Armytage Smith. The assimilation of social evolutionist theories as a basis from which to launch an economically viable Ireland became apparent in Moran's writings for the Dublin journal, the *New Ireland Review*, from 1898-1900. The series of six articles were collected and published by Dublin publisher James Duffy in 1905 and were titled *The Philosophy of Irish Ireland*. In these writings Moran applied his newly garnered knowledge to the age-old problems of his homeland.

The thesis expounded in the work reveals Moran's knowledge of mainstream social evolutionist thought and an Irish interest in the notion that the British had a special race destiny. It seemed obvious to Moran that the Irish must improve their national stock by developing a uniquely Irish environment in which future generations could grow as distinctly Irish rather than standard British. His analysis of his people had its basis in the attitudes of eugenicist theorists in the matter of Irish rootstock. He saw that the Irish towns based themselves on English fashions in language, dress and social etiquette and were content to live their lives in imitation of the English lower middle classes: 'Though the great shop-keeping classes have nearly everything which riches can give, particularly the veneer of manners and gentility, which costly surroundings are calculated to impart to a mere Caliban.'[2]

The effectiveness of the Irish race in striving to fulfil its destiny, would depend on the encouraging of those things which, he deemed to be indigenous Irish characteristics; whether good or bad; although to give Moran his due, the strict morality of the Irish Ireland cult was intended to produce God-fearing citizens. Moran's concerns about the falsity of a life of imitation had as their basis the fear that the Irish would fare no better than the average Negro did, in a distant British colony. The fact is that many English political cartoons and some Anglo-Irish novelists did portray the Irishman as sub-species of the human race. This began with the portrayal of the Irish as a slave race or white-Negroid, a circumstance with which Moran lashed his fellow Irishmen:

> The shifts, and twists, and turns of the respectable Irish to behave after their absurd second-hand conception of English ladies and gentlemen-the antics they play…the most disagreeable thing about all this cringe is its needlessness and absolutely false basis … it is sad to see an unfortunate wretch whining under the lash of a whip; it is, however, natural to whine in such circumstances. But it is revolting to see a people whining for no

2 D.P. Moran, *The Philosophy of Irish Ireland* (Dublin 1905) 45.

adequate reason whatsoever. And why do we whine? Because we have lost all our national pride.[3]

Towards the end of the last century, newspaper commentaries commonly portrayed the Irish as having slipped even further down the highly imperialistic evolutionary scale. As evolutionary fever hit English society, Anglo-Saxon superiority became a tangible thing evidenced by the spread of the Empire in India, Africa, Australia and Canada. The Irish were increasingly viewed, through reports of agrarian unrest and Fenian activity, as anthropoid apes. Moran was aware of the might of the British Empire, militarily and politically, and his return to Ireland in the midst of the celebrations of the 'glorious' revolution of 1798, only served to point out the precarious position in which Ireland stood; especially now that science had seemingly supplied hard proof that the Irish were a lesser breed. The simianization of the Irish in the English mind was of less concern to him, however, than the psychological effect this line of scientific enquiry was having on the will to be Irish at home:

> Even if the Anglo-Saxon race … the English-speaking race stopped where it is we could not keep on in our present way without disaster. But the English-speaking race, in the meshes of which we are interwoven by a thousand material and immaterial ties, is making the pace and we must either stand up to it-which I fear we cannot; isolate ourselves from its influence-which we largely can do; or else get trodden on and be swallowed up-which, it appears to me, is, if we keep on as we are going, inevitable.[4]

This plan for dissension and an all-out-battle for Irish evolution in a free market would see inherent Irish character and personality, which, he felt could 'by conscious effort, be moulded and changed'[5] rapidly evolve to the same or better levels of intelligence, virility and business savvy which, he had observed in England:

> Irishmen are now in competition with Englishmen in every sphere of social and intellectual activity, in a competition where England has fixed the marks, the subjects, and has had the sole making of the rules of the game … England has been a great commercial and industrial country for centuries, and within her borders there has been, broadly peaking, free competition and, the population has, as a consequence, undergone a rough sifting process. The greater part of what was strenuous, fighting and capable has long since gone to the top. To assert that the poorer classes in England are only the dregs, would be too sweeping, but anyway they are largely composed of the dregs of their race.[6]

3 Ibid. 49   4 Ibid. 11   5 Ibid. 75   6 Ibid. 44-5

This scientific control of man and nation became known as social Darwinism later in the century but for Moran, it was part of the cosmic process and he gambled on the fact that the time for the regeneration of the Gael had come. The past glories of Irish myth and legend were a much more fitting history lesson for the neo-Gael than Irish political history from 1782. Moran attempted to wipe away the current picture in the Irish mind of their ancestors as 'undesirable aborigines, speaking gibberish…a low multitude'.[7] Moran's late discovery of the Irish language convinced him that the Irish had something with which to bring about the change of character: 'We must be original Irish, and not imitation English. Above all we must relearn our language, and become a bi-lingual people. For the great connecting link between us and the real Ireland, which few of us know anything about, is the Gaelic tongue.'[8]

Moran determined that the white-collar workers in the Irish towns would be his primary targets, as he deemed this class of person to be of the most value in the setting of new fashionable trends. He saw that the Gaeltacht areas by virtue of their geographical position had been bypassed by life and had become a sort of evolutionary cul-de-sac; isolated, antiquated and despised by the fashion-conscious towns as evidence of their low origins. With the advent of *The Leader* in 1900, he began his attempt to regenerate or recreate the Gael.

The venture began as a review of 'Current Affairs, Politics, Literature, Art and Industry' with science being conspicuous by its absence. The setting up of a rival paper to the Gaelic League's *An Claidheamh Soluis*, was, despite the blessing of some major League worthies, a risky business. Still more risky was Moran's combining of Catholicism and evolutionary theory. The example surely before Moran's eyes was the fate of the Catholic scientist St George Jackson Mivart, a friend of Lady Gregory, who had felt the full wrath of the Church's difficulty with new advances in science. Moran was a devout Catholic and it is hard to imagine that the influence he had on the Irish Catholic clergy and the high esteem, in which they held him, developed in ignorance of his aim and purpose.

The first subject that *The Leader* dealt with was certainly one of the Church's abiding concerns: emigration. Moran reasoned that in Irish society at present the man or woman with initiative was to be found at the head of the queue for the emigrant ship and that the country was subsequently losing its human wealth to the benefit of other lands. If his neo-Gaelic race were to evolve then the endless flow of emigrants, mainly from the poor rural areas, would have to be halted. He analyzed the problems of these young people and came to the conclusion that their environment had become unnatural. On an economic basis, Moran reckoned that incomes from young adults who had left for the New World were replacing initiative in those left behind. This resulted in economic disaster, as the free flow of money in these communities had become unfeasibly erratic. His

7 Ibid. 38   8 Ibid. 26

endorsement of technical education for the young would go a long way to reduce the sterility of existence among Ireland's youth whom, once trained, instead of leaving Ireland, could either find or create work in their own areas. There was another area which, was of some concern to Moran and his plan for the re-population of Ireland. He hoped that greater numbers of people would generate an increase in pressure and competition for survival in the business world so in a sense an increased population was one of the strongest impulses towards evolutionary change:

> The more we struggle amongst ourselves and compete against one another the better for the commonweal ... there will be an apparent waste of energy at which many a shallow mind will be dismayed ... the net benefit to the Gaelic Revival of all this energy let loose in free fields will be comparatively enormous. Uniformity is soul destroying, and leaves more than half the faculties of a man dormant. It is in strife of all kinds that men are drawn out for all they are worth, and free play for strife and competition is an essential condition if we are to get the greatest net amount of energy out of any community ... papers and people will often hit below the belt, and good men will be misrepresented.[9]

One of his first tasks in this area was to reprimand the Church for its part in the problem. Moran lamented the loss of ordinary and natural socializing between the sexes at dances and other everyday meeting places, in the poor rural areas. He felt that an overzealous clergy were partly to blame. Their efforts to rigidly enforce strict moral behaviour on their flock had literally killed the natural means of the young to meet each other, marry, and eventually procreate the species. Moran did not believe that rural Ireland should be left as some sort of shrine to tradition as he feared that population decline would wipe out the Gaelic gene along with the last traces of Gaelic civilization. He called for an upgrade in living standards so that modern pro-gressive thought could replace backward obeisance and ordinary social intercourse could become natural one again:

> We think we are right in stating the proposition that the measure of civilization of any country is to be read from the social relations of the sexes. Rural Ireland is not very advanced in civilization, if we judge it by this standard. Even in the church there is frequently, if not always, a 'men's side' and a 'woman's side'. Of course, among the well-to-do, social inter-course between the sexes is more general, while in 'society' such social commingling appears to be the begin all and end all of existence. That the cross-roads dance may be abused is no reason why the institution itself

9 Ibid. 77-8

should be swept away. We have swept the institution away and the people are leaving, too: and if they are denied the cross-roads at home, they may be caught in the low-dancing saloons of London or New York.[10]

It was not by accident that Moran chose to target the lower middle classes as they were regarded by eugenicists as the economic seedbed for future capitalist stock. His disillusionment in the 1920s was due jointly to the last eventful decade and his annoyance at state interventionism in his chimerical ferment of commerce. In 1923 as Moran contemplated the effectiveness of his Irish Ireland campaign the disappointment in his judgement of cosmic processes became evident:

> In our very young days there was a lot of talk about the theory of evolution. The nineteenth century was the last thing in civilization. In the Middle Ages, in the times of Cromwell … things were done that were impossible in the nineteenth century. The human race was evolving to higher things. Read any daily paper about the doings in Ireland and Europe today, and the bottom is knocked out of all that cant and rant. The devil is as active today as he was in the middle or any other ages. The world war and its after effects have put Darwin in his grave. We are the same old human race today as we were a thousand years ago. Even though today we have air-ships, motor-cars, telephones, and other inventions.[11]

The recitation of the technological advances that accompany war in all ages give Moran the air of a disillusioned technophobe, but it is hard not to feel that his greatest disappointment was with the human race. Moran's gamble on the regeneration of the Gaelic gene did not appear to come to fruition during his lifetime and he came to regret his earlier bullishness in claiming the right to the title of cosmic conductor.[12] 'Mr. Leader, a modern scientist'[13] may not have witnessed the modernized and inventive economy, teeming with business-orientated white-collar workers and entrepreneurial commercial enterprise that he had worked for, but he did supply the vision.[14]

10 D.P. Moran, 'Rural Amusements', *The Leader* (22 June 1901). See also F.H.O'Donnell ,'The Cause of Irish Depopulation', *The Leader* (23 March 1901).   11 D.P. Moran, 'Current Affairs' in *The Leader* (14 April 1923).   12 D.P. Moran, 'Current Affairs', *The Leader* (6 February 1909), (13 September 1902).   13 The Showman, 'The Wild Beast Show', *The Leader* (17 August 1901).   14 Morans' economic ideals are cited as the 'blueprint' for the Lemass era of leadership in John Horgan, *Sean Lemass: Enigmatic Patriot* (Dublin: Gill and Macmillan, 1997) 9.

Yeats' Endgame: *Postcolonialism and Modernism*

MICHAEL MCATEER, THE QUEEN'S UNIVERSITY OF BELFAST

In this paper I wish to offer some rudimentary comparison between a late play of W.B. Yeats, *Purgatory*, and Samuel Beckett's *Endgame*. The purpose of this is to open a discussion on the extent to which the context of European modernism both problematizes and is affected by postcolonial interpretations of twentieth century Irish writing. I will suggest how both plays are differentially linked into the specifics of an Irish historical situation that is itself intrinsic to the political culture of modern Europe, and that the blurring of this context in interpreting Irish literature is a potentially dangerous exercise in legitimizing critical positions inimical to a rigorous critique of naturalized ideology.

Initially, these plays might seem to offer very little by way of comparison. Beckett's is clearly identifiable with the absurdist movement of mid-20th century French drama, whilst Yeats' play comes at the end of a dramatic movement thematically pre-occupied with Ireland within which the Abbey Theatre was born. One might speculate on the 'French Connections' in the Irish dramatic movement as a tenuous point of connection here—Yeats meeting Synge in 1898 Paris and (reputedly) pointing him to the rooted West of Ireland to find his themes for drama there; the general influence of Baudelaire on 1890s symbolist drama and the pretext of symbolism for Yeats' theatrical endeavors after 1900; or even Ernest Renan's imaginative, irrational Celt as a pretext for the Celtic Twilight. Such connections are not without significance and convey the sense that neither the cultural nationalist dramatic movement in Ireland nor avant-garde drama in France fell suddenly from the Heavens. However, they may be misleading if employed to explain away certain primary formal tendencies distinguishing both types of drama. Whatever we might say about formal experiment in Yeats, we never get a raining down of limbs on stage, nor a prostitute biting the wrist of God, as in Antonin Artaud's *The Spurt of Blood*. And perhaps the closest we get to Eugene Ionesco's Rhinoceros is the woman with the crow's head, the Morrigu, who appears in *The Death of Cuchulain*.

Nevertheless, Yeats' *Purgatory* and Beckett's *Endgame* can be compared in ways that illuminate the complex situation of modern Irish culture in relation to Europe and to colonialism. It is now yawnfully axiomatic to observe that both authors were members of the southern Irish Protestant community who had complex and strained relationships to the country in which they were born. Yeats chose to make of Ireland the primary subject matter of his literary career but how he understood Ireland and his relationship to it were often at variance with conventional notions of Irishness. Beckett, on the other hand, appeared to reject Ireland definitively in choosing to immerse himself in the cultural life of Paris, yet much of his writing turns to Irish characters and Irish dialect. One thinks of Neary headbutting the buttocks of Cuchulainn's statue in *Murphy*, *Molloy*, Malone who Dies, Dunlaoghaire Pier in *Krapp's Last Tape* to name but a few instances.[1] Certainly, in *Endgame* we hear Irish dialect in Nagg's shout to Hamm 'Me Pap' or 'Me Sugar-Plum'. Of *Endgame*, Theodor Adorno writes 'Understanding it can mean nothing other than understanding its incomprehensibility, or concretely reconstructing its meaning structure—that it has none.'[2]

Why, in such a play, does Beckett choose to include Irish dialect? Consider one significant instance in the play:

> Nagg: Me pap!
> Hamm: Accursed progenitor!
> Nagg: Me pap!
> Hamm: The old folks at home! No decency left! Guzzle, guzzle, that's all they think of.[3]

Nagg is Hamm's 'Accursed progenitor'—he perpetuates the agony of an existence defined by pain alone. An allusion to the agony of existence in Yeats' *Purgatory* is obvious here, but before going to that, it's worth considering Nagg's 'Me pap' further. In reading 'Pap' as baby food, Nagg may be heard to cry with the babble of a baby—but also with the idiom of an Irish accent. Hamm responds in lofty speech 'accursed progenitor,' echoing his line 'Can there be misery—loftier than mine' from the beginning of the play. The resonance of Strindbergian lofty suffering is felt, but also the lofty suffering of Yeats' lonely hero Cuchulainn, railing against destiny and the ignominy of 'the filthy, modern tide' throughout the Cuchulainn cycle of plays. There is surely a trace of the father-son conflicts of *On Baile's Strand* and *The Playboy of the Western World* in this Nagg-Hamm exchange. Adorno comments: 'Hamm lets his stumps of parents completely starve, those parents who have become babies in their trashcans—the son's triumph as a father.'[4] If this is so, then it is also the case that the father has become the child. Thus, the phrase 'Me pap' suggests three identities for Nagg simultaneously—I am the father, I am Irish and I am a baby. If we think of the relationship between these identities as a necessary one, then something interesting for our understanding of Beckett in postcolonial terms happens. Irishness becomes the vehicle for revealing the dialectic of authority and servility through which the play is structured: a dialectic constitutive of its modernist aesthetic.

At this point one immediately senses the possibility of various modes of critiquing the play in postcolonial terms—Ireland as childlike, imaginative, pre-

---

1 John P. Harrington provides one of the most illuminating studies of Beckett's Irishness in recent years. See *The Irish Beckett* (Syracuse, NY: Syracuse UP, 1991).   2 Theodor Adorno, 'Trying to Understand *Endgame.*' *The Adorno Reader*, ed. Brian O'Connor. (Oxford: Blackwell, 2000) 322.   3 Samuel Beckett, *Samuel Beckett: The Complete Dramatic Works* (London: Faber, 1986) 96.   4 Adorno 336.

Oedipal, pre-rational, subject to the law of the father, itself Saxon, modern, rational; or equally Ireland as father, patriarchal, communalist, perpetuating tradition through purified kinship. Just as soon as these modes of critique come to the surface, however, they immediately begin to hover, lose confidence, and precisely for the very reason that allows for their possibility in the first place. By refusing the audience the comfort of transparent meaning, language is used in the play in a way that reveals how language works to allow for the production of and prevention of meaning. Cognisance of the prison-house of language and the view of communication as simulation, emerging in Saussure, Wittigenstein and reaching its zenith in Derrida, is itself a sign of the specifically European modernist form of *Endgame* that simultaneously gives rise to and cuts off Ireland as interpretative vehicle for the meaning of the play as a whole.

What then of *Purgatory* in relation to of this? How can a play written within a dramatic corpus that prioritises the question of nationhood relate to a play that refuses the forms of identity and communication that nationhood would seem to assume? First, there is the obvious yet important point that both plays are separated by the Second World War. *Purgatory* is first produced in 1938 and *Endgame* in 1957. Those years are separated by the cataclysmic events surrounding the Second World War, in particular the Holocaust and the dropping of the Atom bomb, and it might be argued that the destruction wrought by racialist nationalism during these years measures the distance between both plays: Yeats' anticipating the slaughter that was about to erupt, Beckett's a testament to its aftermath. To accept this is to observe that both plays are saying some unpalatable things about the category of nationhood itself, but in quite different ways. The titles of both plays are suggestive in this regard: *Purgatory* is an Endgame in a literal sense, a place where in the Catholic tradition, the dead live on in the restless agony of damnation but with the perpetual hope of salvation. Interestingly, Yeats chooses one of the most important theological differences between Catholicism and Protestantism for the title of this play, for it is out of the doctrine of Purgatory that the history of plenary indulgences emerged— the souls in Purgatory may be assisted to Heaven through prayer, the giving of alms and the offering up of the sacrifice of the mass.

W.J. McCormack has noted that the evidence of the play's genesis specifies its assumption of the Protestant/Catholic antagonism as tribal if not racial, as the operational field of taboo and totem. For McCormack, a crucial structural aspect of the play is the suppression of this specific context in the canonical text.[5] From this perspective, the play would appear to be firmly situated within the general framework of European history since the Reformation and its violent impact on Irish history in that period. But the presence of this historical sense in *Purgatory* is *hauntological* rather than ontological, in Derrida's sense—history itself is

5 W.J. McCormack, *From Burke to Beckett: Ascendancy, Tradition and Betrayal in Irish Literary History* (Cork: Cork UP, 1994) 343.

subject to those historical forces McCormack alludes to—the play locates itself in a history that has no longer become bearable and consequently collapses in upon itself.[6] Thus, the play's title simultaneously invokes and revokes history— if Purgatory is emblematic of the primary site of conflict in Europe since the Reformation and the weight of those modernising processes accelerated through that conflict, it equally symbolises the spectrality of such history, the destruction of the ontology of self-presence that is this history's pretext. This brings us to a very difficult place, however. The destruction of the ontology of self-presence, signified by spectral absent-presence throughout nineteenth-century Irish literary history, has been identified by David Lloyd and Seamus Deane as evidence of Irish colonial experience and the point from which a *jouissance* of postcolonial hybrid identity might be realised.[7] Yet the proximity of the destruction of logos by which Yeats' play takes the shape of, in McCormack's words, 'the self-regulating modernist art-work,' to Martin Heidegger's destruction of classical ontology in *Being and Time* (1927), itself the pretext for Derrida's programme of deconstruction, is significantly ignored.[8]

In one sense, what we get in *Purgatory* is precisely what Heidegger advocated and what Adorno condemned in him as fascist—a return to authenticity, to the pre-Socratic philosophy of Thales and Empedocles. This comes through in the play in the destruction of a linear, progressivist chronology in which time is instrumentally externalised (McCormack points out that 'the agony of the different generations in *Purgatory* has only the appearance of sequence; dramatically, the Old Man and the Boy go through their violent ritual simultaneously with the Bride and Groom'). It also manifests itself in a return to sacrificial purification, exemplified in the play in the Old Man's murder of his father, a man who burnt down their house when drunk, and of his son, whose mentality is presented as parsimoniously pecuniary.[9] Equally, however, Yeats' play remains more Nietzschean than Heideggerian because it is unwilling to turn away from the violent consequences following from the destruction of ontology and because of its recognition of that destruction's intrinsic relation to the very processes of modernization against which it is defined. The fascist charge against this play is disrupted by the fact that simultaneous with the assertion of values of racial purity is the destruction of the genealogical line of descent upon which that purity is based.[10] The Old Man looks to his mother for a

---

6 For Derrida's thesis of hauntology see *Spectres of Marx: The State of the Debt, The Work of Mourning and the New International,* trans. Peggy Kamuf (London: Routledge, 1994) 3-29. 7 David Lloyd, *Nationalism and Minor Literature: James Clarence Mangan and the Emergence of Irish Cultural Nationalism* (Berkeley: University of California P, 1987). Seamus Deane, *Strange Country: Modernity and Nationhood in Irish Writing since 1790* (Oxford: Clarendon, 1998). 8 For Derrida's indebtedness to Heidegger's conceptual discourse see Derrida, *Of Spirit: Heidegger and the Question,* trans. Geoff Bennington & Rachel Bowlby (Chicago: Chicago UP, 1989). 9 McCormack 348. 10 Marjorie Howes' claim that a positive argument is made for a eugenic model of nationality in *Purgatory* is somewhat misleading. It is more appropriate to view the kindred politics of the play as an expression of its formal-thematic crisis rather than a response to this crisis on Yeats' part. Howes' argument is stronger when she claims that Yeats' kindred politics in

trace of purified racial bloodline exhibited in her loftiness and generosity, but on realising its contamination, he kills both father and son in order that he would not have 'passed pollution on'. The tree in the play, certainly an emblem of Japanese Noh influence (anticipating the tree of *Waiting for Godot*), is a symbol for so much in Yeats' thought, but perhaps most importantly, genealogical inheritance. After the old man stabs his son, he looks to the Tree as if it has been renewed, 'like a purified soul' but only to realise that his murderous repetition has failed (as it must) to reinstate genealogical continuity: 'Twice a murderer and all for nothing.'[11] If the murders have been acts of purification, they have also been acts of base destruction.

If *Purgatory* and *Endgame* are amenable to postcolonial analysis it is at the level of the historical mutation of history. Adorno recognizes in *Endgame*, a transcendence of the devouring of history in French existentialist drama. He comments 'History is excluded, because it itself has dehydrated the power of consciousness to think history, the power of remembrance. Drama falls silent and becomes gesture, frozen amid the dialogues. Only the result of history appears—as decline.'[12] For McCormack, *Purgatory* is the 'focus of a critique directed at the romantic reading of history. Modernism as the culmination of romantic philosophy is its proper context.'[13] Significantly, Adorno's comments are made as a gloss on the following dialogue between Hamm and Clov:

> Hamm: The waves, how are the waves?
> Clov: The Waves? (He turns the telescope on the waves.) Lead.
> Hamm: And the sun?
> Clov: (looking) Zero.
> Hamm: But it should be sinking. Look again.
> Clov: (looking) Damn the sun.
> Hamm: Is it night already then?
> Clov: (looking) No.
> Hamm: Then what is it?
> Clov: (looking) Grey. (Lowering the telescope, turning towards Hamm, louder.)
> Grey! (Pause. Still louder.) GRREY![14]

Certainly, grey is the colour of an existence at the edge of annihilation here, but it also recalls the grey twilight of Yeats' 'Celtic Twilight' poetry and the fisherman 'who goes/ To a grey place on a hill/ In grey Connemara clothes.'[15] If this localizes the modernist universality of Beckett to an Irish context, it equally universalises the

Purgatory is useful in revealing the unpalatable aspects of nationalism 'that often lurk behind the facades of more attractive versions of the nation.' Marjorie Howes, *Yeats' Nations: Gender, Class, and Irishness* (Cambridge: CUP, 1996) 185.   11 W.B Yeats, *Collected Plays* (London: Macmillan, 1952) 679.   12 Adorno 326.   13 McCormack 359.   14 Beckett 107.   15 W.B Yeats, *Collected Poems*, ed. Norman Jeffares (London: Macmillan, 1989) 251.

specifically Irish context of Yeats. The spectral greyness of history in ruins is exclusive neither to the decrepit cottages and burnt-out Big Houses of rural Ireland, nor the echoing, empty gas-chambers of Auschwitz, but somehow traces a connecting thread between these.

In conclusion, I want to turn Seamus Deane's essay 'Boredom and Apocalypse' to suggest a discursive point of departure for the issues I've been raising. Deane hypothesizes that Irish history was too disturbed up to and into the nineteenth century to allow for a 'Whig interpretation' (scientific, rationalist, teleological) of history, resulting in the exoticization of the country as strange in English writing after the famine, an exoticization taken up by Irish nationalism and made into a virtue, a basis for separation rather than integration. As one consequence of this, he sights the tourist perspective of Ireland as unreal, an imaginative fantasy. For Deane, this is productive of boredom, in that the Irish themselves become 'endlessly entrapped between representing [Ireland] as a quaint other to imperial normality, or as a radical otherness for which no canonical system of representation is sufficient.'[16] But boredom also carries the more mundane sense for Deane, of the repetitive nature of experience systematized and rationalized through modern bureacracy. For Deane, Yeats is apocalyptic, the dialectical antithesis of this form of boredom—if Yeats is boring, it is in terms of endless entrapment in the eccentric circularity of occultism. Perhaps Deane is theoretically glossing the sentiment expressed in Eric Bentley's jocular yet revealing observation that reading Yeats' plays might lead one to lose interest in life. This is all very well, though it is significant here that the best Irish writer on boredom (some might claim the most boring Irish writer) Samuel Beckett, commands only one paragraph in Deane's essay. One wonders why, in an essay in which Flann O'Brien receives so much attention. Leaving this aside, something happens in Deane's essay when he gets on to historical revisionism—the dialectic gets dumped. For Deane, because revisionism is updated 'Whig interpretation,' 1916 can never really be understood. As apocalypse, it remains recalcitrant to the boredom of administrative rationality. However, to valorise it as such, to embrace its counter-modernising impulse, is not simply to be seduced by its aura of authenticity, of Dionysian spontaneity breaking through the mask of Apollo. It is to efface its structural interdependence with the systematic rationalization of identity it defines itself against. Such a move is Heideggerian and a question for postcolonialism is why Deane makes it at the end of a strongly dialectical essay. Might it be another Endgame?

16 Deane 156.

Urban Hymns: The City, Desire and Theology in Austin Clarke and Patrick Kavanagh

JOHN MCAULIFFE, TRINITY COLLEGE, DUBLIN

The city has rarely been central to poetry in the Irish republic. Patrick Kavanagh, the laureate of the Free State, is primarily read for his early lyrics, the canal bank poems and 'The Great Hunger', poems that are at the heart of a still-thriving pastoral tradition in Irish poetry. Austin Clarke's poetic character is more difficult to establish; he is usually read as either the Anglo-Gaelic poet of 'The Lost Heifer' and 'The Blackbird of Derrycairn', or as one of the State's most effective but erratic satirists. While neither man has been much considered as an urban poet, I will argue that reading both in an urban context clarifies critical ideas about their central pre-occupations. I will focus on their work in the mid-1950s when, for the first time, they both lived and published poetry in the same city.[1]

Although both men wrote about London and New York, Dublin is the central metropolis in their work. This is the Dublin of Archbishop John Charles McQuaid, a man with whom both poets had connections. Clarke's mother famously disin-herited her anti-clerical son by willing the family home to the Dublin diocese; on the other hand, McQuaid intervened to find Kavanagh a job first in the 1940s as a film reviewer and later as a UCD lecturer, in addition to granting him irregular financial assistance, probably McQuaid's greatest contribution to Irish intellectual life at this time.[2] Otherwise, an exacting, abstract city of god loomed over Dublin, shadowing every corner of the city, as is most evident in the Marian year 1954. This was a starting point for an intensive church-building programme and also led to the institution of the Angelus bells on RTE radio. In a recent essay, the poet Thomas McCarthy points out that, although it was originally a one-year honour to the virgin which RTE took off the air at the end of 1954, the angelus broadcast was re-instituted due to public demand in 1955 and is still with us.[3] So, during Clarke and Kavanagh's lifetime, the city of Dublin is primarily defined by the increasingly powerful presence of Catholicism. The church dominates Ireland's cultural discourse as well as its political life and physical landscape. There is not much sign of a counterculture—with the passing of Yeats' generation, both poets describe the city's literary culture as impoverished and in constant retreat.

However, they respond very differently to this social situation. In effect, though hardly in intention, Kavanagh's poetry after 'The Great Hunger' is recep-

---

1 All quotations from poems are taken from Austin Clarke, *Collected Poems* (Dublin: Dolmen, 1974) and Patrick Kavanagh, *The Complete Poems* (Newbridge: Goldsmith, 1991). Further references are to these editions and are cited in the text. 2 John Cooney *Archbishop John Charles McQuaid: Ruler of Catholic Ireland* (Dublin: O'Brien, 1999) 142, 459. 3 Thomas McCarthy, *Gardens of Remembrance* (Dublin: New Island, 1998) 196.

tive to if not supportive of Ireland's and Dublin's Catholicization. This will be clearer after an examination of those poems that take an urban theme. The city is present even in Kavanagh's earliest lyric poems, written in Monaghan. In 'Gay Cities', Kavanagh imagines himself in the city, 'crushed and shoved in the rude / unknowing throng'; in 'Ascetic', he sees the poet searching the 'slums of Mind' for the invaluable, elusive material for poetry (11, 5). In 'At Noon', the city is identified with self-destructive desire:

> Now at the passionate noon
> The no-good dames
> Tatoo my flesh with the indelible
> Ink of lust.
>
> What are these dim rooms
> And red ghost-lamps?
> Tell me this city's name,
> New York or Paris?
>
> Heaven was somewhere about
> A child ideal.
> Ah! The disillusioned one cried,
> You have come too far (22).

In the well-known 'Memory of my Father', this sense of displacement in an anonymous, amoral, brutal urban world is also present: 'Every old man I see / Reminds me of my father', he begins, as he walks down London's Gardiner Street, and the poem concludes

> Every old man I see
> In October-coloured weather
> Seems to say to me:
> 'I was once your father' (69).

Again the city is a place where man wanders, lost and orphaned, without community or family. For Kavanagh, this is no liberation, and there is a constant desire to return to the more secure identities of rural life, however harsh that life may be.

For Kavanagh, the city is never a subject in itself; the poems are grounded in a formulaic opposition where the city is always present as the flipside of a child's rural life. The poems are 'The Lake Isle of Inisfree', rewritten time after time, setting up a simple opposition: the world of pavements, roadways and adulthood against the field, the lane and childhood. The poems ignore current political usages of that rural vision, images that culminate in de Valera's famous 1941 St Patrick's Day speech. They also ignore Yeats' own complication of that rural scene, they ignore Clarke's epic revisions of that Irish landscape which see it as an arduous stage for the humbling of man, and later, they ignore his own 'The Great Hunger', the great poem that he spent much of his career repudiating.

At this point, it is worth noting that, and this may be already clear, much of Kavanagh's least interesting poetry is on an urban theme. When he does attempt to transform the city, to see it as a viable place for writing, he writes an utterly odd poem like 'Phoenix' that attaches his characteristic redemptive conclusion to the grim and clichéd image of the urban scrap-yard,

> A Leeds furnace
> Is the Phoenix
> From whose death-wings on this scrap-heap
> Will rise
> Mechanic vigour.
> We believe.
> Now is the Faith-dawn (6).

This oddity apart, an anti-modern posture continues to predicate all of Kavanagh's poetry, although other, more concrete urban spaces are introduced and consistently examined in the 1950s. The city at mid-century is characterized by two settings, the pub and the street—the former is the court where Kavanagh judges his contemporaries and bewails the unParnassian nature of city life and the problem of 'literary gloom'. (In poems like 'If you ever go to Dublin Town / Look for me on Pembroke Road', Kavanagh is dying to be remembered, and dying to be gone too). Many of these poems take the form of ballads and verse drama and have been clearly discussed by Antoinette Quinn in her account of Kavanagh's self-representation as a heroic figure.[4]

The other kind of city poem is set on the street, usually the site of the opportunistic male gaze. In 'The Rowley Mile', a poem that imitates the disconcertingly uncomfortable trajectory of 'On Raglan Road' (187), 'Grafton Street Admiration' (130), 'Good By Ladies' (209), and 'Along the Grand Canal' (297), the poet approaches a woman after an exchange of glances, only to be rebuffed:

> The street was full of eyes that stared
> At something very odd.
> I tried to imagine how little means
> Such a contretemps to God.

---

4 Antoinette Quinn, *Patrick Kavanagh: Born Again Romantic* (Dublin: Gill and Macmillan, 1991)

I followed her a few slow yards
'Please just one minute stop'
And then I dashed with urgent tread
Into a corner shop.

As I walked down that sunny street
I was a broken man
Thanks to an Irish girl
But is true to the plan
Taught her by old Gummy Granny—
You must try out your power with a smile,
But come to the test hard reality must
Make the pace on the Rowley Mile (260).

The city street, as in his earliest poems, is the occasion of desire but only ever provides frustrating glimpses of another lifestyle that can never be realized. But even when successful, the city can get in the lover's way, intruding as the despoiler of innocent nostalgia: in 'Love in a Meadow',

She waved her body in the circle sign
Of love purely born without side;
The earth's contour, she orbited to my pride,
Sin and unsin.
But the critic asking questions ran
From the fright of the dawn
To weep later on an urban lawn
For the undone,
God-gifted man (289).

Love and art can only be contained and sustained in the unthinking, stable setting of rural life and Kavanagh's vision of love and the good life is always the backward, northwestern look. In poems like 'Miss Universe' where the body is actually graphically *mentioned*, it is never in an urban context and religious prescriptions are never more than a couple of lines away:

O the sensual throb
Of the explosive body and tumultuous thighs!
Adown a summer lane comes Miss Universe
She whom no lecher's art can rob
Though she is not the virgin who was wise (291).

When he writes positively of the city, in the canal bank poems, it is a domesticated city, connected to the rural world—'the barge comes bringing from Athy / And other far-flung towns mythologies.'[5] Or, it is a city whose sense of community is comically rural and familial in its intimacy: 'And be excited to meet old acquaintances such as / A branch in the water and a cocksfoot of this year's growth / And be able to say I knew your father and your mother both.'[6]. In a fine early poem like 'The 6:40 from Amiens Street', reader and protagonist are soon transported into the pastoral scene where Kavanagh's lyrical intensity safely retreats from the problematic conservatism of contemporary Catholicism. That poem begins:

O is it 1940
Or a thousand years ago
We are not going home by train
We are riding through the snow (75).

Where Kavanagh retreats from the ruins and rubble, the transformations and the multiplicity of city life, Austin Clarke celebrates the unsettling power of the urban to produce disorder and change. Clarke was born in Dublin's North inner city and he received his primary and secondary education there and in Limerick—he completed a BA and an MA at UCD, where he taught for a short time; he then spent 15 years working as book-reviewer in London. The city, however, does not appear as a subject in Clarke's work until late in his career, with the publication of the short book of satires *Ancient Lights*. In 1955, at the age of 59, Clarke approaches the city of Dublin and its governance. Gone is the harsh, wet and windy natural landscape of the early work, gone too is the recourse to Gaelic myth and symbol; in its stead is an urgency that insists on the modern city as the battleground of civilization. Clarke, to paraphrase Eavan Boland, passes on myth and moves into history. It is telling that the first poem in the collection, 'Celebrations', takes its form from the ballad 'Who fears to speak of '98?': Clarke's poem begins 'Who dare complain or be ashamed / Of liberties our arms have taken?' (195). The ballad form and Clarke's role as satirist, both ashamed and complaining about the state, clearly announce the new turn his poetry has taken. After 1955, Clarke consistently refers to urban life and contemporary political and religious intrigue—his satires will be a reliable map to the changing state. As Thomas McCarthy puts it: 'in the 1950s faith had a vibrant streetlife. Clarke follows this life around the Free State like a well-rehearsed heckler.'[7]

In the title poem of *Ancient Lights*, he meditates at length upon his radical decision to write poetry that is specifically grounded in an urban environment. It is a central poem for any understanding of Clarke's later work, as a close reading illustrates.[8] The poem's title is typical of Clarke's rich contextual subtlety—it

5 'Lines Written on a Seat ...' (295). 6 'Cool Water Under Bridges' (296). 7 McCarthy 196. 8 This close reading is indebted to other readers of the poem, including Maurice Harmon, *Austin Clarke: A*

refers to the building law that allows tenants to object to any new building that obstructs daylight naturally entering their windows. Until recently, objectors had only to chalk the words 'Ancient Light' on the house wall to protect their right. Clarke's poem is an equivalent writing on the wall, defending the natural light of the protagonist from the construction that the church places on his words and his place. Crudely expressed, the poem's theme is the Church's domination of the young poet's mental and physical landscape. Clarke begins:

> When all of us wore smaller shoes
> And knew the next world better than
> The knots we broke, I used to hurry
> On missions of my own to Capel
> Street, Bolton Street and Granby Row
> To see what man has made.[9]

The stanza immediately concerns itself with spatial definition: Clarke contrasts the well-known 'next world' (of heaven and hell) with the actual living reality of which the terrified child is hardly aware. Line 5 ironically contrasts the shopping streets of Capel et al ('what man has made') with the divinely authorized church. The boy's obsessive concern with other worldly knowledge is evident in the pun of the third line where he 'breaks the knots' of shoelaces and also, unknowingly, the 'thou shalt nots' of the ten commandments. A further pun on 'missions' contrasts the errands on which children are sent with the religious Missions to the non-Catholic world.

The stanza continues

> But darkness
> Was roomed with fears. Sleep, stripped by woes
> I had been taught, beat door, leaped landing,
> Lied down the banisters of naught.

The darkness of the night (and later the Church and its confessional) is imbued with fear, due to the taught 'woes' that populate his imagination. Then, Clarke puns on 'landing', denoting the top of a staircase but also the groundedness of human life that eludes him since he has entered the fantastic world of super-stition and fear. The 'lying' on the banister sends him on a rollercoaster ride out of the physical world and describes the child's utter rootlessness in the arcane unreality of dogma: the 'naught' from which he cannot escape into reality.

Critical Introduction (Dublin: Wolfhound, 1989) 154-9; and W.J. McCormack *Austin Clarke: Selected Poems* Dublin: Lilliput, 1991) 234-5. 9 'Ancient Lights' 199-201. All further quotations are from this text.

The next two stanzas describe the reason for the child's terror, the false confession where he unwittingly confessed to sins of the flesh, 'immodest look ... unnecessary touch.' The fourth and fifth stanzas recount a liberating incident outside the church, when the child witnesses a cage bird devoured by sparrows, an event that he is unable to prevent. Confronted by mortality, the child despairs, but moments later a 'bronze bird' attacking the sparrows is distracted by the child's shouts. The 'lesson' is this: 'Pity / Could raise some littleness from dust,' a striking thought that grants agency and a sacrilegiously godlike power of resurrection to the young child. The next stanza relates this notion to the adult world that Clarke now inhabits, 'among the hatreds of rent Europe', and praises freethinkers, Martin Luther and Clarke's namesake, St Augustine.

The final stanzas again return to the moment of liberation that freed his childhood from oppressive religious strictures, and the scene is again the city street, where the child takes shelter from a downpour in the doorway of the heretic protestant church, (the Black Church where, superstition has it, if you walk twice round, after dark, you will meet the devil himself).[10] The city, undogmatic, open still to accident and dialogue offers Clarke salvation:

> Still, still I remember awful downpour
> Cabbing Mountjoy Street, spun loneliness
> Veiling almost the Protestant church,
> Two backyards from my very home,
> I dared to shelter at locked door.
> There, walled by heresy, my fears
> Were solved. I had absolved myself:
> Feast-day effulgence, as though I gained
> For life a plenary indulgence.

Clarke sets out his beliefs and writes that he can and has absolved himself—the location is symbolic, on a busy, rainy street, at the door of the Protestant church, like Martin Luther before him. His use of sacramental language grants the church an almost bridal appearance, the rain baptizes his new fearlessness. By judicious punning the last stanza also recovers for secular use the language of confession (by the poet's apt choice of verb and image for the concluding downpour: he hears 'half our heavens' pass through the street sewer's confessional grille), mass (the pun on 'services') and papal election ('New smoke flew up'). The Catholic Church's dominance of language and the urban scene is fiercely contested and the last stanza also diminishes religion's abstract spirituality, concentrating instead on the physical and human landscapes that underpin and here undermine such Catholic structures.

10 Austin Clarke, *Twice round the Black Church: Early Memories of Ireland and England* (Dublin: Moytura, 1990 [1962]) 22.

The stanza finally forces our attention on mortality, the body, and the excremental street:

> The sun came out, new smoke flew up,
> The gutters of the Black Church rang
> With services. Waste water mocked
> The ballcocks: down-pipes sparrowing,
> And all around the spires of Dublin
> Such swallowing in the air, such cowling
> To keep high offices pure: I heard
> From shore to shore, the iron gratings
> Take half our heavens with a roar.

In 'Ancient Lights', Clarke describes the terrain which his imagination habitually inhabits thereafter, an area familiar to residents of Dublin and readers of Clarke's work. With a typically allusive wit, Clarke illuminates a moment of crisis when powerful forces test the identity of the individual. There is no over-reaching search for closure: rather, Clarke is content to represent characters living in doubt, uncertainty and confusion, a state that is imagined as the babbling city street. The poem's difficulty, the reticence of its style, is itself a rebuke to the kind of preaching and oversimplification that defined the political and religious morality of Roman Catholic Ireland.

To conclude, and to finally refer to this paper's title, neither poet is able to write the kind of conformist urban hymn that the age demanded—Kavanagh's conservative religious sensibility conceives of the city as irretrievably a place of fear, desire and sin. On the other hand, Clarke squares up to his urban situation, but he produces poems that deliberately evade the simplicity that characterizes popular song. Clarke's city is the place where he sings from his own dissonant hymn sheet, where he discovers a way out of the mass devotions that characterized Irish religious practice during his lifetime.

The Shan Van Vocht: *Notes from the North*

ROBBIE MEREDITH, THE QUEEN'S UNIVERSITY OF BELFAST

The North created many problems for nationalists who desired independence and unity in Ireland, whether of culture or politics. Culturally, the North, and especially the city of Belfast, often seemed too hard, too industrial, for Revivalists eager to locate 'Irishness' well away from such urban centres. Hence, for instance,

Yeats' occasional antagonism, his declarations of dislike for the people of Ulster,[1] or insistence on challenging the geographical signified in relation to folklore, asserting that 'a woman from the North would probably be a fairy woman, or, at any rate, a "knowledgeable" woman, one who was "in the fairies" and certainly not necessarily at all a woman from Ulster'.[2] Lady Gregory would make similar pronouncements,[3] while Nora Hopper, in *Ballads in Prose*, asserted the presence of 'pishogues and sheogues in Ireland yet', despite all the mills in Belfast and Armagh.[4]

Yet the image, which Douglas Hyde also provides, of a Saxon north-east corner on a Celtic island, can be deceptive.[5] A glance through the 'Notes and News' columns of *An t-Sean Bhean Bhoct* (the *Shan Van Vocht*) reveals a plethora of movements situated in the vortex of nationalist politics and Celtic culture— for example, the Henry Joy McCracken Literary Society, various branches of the Irishwomen's Association and the Gaelic League, the Belfast branch of the Irish National Amnesty Association, various '98 clubs, and lending libraries of Irish literature. All of these and more were active in 1890s Belfast, and numerous lectures, meetings and concerts held in order to further national culture are also detailed. Prime movers in many of these were Alice Milligan and Anna Johnston, editor and secretary respectively of the *Shan Van Vocht*, who also wrote most of the paper between them.

Alice Milligan was born near Omagh on 14 September 1866, the second of nine surviving children to a middle-class Methodist family, who later relocated to Belfast and ultimately Bangor. Her father, Seaton Forest Milligan, was active in the conservative and influential 'antiquarian' movement in Ulster; one of those Irish Protestants infatuated with the Irish past, usually at the expense of the political present. Milligan's father afforded her not only with literary interests but also the opportunities for education offered by his relative prosperity and the two collaborated on a short work, *Glimpses of Erin*, in 1888.[6] The familiar Gaelicized relations and servants who seem to crop up in the (romanticized) biographies of so many Revival figures, was also informing Milligan's contributions to various national movements and periodicals by the time she met Anna Johnston when the Milligan family moved to Belfast's Antrim Road in 1893. Johnston, better known as a poet, under her pseudonym 'Ethna Carbery', was from a different

1 W.B. Yeats qtd. in Gerald Dawe and Edna Longley eds., *Across a Roaring Hill: The Protestant Imagination in Modern Ireland* (Belfast: Blackstaff, 1985) iv. 2 W.B. Yeats, notes, *Visions and Beliefs in the West of Ireland collected and arranged by Lady Gregory with two Essays and Notes by W.B. Yeats* by Lady Gregory, vol. 2 (New York and London: G.P. Putnam's Sons, 1920) 343. 3 In *Poets and Dreamers*, for instance, she claims that, 'knowledge of charms has usually come from the North, but the North may be taken to mean any strange unfamiliar place.' Lady Gregory, *Poets and Dreamers: Studies and Translations from the Irish including Nine Plays by Douglas Hyde* (Gerrards Cross: Colin Smythe, 1974 [1903]) 274. 4 Nora Hopper, 'Daluan,' *Ballads in Prose* (London: John Lane, Bodley Head, 1894) 103. 5 Douglas Hyde, 'The Necessity for De-Anglicising Ireland,' *The Revival of Irish Literature* (London: T. Fisher Unwin, 1894) 159. 6 Seaton F. Milligan and Alice L. Milligan, *Glimpses of Erin* (Belfast: Marcus Ward, 1888).

religious but similar social background. Her father, Robert, had been a prominent Ulster member of the Irish Republican Brotherhood, but by the 1890s was a timber merchant (and, according to Yeats, a bore), and Anna, a Catholic, was also moving among the various 'national' organizations in Belfast.

In October 1895, Milligan and Johnston were appointed editors of the *Northern Patriot*, the paper of the Henry Joy McCracken Literary Society. A central theme of the paper under their editorship was the ability of Ulster to contribute to the national cause, in order to encourage Northern nationalists, and to assure Southern nationalists about the 'hard' North's ability to contribute to a national Revival. Milligan alluded to these attitudes in the Christmas issue of 1895, arguing that, 'the assertion of Ulster's colonialism is exaggerated vastly. Belfast is not all Ulster, nor even a representative of that province. There is a native North, as thoroughly Celtic as any part of our island.'[7] In example, this claim was followed by an account of 1798 in Saintfield and Ballynahinch.

Milligan and Johnston, however, were removed as editors of the *Northern Patriot* in acrimonious circumstances after only three issues, possibly as a result of their support for Maud Gonne's Amnesty campaign for Irish prisoners in England; the focus on current revolutionaries ahead of romantic historical rebels proving too much for some members of the society. However, the women quickly resurfaced. Using Robert Johnston's business premises in Great George's St. in Belfast as a base, they began to produce the *Shan Van Vocht* at the beginning of 1896.

Many characteristics of the new paper were shared with the *Northern Patriot*, as it took its place in the literary and cultural Revival with a brew of romanticism, folklore and history, yet it also provided a forum for competing ideologies in the Nationalist politics of the 1890s. Milligan and Johnston's primary aim was to ensure that the North was not viewed as barren ground for nationalist culture, and could function as well as the rest of the island as a source of 'national' literature, politics and history. The method may be classically Victorian and bourgeois—an energetic journal forwarding educational propaganda, combined with reading circles celebrating the heroes (and heroines) of the Irish past—but the object was to increase Northern national knowledge and pride, not to incite revolution.

In terms of the writing published in the monthly, a familiar Revival dilemma was faced. A balance had to be found between a literature dominated by political considerations—the kind Yeats would later scorn in *The Trembling of the Veil* in which, 'all the past had been turned into a melodrama with Ireland for blameless hero and poet'[8]—and writing seemingly detached from explicit nationality in a way that was anathema to many nationalists. Admittedly, much of the writing in the *Shan Van Vocht* veered into the 'Cuchulainoid' modes later ridiculed by Joyce,[9] but it is important to note the promotional context of *The Shan Van Vocht*,

7 Iris Olkyrn [Alice Milligan], 'The Boys who are true to Erin Oh!' *Northern Patriot* 3 (1895) 33. 8 W.B. Yeats, *Autobiographies* (London: Macmillan, 1992 [1955]) 206. 9 James Joyce, 'The Day of the

bringing Irish history and literature into the public realm in populist form in order to compensate for perceived deficiencies in state education. Addressing the Belfast Natural History and Philosophical Society in 1893, Milligan had stated that, 'in the excellent schools of Belfast and its flourishing college every branch of science and literature is taught, but no provision is made for teaching the youth of Ulster the past history of their famous province.'[10] Her own interest in Ulster had been stimulated by her father's antiquarianism, rather than her schooling at Methodist College.

As can be expected from the number of central Revival figures who contributed to the paper—Standish James O'Grady, Douglas Hyde and Stephen Gwynn, among others—and Milligan and Johnston's involvement in 'national' organizations, most of the literary writing in the *Shan Van Vocht* amplifies a number of themes and ideas articulated in the Revival. The writing published was mainly vernacular 'history', employing folk motifs, allegory, notions of collective memory and popular justice, in order to represent an Ulster Gaelic identity. Familiar critiques also surfaced. In the 'Notes and News' column of the September 1896 issue, for example, the paper's hitherto comparative silence on contemporary party politics was justified by the well known reading of the nation turning from politics to culture post-Parnell,[11] and the Dublin press were berated for ignoring native movements in favour of 'London crime ... the society beauty, the music hall favourite, the Royal Derby winner.'[12] Later articles would similarly deplore the prevalence of English drama, vaudeville and novels consumed in Ireland.

The hero, bringing pride and dignity to the national character, was an important Revival response to the felt vacuity of these seemingly 'imported' forms, and *The Shan Van Vocht* attempted to contribute Northern candidates for this status. Of course, this heroic fascination is partly an admission of present impotence and medi-ocrity; that, in Milligan's words, 'Tara Hill is of Kings forsaken,'[13] and the present generation were to be inspired to change this. There were therefore numerous articles based on 1798. Samuel Neilson, the editor of the *Northern Star*, was depicted helping a Catholic printer to escape the hangman's noose,[14] and other 1798 figures, such as John Tennant or Wolfe Tone, became the subject of stories, poems and plays.[15] Other writing forwarded exemplary women of the period, including Rose Hope, Lady Edward Fitzgerald, Mary McCracken, Rose McGladdery, Anne Devlin (Robert Emmet's servant), and the heroine of the battle of Ballynahinch, Betsy Gray (an excursion was organized to decorate her grave). Of a later generation, Jane Francesca Elgee, better known as Lady Wilde or 'Speranza', was celebrated as a free

Rabblement,' 1901, *The Critical Writings of James Joyce*, ed. Ellsworth Mason and Richard Ellman (London: Faber and Faber, 1959) 68-72.   10 Alice Milligan qtd. in Brighid Mhic Sheáin, *Glimpses of Erin* (Belfast: *Fortnight* Educational Trust, n.d.) 9.   11 The best example of this, still widely held, belief is provided by Yeats at the beginning of his Nobel lecture to the Royal Academy of Sweden on 'The Irish Dramatic Movement,' *Autobiographies* 559.   12 'Notes and News,' *Shan Van Vocht* 1.9 (1896) 178.   13 Alice Milligan, 'Tara Hill is of Kings Forsaken,' *Shan Van Vocht* 3.7 (1898) 131.

thinking role model who challenged the ideologies of her upbringing in order to write and promote Irish culture, and John Mitchel and his mother were also lauded. Mitchel, in fact, has a lot to answer for: the very presence of his *Jail Journal* on a bookshelf can cause seemingly good Anglo-Irish girls to mutate into fanatical Republican women, at least if their quasi-autobiographical writings are to be believed (but that's another paper). The intense focus on 1798 was partly due to the aim of encouraging Northern Protestants to identify with the dynamism and ideals of nationalism, even if some of its methods were anathema. The idea of unionism resenting union was, to Milligan and Johnston, evidence of a greater national unconscious, if only Northern Protestants could dig deep enough to find it. The fictional representations of the various female heroines also had the happy side-effect of countering some of the execrable male Gael-gaze fantasies which appeared frequently in the paper, such as T.C. Murray's 'The Brown Haired Girleen from Dunloe', which surprisingly hasn't yet been covered by Daniel O'Donnell.[16]

Further, in common with other Revivalists, writers in the *Shan Van Vocht* tended to use local folklore as a basis for fiction, glorifying versions of the Irish Gaelic past and leaving contemporary realism in short supply. The most common writing utilized local Ulster folklore and myth as a basis for fictional episodes in order to provide an alternative 'vernacular' history to challenge both the dominant British ideologies in Ulster and the southern view of the North as hostile, industrial and utilitarian. Ulster is portrayed as providing distinctive regional narratives which take their place in the political purpose of the greater national narrative.

This is evident in Ethna Carbery's 'In the North Countrie' series. This collection of sentimental, tragic and mystical short stories set in the recent past depicted a Celtic north of apparitions, Catholic mystics, romantic poets, picaresque peasants and innocents. In addition, Milligan contributed several pieces emphasizing that Ulster had been populated by a highly sophisticated Gaelic pre-conquest civilization. In one piece, Hugh O'Neill was depicted at the Donegal landmark of Aileach to mark the possibility of an Ulster warrior king and redeemer liberating the land,[17] while in the poem 'The Harper of the Only God' she used the Ulster cycle at a comparatively early stage of its recognition in the Revival, in order to emphasize Cuchulain as a resolute defender of Ulster, refusing 'Rome's proud Ard-Righ' and dying with 'sword in hand/ and his face to the foes of the Northern land',[18] which contrasts with Lady Gregory's later presentation of his Northern identity as diluted.

The 'Ulster Revival' also forwarded alternative locations for the peasant west. Various articles upheld the party line of an authentic Ireland situated in

14 'Willie Kane of the *Northern Star*: How he escaped the Scaffold,' *Shan Van Vocht* 1.2 (1896) 26-8.   15 For instance, Alice Milligan, 'The Green Upon the Cape,' *Shan Van Vocht* 3.4 (1898) 57-9.   16 T.C. Murray, 'The Brown Haired Girleen from Dunloe,' *Shan Van Vocht* 1.3 (1896) 58.   17 Iris Olkyrn, 'The Horsemen of Aileach,' *Shan Van Vocht* 1.7 (1896) 135.   18 Iris Olkyrn, 'The Harper of the Only God,' *Shan Van Vocht* 1.12 (1896) 224.

Connaught or the Aran Islands. One of the regular correspondents, Thomas Concannon (later to marry Helena Walsh) was an Aran 'ex-pat', but Milligan frequently situated the authentic west, that source of heroism, mystery, violence and romance, in Donegal, 'the land of the Northern Gael', portrayed in stark contrast to 'Derry of the landowners'.[19] Gaelic antiquity was not only situated here, however. Cave Hill was also revered, not only for 1798, but as the site of the ancient McArt's fort. The North too could be holy and haunted; Greater Belfast provided locations for a mythology more historically recent than that of most other Revival folklore, that of 1798. In the run-up to the centennial, the paper was filled with writing based on 1798 in Ulster. For writers like Margaret Pender, Tone, McCracken and Hope were the giant shadows against whom the present generation was measured, and the equality of 'the tough Northern planter, the fiery Southern Celt' was contrasted to the self-interest and corruption of the Patriot parliament.[20]

The centennial, however, would expose the deep divisions within Irish nationalism, but, in contrast to the supposed stance of the earlier *Northern Patriot*, the *Shan Van Vocht* increasingly gave space to nationalists from different camps to state their case. Milligan herself had broadly Parnellite sympathies—in a typical Revival gesture, she asserted the appearance of lightning in the sky over Bangor on 6th October 1891, the day of his death. However, the 'Other People's Opinions' column, established in November 1896, allowed a variety of writers to debate the strategies available to Irish nationalism, and what exactly could be done in the name of Ireland.

For example, James Connolly developed a distinctive thesis in a series of articles published in 1897. Critiquing the literary movement, Connolly argued that the 'neglect of vital living issues … may only succeed in stereotyping our historical studies into a worship of the past, or crystallising nationalism into a tradition.'[21] An Irish socialist republic would, therefore, only come about through a moral and ideological insurrection preceding a military one. To this end, Connolly argued that Irish republicans should sit in Westminster in order to counter the inherent loyalism, as he saw it, of Irish political opinion: 'it is indeed a pity that the whipped hounds can only whine in their master's hall but it requires more moral courage to do even that than it does to sulk in our own kennels.'[22] Milligan opposed this, fearing an alliance with the English labour party would result (even though this had been favoured in her earlier novel, *A Royal Democrat*, and she had defended Connolly from attacks by other correspondents). Her editorial democracy, in a sense, complies with T.W. Rolleston's assertion that the highest of Revival principles was, 'that accepted conventional beliefs should be challenged and made to justify themselves … The mind of Ireland is absolutely stagnant under this crust of accepted beliefs which are stamped patriotic and set up for unquestioning reverence.'[23] To this

19 Alice Milligan, 'Rambling Reminiscences,' *Shan Van Vocht* 3.7 (1898) 126. 20 M.T. Pender, 'Some Men and Episodes of '98,' *Shan Van Vocht* 2.7 (1897) 123-6. 21 James Connolly, 'Nationalism and Socialism,' *Shan Van Vocht* 2.13 (1897) 7-8. 22 Connolly, 'Other People's Opinions,' *Shan Van Vocht* 2.10 (1897) 188. 23 T.W. Rolleston, 'Other People's Opinions,' *Shan Van Vocht* 1.11 (1896) 210.

end, Rolleston contributed an article which sprang to the defence of Oliver Cromwell!

The Shan Van Vocht also emphasized just how much women were involved in Irish culture and politics. The paper gave an opportunity to a number of women to publish. Some names are familiar, some appear within its pages alone and the paper also mentions numerous female speakers, singers and 'national workers' whose names are otherwise lost to history. Ironically, the editorial democracy exercised by Milligan and Johnston would prove the paper's downfall. The final issue appeared on 3rd April 1899, its demise probably due to a refusal to align with any specific political faction. The subscription list went to Griffith and Rooney's *United Irishman*.

In conclusion, and taking *The Shan Van Vocht* as representative of the dynamics of Northern cultural nationalism in the 1890s, I'd like to posit briefly some possible implications for dominant critical perceptions of the Irish Literary Revival. *The Shan Van Vocht* illustrates the relative heterogeneity of Irish nationalist culture during the period, indicating the ways in which the ideals formulated by the 'Dublin school' at the centre of the Revival influenced Irish writers from diffuse geographical and social backgrounds. Milligan and Johnston, among others, initiated a distinctive strand of Revivalism in response to their Northern context.

Too many critical accounts which look back to Irish writing in the period of the Irish Literary Revival construct a literary history which wrestles with the Revival as a duplicitous Ascendancy project; a literature inscribing an imaginative relationship with the people nation in order to compensate for perceived Anglo-Irish social and religious isolation. The Revival is commonly depicted as 'a desperate strategy adopted by the more liberal unionists who knew that their backs were to the wall,'[24] an attempt to avert the rise of aspirant Catholic Ireland. Critical attention usually focuses on Yeats as an exemplar of this 'literary union-ism'. Although one of the contexts for the Revival was certainly an awareness, on the part of some Anglo-Irish intellectuals, of the perceived erosion of social supremacy for which cultural supremacy could be a compensation, too many critics, in fighting with Yeats' 'extraordinary ability to impose his view of how things should look to people later on,'[25] ignore the relative diversity of the desired 'unity of culture'. Much of the writing of the period cannot be placed in a tradition of marginality or adherence to the perceived social mission or aesthetic ideals of, to make a crude distinction, the 'Anglo-Irish' or 'Irish-Irish' Revivals.

The Shan Van Vocht is testimony to the ways in which a number of writers grappled with the dominant and emergent literary, cultural and political ideolo-

24 Declan Kiberd, 'The Perils of Nostalgia: A Critique of the Revival,' *Literature and the Changing Ireland*, ed. Peter Connolly (Gerrards Cross: Colin Smythe, 1982) 17. His later survey, *Inventing Ireland: The Literature of the Modern Nation* (London: Vintage, 1996 [1995]) is more appreciative of the complexity of the movement. 25 R.F. Foster, 'Thinking from Hand to Mouth: Anglo-Irish Literature, Gaelic Nationalism and Irish Politics in the 1890s,' *Paddy and Mr Punch* (1993. London: Penguin, 1995) 280.

gies which enmeshed Irish life during the era. Revival ideals are utilized and advocated, but often partially. This awareness complicates homogeneities, expands critical categories and raises 'troubling questions' which ensure that notions of wholeness or completeness cannot be advanced. To use one example of another neglected writer from the time, Jane Barlow, the Dublin novelist, is (nominally) a Protestant unionist, but cannot be contained within a critical discourse which reads Anglo-Irish interest in cultural nationalism in terms of a dishonest attempt to maintain a discredited authority. The editorial democracy practised by Alice Milligan and Anna Johnston, and the diversity of writing contained in *The Shan Van Vocht*, emphasizes the myriad of contexts for Revival aesthetics.

A Celtic Resurrection: Perspectives on Yeats' Generation in the Fin de Siècle

KATY PLOWRIGHT, EXETER COLLEGE, OXFORD

In Yeats' play *The Resurrection*, he writes that the fanatical mob in the street 'sing of the death of the god and pray for his resurrection'.[1] The hysterical and fervent crowd causes fear amongst the on-stage characters, confined to a single room and anxious about what physical form the dead Christ will take. Yeats was not the first poet to find the idea of resurrection appealing; the personification of Celtic identity had been a politically charged practice within precisely the kind of nervous and defensive culture which Yeats described in his maturity as resurrective.

In 1886, Yeats' poem 'The Two Titans: A Political Poem' mediated resurrection in a resonant rethinking of an identifiable Victorian image; it reveals Yeats beginning to discover the possibilities of using a conventional set of poetic techniques to disquiet the anticipated political meaning.[2] The poem was published in March 1886 in the pages of the then recently established *Dublin University Review*, just two months after the founding of the Ulster Unionist Party, a single month after Gladstone's return to power, the same month as Chamberlain and Trevelyan's resignations from the Liberal Party. It anticipated the first Home Rule Bill by only a month; Yeats' subtitling of his poem as 'political' was a marker that it should be read as a commentary upon modern events. This superficial flag-posting, however, masked some deeper levels of political resonance within a specific line of thought in Victorian Irish writing, especially that which sought to employ the social discourse

---

1 W.B. Yeats, *The Resurrection* (1931), in *The Variorum Plays of W.B. Yeats*, ed. Russell K. Alspach (London: Macmillan, 1965) 915.   2 Yeats, 'The Two Titans. A Political Poem', in *Dublin University Review* 2 (March 1886) 265-6.

of the revolutionary mid-century. 'The Two Titans' is significant as Yeats' most polemic early poem, despite is subsequent neglect within the canon; it reveals Yeats expertly manipulating this particular nineteenth-century concept of Irish political identity.

The poem describes a violent scene between a sibyl and a youth, against a distinctively Romantic landscape: 'The vision of a rock where lightnings whirl'd.' The Titans are seen as

> Two figures crouching on the black rock, bound
> To one another with a coiling chain;
> A grey-haired youth, whose cheeks had never found,
> Or long ere this had lost their ruddy stain;
> A sibyl, with fierce face as of a hound
> That dreams.

'The Two Titans' effectively stages for a fin de siècle audience the metaphorical conventions of resurrection. To read the poem in the light of the resurrective image in both English and Irish culture is to reassess Yeats' sophistication at the age of just twenty-one.

Resurrective thought had a strong tradition as an image of the reinvigoration of Ireland, then, decades before the fin de siècle. It imported a spiritual dimension to the debates and the idea of 'the Irish problem' taking a supernatural yet human form was influential. Thomas Carlyle was among the first to use it in this context, in his *Latter-Day Pamphlets* (1850):

> An Irish Giant, named of despair, is advancing upon London itself, laying waste all English cities, towns and villages I notice him in Piccadilly, blue-visaged, thatched in rags, a blue child on each arm; hunger-driven, wide-mouthed, seeking whom he may devour: he, missioned by the just Heavens, too truly and too sadly their 'divine missionary' come at last.[3]

Carlyle's perception of the Irish, shaped by his experiences in Ireland in the summer of 1849, took a personified form: his metaphor clearly implied that the social responsibility of English misrule would infiltrate to the very centre of empire. This 'divine missionary' figured Irish survival through suffering and despair, at the expense of humanity; Carlyle described a cultural malady which deadened the humanity of the Irish. This was a grotesque messianism, the image of the Promethean race implying a *lack* of internality very different to its usual Romantic incarnation.

In the aftermath of the European uprisings of 1848, the rehabilitation of the resurrected giant began in earnest among those seeking to embolden the political

3 Thomas Carlyle, *Latter-Day Pamphlets* (1850), *The Collected Works of Thomas Carlyle in Thirty Volumes* (London: Chapman and Hall, 1898) 1: 93-4.

will of radicalism. The image of the relentlessly encroaching and rebellious giant was already associated with the resurrective disruptions of normal life patterns, being imagined to exist in a stormy cycle of rebellion, punishment, defeat and resurrection. It was used primarily by youthful, idealist radicals. Yeats was in his twenty-first year when he engaged with the tradition; similarly, the Chartist poet Gerald Massey was only twenty-three when he wrote his poem 'The Men of Forty-Eight' (first published in 1851):

> The Kings have got their Crown again,
> And blood-red revel cup;
> They've bound the Titan down again,
> And heaved his grave-mound up!
> But still he lives, though buried 'neath
> The mountain,—lies in wait,
> Heart-stifled heaves and tries to breathe
> The breath of 'Forty-eight'.[4]

Massey places the mythical rebel in the tomb only to anticipate his inevitable rise. The Christian transitions from life to death, from earthly toil to heavenly rest, are disrupted by those who seek to bury the revolution; like Yeats' Dionysian revellers in *The Resurrection*, the kings exult in their bloody legacy, but, Massey exclaims, the Titan spirit is patiently biding its time beneath the surface. This was a rousing call, expressed in particular terms: as Carlyle had argued the previous year, the time of overthrow was not now, but was fast approaching.

By the 1850s, then, the encroaching figure of the Giant or Titan was a familiar image through which to align the complementary revolutionary spirits of social reform and Irish nationalism.[5] Carlyle's 'divine messenger' represented in graphic form the responsibility of English government to address the human disaster of the Famine; when Ernest Renan joined the debate in 1854, writing of a militant 'Celtic Messianism', he described precisely this inherently political potential for revolt, which he described as a 'belief in a future avenger.' Renan put his case in terms which set the religious tone as an aggressive recuperation of national strength, from a background of historical wrongs:

> It is thus that little peoples dowered with imagination revenge themselves on their conquerors. Feeling themselves to be strong inwardly and weak outwardly, they protest, they exult; and such a strife unloosing their might, renders them capable of miracles. Nearly all great appeals to the supernatural are due to peoples hoping against hope.[6]

4 Gerald Massey, *Voices of Freedom and Lyrics of Love* (London: J. Watson, 1851) 59-60.   5 See Ian Haywood, ed., *The Literature of Struggle: An Anthology of Chartist Fiction* (Aldershot: Scolar Press, 1995) 10.   6 Ernest Renan, *The Poetry of the Celtic Races, and Other Studies* (repr. NY & London, 1970; 1896

The nation's inner strengths transform into an exultant frenzy of self-assertion, a proto-Nietzschean emphasis on *sturm und drang* and Carlylean recognition of the power that came with might.

Renan's reputation in England was unarguably made through Matthew Arnold's *On the Study of Celtic Literature* (1867).[7] Yet it was actually through the resurrection image that Arnold mediated Renan's ethnic categories. Arnold's thinking about Celticism as 'the indomitable reaction against the despotism of fact' was a quite deliberate response to the monstrous messianism of the social debate.[8] His famous claim that the Celt was in 'passionate, turbulent, indomitable reaction against the despotism of fact' is sometimes taken out of context as a statement of some essentialized Celtic character in its own right. In fact, Arnold claimed that it was precisely through the 'Titanism of the Celt' that this rebellion took effect, making a contextual allusion to the alignment of social and national unrest which had been recognized as part of romantic nationalism in the 1840s.

Arnold had initially employed the Titan image as a heroic figure for English industrial enslavement in the interests of empire—essentially anti-poetic in spirit, dehumanised and inexorable, moving towards the global scale:

Yes, we arraign her! but she,
The weary Titan, with deaf
Ears, and labour-dimm'd eyes,
. Regarding neither to right
Nor left, goes passively by,
Staggering on to her goal[9]

Arnold replayed the messianic metaphor, aligning national identity and the social organization that constituted it. Again, the modern age was inimical to the poetic life, removing the internality necessary to culture.[10] The dynamic yet deadened Titan, then, could represent both the English nation with its spirit of independent thought effectively humbled by the grind of labour, and also the Promethean figure of the revolutionary, whose uprising has been quashed but whom the poet believes will revive in the future.

In the charged atmosphere of the 1880s, with coercion and land war on the agenda and Arnold's Celticism well established, the spectre of the Celt rose once more with Parnell as its pivotal imaginative influence. The strong rhetoric of the

edition), 10. Emphasis in original. 7 For various perspectives, see Frederic Faverty, *Matthew Arnold, Ethnologist* (Evanston, Ill.: Northwestern UP, 1951); Rachel Bromwich, *Matthew Arnold and Celtic Literature: A Retrospect, 1865-1965* (Oxford: Clarendon, 1965); Seamus Deane, *Celtic Revivals: Essays in Modern Irish Literature 1880-1980* (London: Faber, 1985); Terence Brown, *The Life of W.B. Yeats: A Critical Biography* (Oxford: Blackwell, 1999). 8 Matthew Arnold, *On the Study of Celtic Literature* (London: Smith, Elder and Co., 1867). 9 Arnold, *Matthew Arnold: A Critical Edition of the Major Works* ed. Miriam Allott and Robert H. Super (Oxford: OUP, 1986) 232-3.

land war led to a newly invigorated 'divine' imagery for the new decade. Standish O'Grady invoked the image of the silent but deadly Irish revolution in terms which also clearly borrowed from Carlyle's silently dynamic Irish giant: 'The fierce oratory of the incipient revolution is no longer heard, or heard only in muttered curses and the rifle-shot at midnight; but the revolution goes its own way, if silently, then with swifter steps, and breathing fuller strength.'[11] O'Grady imagined revolution advancing upon English prosperity in a potent alignment between the conceptual and personified, haunting the ruling country with the spectre of its failure in its duty to maintain the welfare of its Irish population.

This personification was a populist trope: Grant Allen, the promoter of Spenserian naturalism and himself a vigorously self-proclaimed Celt, also wrote in Carlylean terms of infiltration: 'Mac's and O's are as common in London as in Perthshire and Mayo'.[12] Allen rejoiced in the militant radicalism of men such as Morris and Shaw (Welsh and Irish respectively): 'We Celts now lurk in every corner of Britain; we have permeated it with our aspirations; we have roused the Celtic remnant in the south-east itself to a sense of their wrongs; and we are marching today, all abreast, to the overthrow of feudalism'. If we listen to the language Allen used there—leading, lurking, permeating, rousing, marching, overthrowing—it is clear that his polemic aimed to refresh the Titan's role within modern culture. This was recognizably the established post-1848 approach, but with the key adjustment that if the Celts were causing the disintegration of the social fabric by their encroaching presence, this necessarily entailed definite, immediate and far-reaching reform.

After the failure of the first Home Rule Bill, cultural commentators and writers of all shades of opinion were forced to adjust their messianic treatment of the increasingly attenuated Liberal-IPP relationship. The approach became defensively entrenched, against the background of accusations over Parnellite criminality and murderous intent; the image of resurrection came to the fore again to turn the negativity of unionist and liberal disillusionment into positive terms. When the critic and Bedford Park resident Arthur Galton stated in 1887 that 'We are on the eve, not of a Celtic Renaissance, but of a Celtic Resurrection', his words struck into this established tradition of the transfigured, resurrecting Celtic Titan. A year to the month after the introduction of Gladstone's first Home Rule Bill in Parliament (April 1887), Galton's championing of Celtic militancy was timely. Further, that he published his comment in the *Hobby Horse*—the influential journal of the aesthetic community at Bedford Park—was significant. For the approaching fin de siècle brought with it a millenarian way of thinking which gradually shifted from its roots in Carlyle and Arnold, and raised some distinctly fin de siècle concerns. Galton continued,

10 This is a standard view of Arnold's poetic life itself. See Ian Hamilton, *A Gift Imprisoned: The Poetic Life of Matthew Arnold* (London: Bloomsbury, 1998).   11 Standish O'Grady, *The Crisis in Ireland* (Dublin: E Ponsonby; London: Simpkin, Marshall & Co., 1882) 4.   12 Grant Allen, 'Our Ancestors— IV. The Final Mixture', *Knowledge* 2:31 (2 June 1882) 4.

This is the hour of the Celts in politics; they have us by the throat; and may their grip never be loosened until they have forced us into the path of justice and lucidity. The Celts' immortal youth seems destined to vanquish even the despotism of facts ... He will be the most winning artist, especially will he be the most winning poet, who can learn how to fascinate our over-taught, thought-wearied generation with the young-eyed freshness, the entrancing rapture of Celtic Naturalism.[13]

The period from the mid-1880s to the turn of the century witnessed a boom in messianic discourses (produced in the main at Edinburgh, which also published the primary texts of pan-Celticism).[14] Two major strands of this period had cultural currency: the first, like Carlyle's Irish giant, aimed at embodiment, while the second took the form of metaphors of disintegration and disembodiment. Observers of contemporary Anglo-Irish relations saw the union reaching crisis-point, then, and this filtered into the persona of the Titan *and* into an abstracted decadent disintegration.

The engagement with Celticism revived at a time when it again seemed appropriate as a charged cultural response to the political moment. Erstwhile supporters of Home Rule, such as the former *Daily News* editor Frank Hill, wrote that Gladstone was the 'idol of the domestic oppressors who affect to be the nation which their terrorism silences', and critics of Irish nationalism, such as Goldwin Smith and A.V. Dicey, entitled their works *Dismemberment No Remedy* and *A Leap in the Dark*, to portray the modern state's fractured and nebulous condition.[15]

Embodiment and dissolution were not sealed discourses, independent of one another; in 1887 for instance, Dicey warned of the Liberal 'alliance with revolutionists or conspirators'.[16] The element of Carlylean personification remained a feature in images of Gladstone as the Irish champion, despite the increasing distance between the Liberal leader and Parnell as notoriety dogged the IPP into the late 1880s.[17]

However, the metaphor of dissolution through which the resurrection debate was commonly expressed, also received a boost in the late 1880s and early 1890s through the support of figures at the forefront of radical and unionist propaganda. Grant

---

13 Arthur Galton, 'Ancient Legends of Ireland. By Lady Wilde,' *Centenary Guild Hobby Horse* 2:6 (April 1887), 67-74; 68.   14 T. and T. Clark were the primary publishers of messianic analyses in the *fin de siècle*, publishing Franz Delitzsch, *Messianic Prophecies in Historical Succession*, tr. Samuel Ives Curtiss (Edinburgh, 1891). A major text of Celticism was Elizabeth Sharp's *Lyra Celtica: An Anthology of Representative Celtic Poetry* (Edinburgh: Patrick Geddes & Colleagues, 1896).   15 Frank H Hill, 'Home Rule and the Opposition Question', *Universal Review* 1:2 (15 June 1888) 169; Goldwin Smith, *Dismemberment No Remedy* (London etc., 1886); A.V. Dicey, *A Leap in the Dark, or, England's New Constitution* (London: John Murray, 1893).   16 A.V. Dicey, *Why England Maintains the Union: A Popular Rendering of 'England's Case against Home Rule'* (London: John Murray, 1887) 190.   17 See Margaret O'Callaghan, *British High Politics and a Nationalist Ireland* (Cork: Cork UP, 1994) on criminality and the changing nature of the Liberal-IPP relationship. Frank Huggett's *Victorian England as seen by Punch* (London: Sidgwick and Jackson, 1978), reproduces images of Gladstone in an earlier, heroically muscular incarnation, fighting the

Allen continued to promote his ideal Celtic England in increasingly defiant tones. In 1891 he celebrated the 'fresh forces' which Celts brought to the political life of England.[18] Again, in 1894, in the month of Gladstone's resignation over the second Home Rule Bill, 'We have never been conquered, and ... to our unconquered state we owe in the main our Radicalism, our Socialism, our ingrained love of political freedom.'[19]

Meanwhile, Dicey also intensified his campaign with *A Leap in the Dark* (1893), which concentrated from first to last on images of stability and collective identity: he warned 'the people of England against a leap in the dark'. He relied upon the idea that the Home Rule agenda was unstable, fragmentary in its aims, and unknown, an absence rather than a describable entity.[20] For Dicey, the reformist impulse was an *absence*—an unregulated chaos which lay beyond the safe workings of constitutionalism—and as a kind of identity vacuum, pre-empting the 'proper dark' of Yeats' late vision.[21] The Irish threat was *more* threatening when described in vague terms which directly reflected its nebulous nature. Against this background, we might expect that Irish writers who employed implicitly resurrective models of Celticism in the *fin de siècle* also did so in time with the stresses and fractures of the 'Irish problem'. By 1893-4, then, both radical and unionist thinking were regularly using the emotive images of encroachment and combination, in the interests of change or consolidation.

To return to Yeats' 'The Two Titans', it is clear that the poem registers this strongly political Victorian debate. The poem asks to be read within the context of the debate about the nation's future, through Carlyle, Arnold, and the other resurrectionists. Yeats works through an intricate set of verbal resonances, which are more suggestive than explicit. He does not simply imitate, but echoes the debates in visualized form.

The poem, as mentioned earlier, presents two embodiments of the Celtic Titan: the first Titan is the lyrical youth of Ireland, voluntarily yet compulsively attracted to the dominant second Titan, who represents 'Failure'. Like Carlyle's Irish giant, the youth does not show the physicality of his age: he is 'grey-haired'. Yeats removes the natural signs of youth, and replaces them with what Carlyle had called the giant's 'blue-thatched visage'. The Genii which surround the youth are akin to his physical identity, increasing the effect of the supernatural rather than humanity:

> And when once more the lightning Genii passed,
> Strewing upon the rocks their steel-blue hair ...

Galton had written of the 'young-eyed freshness of Celticism'; Yeats writes that the youth's 'cheeks had never found, / Or long ere this had lost their ruddy stain'.

'Irish devil-fish' of land agitation.   18 Grant Allen, 'The Celt in English Art', *Fortnightly Review* 55 (February 1891) 267.   19 Grant Allen, 'The New Hedonism', *Fortnightly Review* 55 (March 1894) 152-3. 20 Dicey, *A Leap in the Dark*, Preface.   21 W.B. Yeats, 'The Statues', *Collected Poems of W.B. Yeats* ed. Richard Finneran (London: Macmillan, 1989) 337.

Yeats' is a decadent Celt, exhausted and enervated, even while inhabiting the body of a youth. Like Arnold's Titan England, the subservient figure is loaded down but constantly moving:

> I saw him stagger with the clanking chain,
> Trailing and shining 'neath the flickering glare.

Yeats is asserting that energetic, vigorous action is impossible; the scene is precisely the enforced, numbed round of labour which Arnold had described. The female Titan does not give any further hope: the imperious, sadistic woman symbolizes a bartered and decrepit power. Yeats describes the dehumanized relationship, in terms which replay Carlyle's 'wide-mouthed' Irish Giant, alongside Renan's 'Celtic avenger' and Arnold's deadened English Titan: she moves, but it is the dynamism of the decaying grotesque, rather than the fresh forces of Celtic life which Allen heralded:

> She moveth, feeling in her brain
> The lightnings pulse—behold her, aye behold—
> Ignoble joy, and more ignoble pain
> Cramm'd all her youth; and hates have bought and sold
> Her spirit. As she moves, the foam-globes burst
> Over her spotted flesh and flying hair
> And her gigantic limbs.

The poem effectively dismembers the Titanic body. Just as Goldwin Smith claimed that the state was being 'dismembered', Yeats renders the physicality of the Titan as mere particles: eyes, hair, face, feet, mouth, lips. The youth is dragged in front of the sybil, to act out his subservience:

> Bleeding now, his grasp unlocks,
> And he is dragged again before her feet.
> Why not? He is her own; and crouching nigh
> Bending her face o'er his, she watches meet
> And part his foaming mouth with eager eye.

This is a much more dynamic figure than that of Arnold's 'Heine's Grave', with its belaboured industrial giant. Yeats' female Titan seizes the prostrated supplicant; the earlier authors had imagined the Titan as acted upon, thus removing the agency of the resurrected Titan. The giant was commonly figured, like his relation the Frankenstein monster, as simultaneously monstrous and galvanized, human-seeming and yet stripped of internal life.[22]

---

22 Chris Baldick, *In Frankenstein's Shadow: Myth, Monstrosity and Nineteenth-Century Writing* (Oxford: Clarendon, 1987) 92-120.

The final, crucial step which Yeats takes in the poem reveals, once more, the deep connection between the Titan as a combined embodiment of social and national discontent, and the distortion of regular experiential time. The 'Eternal Darkness', Yeats writes, folds around the failing Titan,

> For ever round thy waking and thy sleep
> The darkness of the whirlwind shattered deep.

Again we hear the debate's keynotes: Dicey's chaotic darkness, and Arnold's Celtic glory in failure. The syntactically unsettling final words of the poem—'whirlwind shattered deep'—again envision the fracturing of the natural world which had always been the landscape of the resurrective Titan. The image had been consistently employed as a response to particular political and human events; that Yeats chose never again to publish this poem actually argues the immediacy of its meaning. It was embedded in the nervous, defensive Victorian culture which shaped it, and as such responded not so much to the poetic concern with 'unity of being', but to immediate anxieties about the fracturing modern state.

The next generation of 'Irish Mode' nationalists, despite their willed difference from the 'Celtic Note', would follow Arthur Griffith's explicit appropriation of the dialectic between the resurrected Celt and the dehumanised Titan, the glory of failure together with the consitutional freight of government.[23] Yeats explored the political aspect of Celticism remodelled the relationship as a kind of polemical decadence. That the figure of the Celt had been so variously and dramatically invoked in times of crisis throughout the Victorian era showed just how deeply the crisis was figured within and through Anglo-Irish culture.

The Staging of Protestant Ireland in Somerville and Ross' The Real Charlotte

JULIE ANNE STEVENS, TRINITY COLLEGE, DUBLIN

The promotional advertising picture for Mike Leigh's film, *Topsy-Turvy*, presents a double-headed Japanese man, the Mikado figure, with Gilbert and Sullivan's faces grafted on to his rotund figure. He looks like a child's toy, which if sent spinning across the room would become one animated visage. The picture recalls the two complementary brothers in Robert Louis Stevenson's *The Master of*

23 Arthur Griffith, *The Resurrection of Hungary: A Parallel for Ireland* (Dublin: James Duffy/M.H.Gill/Sealy, Bryers and Walker, 1904), title-page. On this distinction between Celtic and Irish, see Thomas MacDonagh in *Literature in Ireland: Studies Irish and Anglo-Irish* (Dublin: Talbot, 1916).

Ballantrae, the Catholic supporter, James, and the Protestant enthusiast, Henry, a novel Somerville and Ross read while writing their third work, *The Real Charlotte*. A central scene in Stevenson's novel repeats the topsy-turvy pattern Mike Leigh uses in his film on Gilbert and Sullivan.

En route to America from Scotland, on board the *Nonesuch* and during a tremendous storm, the Master of Ballantrae (wild and courageous James) faces the narrator, MacKellar. The pair sit on 'a high raised poop' with the Master 'betwixt [MacKellar] and the side' and in this position in the middle of the storm, with the boat rearing up and down across the monstrous waves, MacKellar comments on the Master's alternating position: 'Now his head would be in the zenith and his shadow fall quite beyond the *Nonesuch* on the further side; and now he would swing down till he was underneath my feet, and the line of the sea leaped high above him like the ceiling of a room.'[1] This topsy-turvy position, where extremes of movement allow for a rapidly successive occupation of polarized locations, may demonstrate, on the one hand, modern ambiguity. On the other hand, it suggests the situation of the split identity, of a person negotiating the polarized positions of a hybrid culture, what Homi Bhabha calls an 'interstitial perspective' and which allows a person to see from the outside as well as the inside: 'identities that "split"—are estranged unto themselves.' Such a perspective originates from the 'interstitial passage between fixed identifications,' says Bhabha, and 'opens up the possibility of a cultural hybridity.'[2]

Topsy-turvydom also allows one to see oneself; it displays the self. Stevenson's boat on a stormy sea creates a swift reversal of perspective that allows MacKellar to see through the Master's eyes. The quick-change demonstrates the arbitrary nature of one particular viewpoint. In the manner of a Gilbert and Sullivan burlesque, then, turning things upside-down draws attention to the process of performance itself. We become aware of the act of imitation, which is, in fact, what Mike Leigh's film is about—stage making. Somerville and Ross' *The Real Charlotte* also draws attention to stage making in Protestant Ireland.

Somerville and Ross' best-known novel, *The Real Charlotte*, exploits burlesque in its depiction of the West of Ireland in the early 1890s. The text displays its artfulness by portraying Irish life and showing that it is doing so. The novel 'stages' Protestant Ireland. The Church of Ireland becomes a kind of playhouse displaying the evangelical mission as a highly self-conscious secularized pursuit. This comic stage set, however, comes charged in the work with a tragic Manichaean vision, a Protestant world view which determines the apocalyptic tremors and Faustian warnings of the text's conclusion.

The landlord's son, Christopher Dysart, becomes interested in the poorest and prettiest occupant of his dominion, Francie Fitzpatrick, and an Anglo-Irish stereotype seems to be confirmed: the wastrel son of excess attempts to debauch

1 Robert Louis Stevenson, *The Master of Ballantrae* (1889; Great Britain: Penguin, 1984) 148.   2 Homi Bhabha, *The Location of Culture* (London: Routledge, 1994) 2-3.

the land's fairest female. When we learn, however, that Christopher's main interest in Francie is her soul, we realize that a hinterland of secularized evangelical thought lies behind his actions. When it becomes apparent that both Christopher and Francie belong to the Church of Ireland, we suspect that there is much more at stake here than a reworking of a colonial stereotype. Christopher's determination to save Francie's soul, to enlighten her understanding and develop her taste, indicates that a Protestant world view adumbrated by large doses of Pre-Raphaelite poetry, rather than an enlarged colonial sexual appetite, fuels his pursuit.

The Real Charlotte is embedded in two traditions that determine its black humour: the workings of the Anglican faith in a secular world and popular farce in the Dublin and London theatres. Although significant issues of contemporary discourse interact with these two traditions, colonialism and New Woman thought in particular; the novel's mainspring originates in the writers' backgrounds.

Somerville and Ross participated fully in a Victorian Anglican upbringing. For much of their early lives, they attended Church twice on a Sunday. Young Violet Martin won prizes at Sunday school in Dublin, and Edith Somerville played the organ in St. Barrahane's Church, Castletownshend, County Cork for seventy years. The Somervilles served Church and Army. In St. Barrahane's, the admirals, brigadiers, and soldiers of the realm, who frequently died in service to Great Britain, have their names inlaid in brass on the lectern, inscribed in stone on the tombs, and covering the plaques mounted on marble walls. St. Barrahane's is as much a Memorial as it is a Church; the names have greater presence than the religious artefacts decorating the altar and nave. In Castletownshend, the Somervilles and Townshends do not merely head the congregation, they are the Church. In St. Barrahane's, the clergy come and go, but the gentry remain and the Protestant parson serves these names in the same way that the poet, Donovan Rossa, served Edith Somerville's grandfather on his return from the Crimean war in January, 1856:

> M artial child of Erin and brilliant son of Mars
> A ll hail and welcome thee to home, from the Crimean Wars.
> J oined hands and hearts are creed and class this meed of praise to shower
> O n one of Ireland's gallant sons, who braved the Russian Power
> R egarding nought but honour bright, no coward though appalled him
> T o make him shrink before the foe when Martial duty called him.
> H ow oft you read the fatal lists, with joy our hearts oft bounded
> O n finding that *one name* was not among the killed or wounded.
> M uch pleasure beamed from every face (and happy felt the Muse)
> A s a respected Father's life depended on the news,
> S o fondly did he love that child, a true and only son,
> S o fatal would the tidings be to *read that he was gone.*
> O h could you picture his despair, thank God 'tis different far,
> M uch joy and peace await him now, as ended is the War.

E xpected shortly is that son, a worthy one of Erin
R eturning to his peaceful home from battling with the Alien.
V alour's representative Skibbereen will proudly greet him
I nclined with feelings of respect she joyfully will meet him,
L oudly to home we'll welcome him, old friends, old scenes—say rather
L ike one arisen from the dead around him we will gather
E njoyed to see that he again has met his honoured Father.³

Ascendancy power within the Anglican Church discovered its greatest chal-
lenge in the Roman Catholic priest, and Somerville and Ross' suspicion of Irish
Catholic priests must be considered in this context. While completing *The Real
Charlotte* in 1893, Martin Ross argued that 'the priests can do as they like with the
Roman Catholic lower classes … they direct them how to vote at every election.'⁴
In *The Real Charlotte*, the Catholic priest lurks in the background as an insidious
figure, ready to snap up lost souls. The Anglican clergy, however, fulfils a social
rather than a religious role.

Terence Brown claims that Irish writing of the modern period tends to present
Irish Anglicanism as 'a series of clichés and programmatic responses.' The Church
of Ireland typically represents one of three things, either the privileged Ascendancy,
or the good cleric, or an 'irresistible decay.'⁵ Yet, *The Real Charlotte* denies any notion
of decay, or special privilege, or even good clergymen in its portrayal of Irish
Anglicanism. The novel is full to bursting with Protestants of all degrees and does
not reflect Irish Protestant reality in the 1890s.⁶ One might conclude that Somerville
and Ross have removed the Catholic element from the Irish equation to demonstrate the dynamics of class relations in Ireland, to show that social position and not
religion gives rise to discontent. By concentrating on a Protestant population, they
attack the basic premise supporting nationalist ideology, that a monolithic group
suppresses the Irish tenantry. The novel demonstrates the disunity of Protestantism
in Ireland.

There is a further reason, however, for Somerville and Ross' concentration on
Irish Protestant characters. The novel traces the process whereby Christopher
Dysart comes to believe he can save Francie's soul.⁷ His particular brand of Pro-
testantism is opposed to the distanced kindliness of his sister, Pamela, a High-
Church advocate. Francie, then, is accustomed to the mixed company of the Dublin
Sunday schools and the visiting evangelicals to her low-church congregations. The

3 Donovan Rossa, qtd. in Moira Somerville, 'Notes on the Background and Early Life of Edith Oenone
Somerville,' *The Edith Oenone Somerville Archive in Drishane*, ed. Otto Rauchbauer (Dublin: Irish
Manuscripts Commission, 1995) B.2.42pp.   4 Martin Ross, letter to anonymous 'sir' in Bristol, 7 Nov.
1893, *Drishane Archive*, L.C.11.a.   5 Terence Brown, 'The Church of Ireland and the Climax of the Ages,'
Ireland's Literature (Mullingar: Lilliput, 1988) 51-5.   6 See Jack White, *Minority Report: The Protestant
Community in the Irish Republic* (Dublin: Gill and Macmillan, 1975) 58.   7 Somerville and Ross, *The Real
Charlotte* (1894; London: Arrow, 1990) 198.

novel shows the characters' religious backgrounds influencing their worldly roles. It addresses what Terence Brown describes as the 'surrogate religiosity' of Victorian literature, 'a transference of evangelical preoccupation, rendered theologically unsustainable by scepticism, to social and aesthetic dimensions.'[8] In *The Real Charlotte*, religious postures become secular poses. We are reminded of the transformation of religious metaphor in earlier Victorian painting, what John Turpin points out in Daniel Maclise's historical studies such as 'Strongbow' or 'Wellington.' According to Turpin, 'religious transposition' in Maclise's work 'is a feature of an age when orthodox religious subject matter almost totally disappeared.'[9] Where did this religious material go? In *The Real Charlotte*, the Irish Anglican ethos exists in a secularized form in the British colonial world.

Christopher Dysart's fatal flaw is his inability to apprehend immediate reality. As an amateur photographer, art translates his reality. When he first looks at Francie, he sees her as a charming picture from the ladies' magazines. When he looks at Ireland, he sees a beloved landscape in the distance. Then, about half way through the novel, a storm like that in Stevenson's novel occurs. In *The Real Charlotte*, however, the boat overturns, and St Christopher Dysart emerges from the waters carrying a half-drowned soul, Francie Fitzpatrick. He begins to believe in the biggest picture of all, the powerful illusion that he can reform Francie's tastes and educate her mind just as the Protestant evangelicals in Dublin have attempted to reform her soul. Vanity driven and unstoppable, Christopher becomes a secular 'Church Militant,' a moulder of souls.

Lady Dysart of Bruff, an English Anglican who has married in to the Anglo-Irish community, has raised a son and daughter who manifest the two strands of Irish Anglicanism. Pamela Dysart's pleasure in the rites of Rome, her 'High Church tendencies', indicates her Anglo-Catholic bent while Christopher's fastidiousness and missionary impulses reveal an evangelical frame of mind.[10] His leanings may well have been fashioned by a childhood steeped in the Sunday-school reading of Mrs. Mary Sherwood and her stories of evangelical family life. Although Christopher's family falls short of the Sunday-school ideal, their *modus vivendi* appears to have been inspired by Sherwood's goody-goody tales.[11]

However, the true source of entertainment in the Protestant world of *The Real Charlotte* is found not in Christopher's inspirational texts but in the theatre. At Bruff House, amateur theatricals liven the summer months. Christopher and Francie chat about the plays they have seen in Dublin's Gaiety Theatre. Mr Lambert, Francie's married admirer, brings her and his wife to *H.M.S. Pinafore* in the Gaiety. The mention of Gilbert and Sullivan's comic opera suggests the authors' satirical intent, which might be best appreciated by considering briefly the novelists' involvement with the theatre.

8 Brown 58-9.   9 John Turpin, 'Daniel Maclise and his Place in Victorian Art,' *Anglo-Irish Studies* 1 (1975): 51-2.   10 Somerville and Ross 85.   11 See M.N. Cutt, *Mrs. Sherwood and her Books for Children* (London: OUP, 1974).

Both Somerville and Ross adored the stage, and they and their families acted in and devised pantomimes. Martin Ross' older brother, Robert Martin, wrote for the Dublin theatres. His big success was *Bluebeard*, the Christmas pantomime at the Dublin Gaiety in 1886,[12] and he was also known for a work called 'Little Doctor Faust.'[13] The story of the doctor who sells his soul to the devil was popular material during this period, and appeared in the Gaiety in various forms during the 80s and 90s—as light opera, burlesque, and pantomime. In fact, Martin Ross herself may have worked on Faustian material in London with her cousin, the playwright William G. Wills. Martin visited him in 1885, before she started collaborating with Somerville, and the Martin/Wills correspondence indicates that she may have worked with him in some capacity.[14] He adapted works like *The Vicar of Wakefield* for Henry Irving at the Lyceum Theatre, and when Martin Ross spent time with him in 1885, he was completing what would be his greatest popular success. Some critics pejoratively described it as a 'pantomime for adults,'[15] and it appeared immediately after Violet Martin left town. It was an expensive reworking of Goethe's *Faust*, a re-enactment of diabolism and described as 'mediaevalism incarnate.'[16]

Edith Somerville preferred light-hearted pantomime and musicals. She wrote a pantomime called *Chloral or the Sleeping Beauty*, which is reminiscent of Gilbert and Sullivan's topsy-turvydom. Somerville was very familiar with their work, having acted in an amateur production of *Sorcerer* and performing in an 1888 English production of *H.M.S. Pinafore*.

This same year, 1888, D'Oyly Carte's Opera Company amused Dublin audiences with its production of the nautical opera, *H.M.S. Pinafore or The Lass that Loved a Sailor*, in the Gaiety. Most likely this is the performance which Francie mentions in *The Real Charlotte*, for on the back of the theatre programme of the performance is a brief advert of the forthcoming engagement of a burlesque, one which becomes the central parody of *The Real Charlotte*. *Little Amy Robsart* is advertised in the Gaiety programme, and in the Somerville and Ross novel, the Dysart amateur theatricals retell Amy Robsart's story. Both burlesques, the real one and the fictional one, are based on Walter Scott's *Kenilworth*. The theatrical material, then, is more than a backdrop to the fiction; rather, there is good indication that the fiction includes the theatrical sources for satirical purposes. After all, the mayhem resulting from the Dysart production, these 'nightmare snatches of *Kenilworth*', turns romantic farce into a kind of mad harlequinade.[17] In the nature of burlesque, the illusion of reality never quite takes hold. Poor Amy Robsart is nearly smashed to pieces in her ottoman/coffin by a heavily bewhiskered Queen Elizabeth while the actors comment freely on their

12 Martin Ross, 'Memoir of Robert,' Manuscripts Dept., Trinity College Library, Dublin, 10884.   13 'Martin Ross,' *Belfast News-Letter*, 24 Dec. 1915.   14 Martin Ross and William G. Wills Correspondence, 1885-90, Somerville and Ross Collection Queen's U Library, Belfast, 876.   15 Madeleine Bingham, *Henry Irving and the Victorian Theatre* (London: George Allen & Unwin, 1978) 215.   16 Edward G. Russell, theatre programme, *Faust*, adapted by William G. Wills, Royal Lyceum Theatre, London, 16 June 1886. 17 Somerville and Ross 204.

work. Like *Midsummer Night's Dream*, the play displays the process of play-making, and we know that in *The Real Charlotte* there were two Gaiety productions which the authors had in mind, *Amy Robsart* and *Pinafore*.

The sea-faring romance of the British Navy in *Pinafore* becomes a lake-locked fantasy in *The Real Charlotte*. Various kinds of boats—steam launches, ferry boats, pleasure yachts—provide a significant part of the novel's setting, and the main event involves the capsizing of a yacht. Although the red-coated young men of the story belong to the British army, their strong affinity for water suggests the Royal Navy. The romantic ne'er-do-well, Gerald Hawkins, possesses a distinctly sea-faring name while Captain Cursiter recalls Captain Corcoran of the popular musical comedy. Charlotte Mullen and her cook, Norry-the-Boat, resemble in grotesque ways Buttercup, the 'Portsmouth Bumboat Woman' of *Pinafore* while Christopher Dysart's nautical skills and monocle provide a topsy-turvy version of the villain, Dick Deadeye.

Given the self-conscious nature of Somerville and Ross' novel and, in particular, its staging of Anglican Ireland, we might ask to what extent the novel demonstrates the increasing isolation of Protestantism in southern Ireland. Though the concrete manifestation of the Church fails Francie, Anglican tradition determines her outcome. The novel records a Protestant ethos, and certain unexplainable things, like Francie's death at the end of the novel are understood within the 'light' of the Protestant world view. The text's Manichaean perspective infused by romantic irony drives Francie to her doom and the novel to a conclusion haunted by Faustian warnings.

Thus, in the latter half of the novel Lady Dysart cannot complete her acrostic puzzle. The final missing word has two letters, a C and a H. She asks Pamela for assistance: '"I shall go mad, Pamela, … if you cannot think of any word for that tenth light. C and H—can't you think of anything with C and H?"'[18] We immediately think of Christopher and Charlotte until Lady Dysart says that the word ends in H. 'Church' may be the missing link of Lady Dysart and the novel's puzzle. When Lady Dysart asks Pamela the word for the tenth lights of her acrostic, she provides her own answer, for the Church *is* the light for the soul in darkness. Ironically, the Dysarts remain unenlightened and unable to recognize the light provided by an uneducated Dublin jackeen, the light-hearted and light-headed Francie Fitzpatrick. This is the Dysart's failure, however, not the embracing Anglican tradition. When Roddy Lambert first sees Francie at fourteen (Margaret's age when Faust first meets her), her high spirits and golden hair brighten Dublin's north side while her gay exploits, running off on a milk-cart with its white horse, delights her Sunday-school pals. Such glorious light is utterly doused by the end of the novel when the black mare, frightened by Julie Duffy's funeral procession, throws her to her death. Anglican thought could explain Francie's undeserved end. The passing funeral procession with

18 Ibid. 376.

its keening women and Norry's sepulchral posture as she flings her arms wide under a billowing black cloak so that she appears as a 'great vulture' conjures up a scene which suggests an Irish Protestant perspective of an Irish Catholic event.[19]

The Real Charlotte expresses an attempt to resolve an Irish Anglican heritage infused with Calvinistic undertones within a secular language. Francie's ruin, her ultimate fall to her death, the light into the darkness, reveals the ambiguity at the heart of the novel. Francie Fitzpatrick is the sacrifice in this satire of cultural enlightenment in colonial Ireland.

In Memoriam James Joyce: *Hugh MacDiarmid and the Tradition of Scottish Multilingualism*

HANNE TANGE, UNIVERSITY OF GLASGOW

My overall theme is the question of multilingualism in Irish and Scottish tradition. I define multilingualism as an awareness of and a willingness to play with language differences. It is my intention to connect the linguistic innovation of the Scottish poet Hugh MacDiarmid with the experimentation of Joyce.[1] Although there are multiple references to Joyce in MacDiarmid's writings, the two modernists never met. In an attempt to compensate for such a lack of communication, Glasgow poet Edwin Morgan brought the two artists together in *The Whittrick*, a 1973 series of imaginary dialogues:

> *Hugh MacDiarmid:*
> Fill yir gless, Icarus! Thae nichts'll no revert!
> The warld, for aa that it's gruppen wi sair decreets
> O physics, stound and steid, will preeve to you and me
> Yon auld camsteerie ghaistlie place Lucretie thocht
> He had exilit fae the nature o things. Nicht
> Will dwine and flee and leave anither you and me
> Happit in relativitie's raggit yestreen.
> Let aa we were and aa we sall be ming and mell
> In this ae lowe o the unfremmit hours, my freen!

19 Ibid. 499.

HANNE TANGE
1 For a more detailed consideration of the relationship between James Joyce and Hugh MacDiarmid, I would like to refer to Edwin Morgan's essay 'James Joyce and Hugh MacDiarmid' in *Crossing the Border: Essays on Scottish Literature* (Manchester: Carcanet, 1990) 169-87.

James Joyce:
Friendly and propitious be the salutation,
Happily lachrymary the candelabra,
Thick the crepuscular phantasmagoria,
The crimson curtain swells: the night-wind's in my glass.
Its golden level tilts, and reason is a dog,
It's had its day. It bays, but now it must obey.
The wild swift wolf its brother loping in the moonlight.
The white-fanged London-jack imagination, leaps
Upon the dusty curtain, slinks by the candles,
Snuffs at the crystal and laps at the fire-water.
Pookahauntus! Nevertiti! Brahan Boru!
A toast to the guthering shadies. Toast the host.
The elements have crossed the Alphs, and Kubla can.²

Edwin Morgan's poem foregrounds the linguistic experimentation that connects the work of Joyce with that of MacDiarmid, and indirectly identifies the poet himself as a heir to their tradition. I shall return to Morgan towards the end of my discussion as I consider him the finest representative of multilingualism on the contemporary scene.

First I want to consider the moment when Scottish writers, inspired by the example of Joyce, started to uncover the potentials of language. And that brings me to Hugh MacDiarmid, who personifies such experimentation within Scottish tradition. The purpose of my paper is, in other words, to argue that multilingualism was something MacDiarmid learned from his reading of *Ulysses* and *Finnegans Wake*, but that it was his enthusiastic response that turned him and fellow-Scots into carriers of the Joycean tradition.

The first aspect of Joycean linguistics which I want to examine, is the author's focus on multilingualism within the English language. To English modernists there was no question whether or not Standard English should be the medium for their art. To Joyce and MacDiarmid, on the contrary, Standard English carried a certain political and cultural agenda. David Pierce discusses in *James Joyce's Ireland* how at an early stage in his career Joyce realized that the notion of linguistic standards was a myth.³ His version of English was a mixture of Norse, Irish and Anglo-Saxon idioms, and such a realization enabled him to explore the diversity contained within his speech. The first manifestations of Joyce's concern with language occur in *A Portrait of the Artist as a Young Man*. Stephen Daedalus enters into conversation with his English dean of studies, but soon their dialogue dissolves into a question of Irish versus Standard English:

2 Edwin Morgan, 'Dialogue one: James Joyce and Hugh MacDiarmid', *Poems of Thirty Years* (Manchester: Carcanet, 1982) 69-87.   3 David Pierce, *James Joyce's Ireland* (New Haven and London:

— To return to the lamp, [the dean] said, the feeding of it is also a nice problem. You must choose the pure oil and you must be careful when you pour it in not to overflow it, not to pour in more than the funnel can hold.
— What funnel? asked Stephen.
— The funnel through which you pour the oil into your lamp.
— That? said Stephen. Is that called a funnel? Is it not a tundish?
— What is a tundish?
— That. The ... funnel.
— Is that called a tundish in Ireland? asked the dean. I never heard the word in my life.[4]

It appears to have been *Ulysses* rather than the *Portrait* that inspired Hugh MacDiarmid to his experimentation, however.[5] MacDiarmid's first vernacular verse appears in 1922, and only a year later he admits that it was in order to obtain effects similar to Joyce he had decided to write in Scots.[6] The immediate differences between Joyce's experimental English and MacDiarmid's literary Scots may seem great. Joyce mixes styles that would not normally converge in a literary text, while MacDiarmid opts for a medium that is restricted to a select group, the Lowland Scots, and the poet thus chooses an exclusive strategy where Joyce is inclusive. Yet the similarities are stronger. Both styles derive from a recognition of linguistic diversity, they are oral in their approach to language, and through an insistence on provincial colloquialisms over national standards they weaken the bulwark that is the English cultural hegemony. One example of the MacDiarmid style is his poem 'The Watergaw' from 1922:

Ae weet forenicht i' the yow-trummle
I saw yon antrin thing,
A watergaw wi' its chitterin' licht
Ayont the on-ding;
An' I thocht o' the last wild look yet gied
Afore ye deed!

There was nae reek i' the laverock's hoose
That nicht—an' nane i' mine;
But I hae thocht o' that foolish licht
Ever sin' syne;

Yale UP, 1992) 21.   4 James Joyce, *A Portrait of the Artist as a Young Man*, ed. Garland (New York and London: Garland, 1993 [1914]) 215.   5 See Morgan, 'James Joyce and Hugh MacDiarmid' 175.   6 See Hugh MacDiarmid, 'Braid Scots and the Sense of Smell' in *The Raucle Tongue: Uncollected Prose by Hugh MacDiarmid*, ed. Angus Calder, Glen Murray and Alan Riach (Manchester: Carcanet, 1996) 73.

An' I think that mebbe at last I ken
What your look meant then.[7]

MacDiarmid's Lowland Scots reminds the reader of the 'funnel' versus 'tundish' discussion of the *Portrait* in the way it foregrounds language differences and destabilizes our notion of Standard English. Through his employment of the vernacular MacDiarmid achieves effects similar to Joyce's, and it is likely Joyce would have exploited it, had Irish English represented a stronger alternative to English. In spite of the strengths of Lowland Scots, MacDiarmid abandons the oral voice characteristic of his first lyrics in favour of a more synthetic diction in the 1930s. In 'James Joyce and Hugh MacDiarmid', Edwin Morgan emphasizes Mac-Diarmid's enthusiastic response to Joyce's *Work in Progress*, and MacDiarmid's 1934 poem 'Water Music' underlines that connection:

> *Wheesht, wheesht, Joyce, and let me hear*
> *Nae Anna Livvy's lilt,*
> *But Wauchope, Esk, and Ewes again,*
> *Each wi' its ain rhythms till't.*
>
> Archin' here and arrachin there,
> Allevolie or allemand,
> Whiles appliable, whiles areird,
> The polysemous poem's planned.
>
> Lively, louch, atweesh, atween,
> Auchimuty or aspate,
> Threidin' through the averins
> Or bightsom in the aftergait.
>
> Or barmybrained or barritchfu',
> Or rinnin' like an attercap,
> Or shinin' like an Atchison,
> Wi' a blare or wi' a blawp.[8]

Towards the end of their careers, both Joyce and MacDiarmid increasingly combine their vision of multilingualism within English with the notion of multilingualism beyond Standard English, and 'Water Music' seems to represent the point where the poet abandons the vernacular in favour of an artificial medium which blends different dictions and reflects a linguistic universalism akin to

7 Hugh MacDiarmid, *Complete Poems 1920–76* (London: Martin Brian and O'Keeffe, 1978) 17.   8 MacDiarmid, *Complete Poems* 333.

Finnegans Wake. 'Wheesht, wheesht, Joyce, and let me hear/ Nae Anna Livvy's lilt,/ But Wauchope, Esk, and Ewes again' the poem begins. Within the opening lines MacDiarmid has rejected the Joycean stream of consciousness, represented by the character of Anna Livia Plurabelle, in favour of more native waters, but though the Scot opts for Scottish airs, his allusion to Joyce acknowledges a debt to the Irishman in terms of approach. The 'polysemous poem', Edwin Morgan argues, 'is planned to move on its different levels, at different rates, with different characteristics'.[9] It must work like a novel by Joyce, Morgan continues, whose 'whole emphasis was again on sonority, rhythm, and verbal play'.[10] MacDiarmid himself observes on the similarities between his own technique and Joyce's:

> By the synthetic use of a language, then, I mean 'the destruction of toothless ratio'—'freedom of speech' in the real meaning of the term—something completely opposed to all our language habits and freely utilizing not only all the vast vocabulary these automatically exclude, but illimitable powers of word formation in keeping with the free genius of any language. Theoretically—and to some extent practically—I go further and agree with Joyce in regard to the utilization of a multi-linguistic medium—a synthetic use, not of any particular language, but of all languages. Personally, I write in English, or in dialect Scots, or in synthetic Scots—or in synthetic English—with bits of other languages. I recognize the values of any language or any dialect for certain purposes, but where I am concerned with the free consciousness I cannot employ these—I must then find an adequate synthetic medium.[11]

MacDiarmid's greatest manifestation of his belief in Joycean linguistics is the giant work *In Memoriam James Joyce* from 1955. The very title of the poem stresses the connection between MacDiarmid's linguistic project and Joyce, and past comparisons between the artists have often centered on the relation of the MacDiarmid poem to *Ulysses* and *Finnegans Wake*.[12] We should not forget that MacDiarmid begun his composition of the work before the death of Joyce, however. The poet would later claim he had written the piece in response to the news of Joyce's death in 1941, but the origins of the work date back to the mid-1930s at the latest.[13] A reference occurs in 1936 to a poem by the name of 'In Memoriam Teofilo Folengo', a sixteenth-century Italian word equilibrist, and MacDiarmid had probably completed most of his Joyce poem by then.[14] He later added an invocation of Joyce here, a reference to Joyce there, but his additions are

9 Morgan, 'James Joyce and Hugh MacDiarmid' 179.   10 Joyce's Italian translator Nino Frank as quoted by Morgan, loc. cit.   11 Hugh MacDiarmid, *The Letters of Hugh MacDairmid*, ed. Alan Bold (London: Hamish Hamilton, 1984) 771.   12 See Carl Freedman, 'Beyond the Dialect of the Tribe: James Joyce, Hugh MacDiarmid and World Language' in *Hugh MacDiarmid: Man and Poet*, ed. Nancy Gish (Edinburgh: Edinburgh UP, 1992) for an example of this.   13 Alan Riach, *Hugh MacDiarmid's Epic Poetry*. Edinburgh: Edinburgh UP, 1991) 60.   14 Ibid. 60.

unlikely to have changed the content of the work radically. The implication is that MacDiarmid reached his vision of world language independent of Joyce. Like the novelist, he had tested the different effects available to him within the English language in his early work. As he developed his poetic vision, he discovered that even the verbal riches of vernacular Scots had their limits, and that brought him to the realization that if language was to reflect his ever-growing ideal, it would have to expand. Only the fusion of all languages into a single, universal diction allowed such continuous extension. 'A Vision of World Language', MacDiarmid subtitles *In Memoriam James Joyce*, and the following passage is representative of his approach:

> Hence this *hapax legomenon* of a poem, this exercise
> In schablone, bordatini, and prolonged scordatura,
> This *divertissement philologique*,
> This Wortspiel, this torch symphony,
> This 'liberal education,' this collection of *fonds de tiroir*,
> This—even more than Kierkegaard's
> 'Frygt og Baeven'—'dialectical lyric,'
> This rag-bag, this Loch Ness monster, this impact
> Of the whole range of *Weltliteratur* on one man's brain,
> In short, this 'friar's job,' as they say in Spain
> Going back in kind
> To the Eddic 'Converse of Thor and the All-Wise Dwarf'
> (Al-viss Mal, 'Edda die lieden des Codex Regius,' 120, I f)
> Existing in its present MS form
> Over five centuries before Shakespeare.
> You remember it?[15]

MacDiarmid's range is breathtaking. The languages he employs include Latin, French, and German, while his literary references cover the thousand year span between the Old Norse sagas and the philosophic writings of Søren Kierkegaard. Yet this is only a tiny section of a piece that takes up well over a hundred pages. The density in linguistic experimentation changes throughout the poem, as does the focus, but everything comes together in a grand vision of universal fusion – a melting-pot ideal that enables the poet to unite all ideas, knowledge, languages and culture into a larger entity. Complete multilingualism has been achieved, the reader is tempted to conclude, but is that really so?

In order to be truly multilingual, we may expect the artist to abandon English in favour of a diction that has no national connotations. Esperanto and Ido represent such media; the vehicles of Joyce and MacDiarmid do not for they never move

15 MacDiarmid, *Complete Poems* 755-6.

beyond Standard English. Critic Carl Freedman has observed how Joycean experimentation depends on an element of recognition. Something in the language must enable the reader to decipher the defamiliarizations, and that makes English a desirable basic structure.[16] Hugh MacDiarmid includes among the quotations that preface the Joyce poem a statement by the Russian writer Vladimir Solovyof: 'The true unity of languages is not an Esperanto or Volapuk or everyone speaking French, not a single language, but an all-embracing language, an interpenetration of all languages'.[17] English, it seems, provides a possible basis for universal speech, but it is an English that is reinforced by borrowings from other languages until it has reached such a state of infiltration that it is no longer recognizable as a national speech. Through their adoption of a multilinguistic strategy, Irishman Joyce and Scot MacDiarmid, in other words, transform the English language from a standard which marginalises the Scottish and the Irish writer in relation to a core culture, into an ever expanding diction inclusive of the artists' universal aspirations.

The twin aspects of multilingualism that have formed the basis of the present discussion have played a key part in the development of Scottish literature in the twentieth century. Before MacDiarmid's vernacular experiment in the 1920s, the Scottish artist had been restricted in his/her choice of language by the biases and anti-biases which were attached to the native idiom; after MacDiarmid there are only few limits for the creative writer who wants to explore Scotland's linguistic resources. The 1999 edition of *New Writing Scotland*[18] thus contains contributions made in all Scotland's three languages of English, Scots and Gaelic, while the fiction of James Kelman and Irvine Welsh, among others, has proven that a Scottish author may employ the vernacular and yet reach a world audience. The drawback behind such a liberation of the national voice is that the author no longer achieves a fore-grounding of language when his Lowland Scots has become accepted as the standard rather than a deviation, and in response contemporary writers have turned to the social or regional codes that exist within Scots. Multilingualism within English has become multilingualism within Scots, and such a development would probably have been welcomed by Joyce and MacDiarmid.

If many contemporary Scottish artists have embraced the potentials of multi-lingualism within English, Edwin Morgan is the only writer that has fully accepted the challenge of world language. Like Joyce and MacDiarmid, Morgan conducts his experiments within English, but he is conscious of the other dictions available to him and eager to explore. In poems such as 'The First Men on Mercury' or 'The Mummy' Morgan plays with the possibility, or impossibility, of linguistic exchange, while his most Joycean piece is probably 'The Loch Ness Monster's Song' where all sense disintegrates into sounds:

16 Freedman 262-3.   17 MacDiarmid, *Complete Poems* 737.   18 Moira Burgess and Donny O'Rourke (eds.), *Friends and Kangaroos: New Writing Scotland 17* (Glasgow: Association of Scottish Literary Studies, 1999).

Sssnnnwhuffffl?
Hnwhuffl hhnnwfl hnfl hfl?
Gdroblboblhobngbl gbl gl g g g g glbgl.
Drublhaflablhaflubhafgabhaflhafl fl fl -
gm grawwwww grf grawf awfgm graw gm.
Hovoplodok—doplodovok— plovodokot—doplodokosh?
Splgraw fok fok splgrafhatchgabrlgabrl fok splfok!
Zgra kra gka fok!
Grof grawff gahf?
Gombl mbl bl -
blm plm,
blm plm,
blm plm,
blp.[19]

In 'The Loch Ness Monster's Song' Morgan takes Joyce's linguistic strategy to its logical conclusion. Nothing remains but a series of sounds, and a few question marks, periods or commas to signify that behind the nonsense there may once have been meaning. Multilingualism has at last enabled the writer to overcome the English language, but the cost of that feat is the loss of all significance. Morgan's message seems to be that the artist may abolish basic linguistic structures in his/her pursuit of world language, but it will be at the expense of readability, and similar conclusions may have compelled MacDiarmid and Joyce from following their linguistic ideal through. As a result, collage, not fusion, becomes the preferred expression of multilingualism, which leaves the reader with the question of whether indeed a universal vision can be expressed within the limits of the English language. James Joyce and Hugh MacDiarmid took it as far as they could, Edwin Morgan tried to go one step further, only to realise the impossibility of world language. Multilingualism seems a desirable poetic philosophy, it has proven unworkable as literary practice, but to its credit, it has brought about an increased awareness of linguistic difference, and it is from such sources much contemporary literature derives its strength.

19 Morgan, *Poems of Thirty Years* 237.

'As the Snake It Shed Its Skin'—or, How the Irish National Ideal of the Irish National Theatre Was Abandoned in Favour of a Corporate Trademark (1902-1906)

KAREN VANDEVELDE, NUI GALWAY

Early in May 1904 Yeats wrote a letter to Frank Fay, stage manager of the Irish National Theatre Society, showing his concern that a company calling itself 'The Belfast Branch of the Irish Literary Theatre' had given a performance of his play *Cathleen ni Houlihan* and of George Russell's *Deirdre*. 'What would you think', he suggested to Fay, 'of putting notice in papers to say Kathleen is copyright by Theatre & that leave can be given on conditions? This would enable us to keep some control of title of societies etc & so prevent confusion.'[1]

The following week, a letter signed by Yeats was published in the New York Irish magazine, *The Gael*, referring to a group of actors performing in St Louis and their borrowing of the name of 'Irish National Theatre.' He argued that 'this choice of names is unfortunate, as a certain number of people will confuse it with the original Irish National Theatre' and concluded that 'the society does not wish to be identified with any other body of players.'[2]

At first sight, Yeats' fastidious attitude towards these two productions of Irish companies in April 1904 might suggest no more than an exaggerated nervous reaction or a certain artistic pride for his own theatre, the Irish National Theatre Society, established in 1902. However, in the context of the early development of this theatre, the commotion over similarity of names, borrowed titles and possible confusion, is symptomatic of a profound change in the function and status of that national theatre. This essay will highlight some of the important structural changes taking place within the Irish National Theatre during the years 1902-6.

First of all, it might be useful to give a very brief overview of the Irish dramatic revival at the turn of the century. As with elsewhere in Europe, Ireland at the close of the nineteenth century also felt the need to confirm its national identity with the establishment of a national theatre. Various cultural figures were dissatisfied with the theatrical fare of foreign plays at the established theatres. As such, in 1899, Yeats, Lady Gregory and Edward Martyn founded the three-year project of the Irish Literary Theatre, proposing to perform 'certain Celtic and Irish plays' in order to show 'that Ireland is not the home of buffoonery and of easy sentiment ... but the home of an ancient idealism.'[3]

---

1 Undated letter from W.B. Yeats to F. Fay, early May 1904. John Kelly, *The Collected Letters of W.B. Yeats Vol. III, 1901-1904* (Oxford: OUP, 1994) 588.   2 *The Gael/An Gaodhal* (7 May 1904) 234; Kelly 590-1.   3 Letter from Lady Gregory, W.B. Yeats and Edward Martyn to possible guarantors of the theatre, quoted in Lady Gregory's *Our Irish Theatre* (Gerrards Cross: Colin Smythe, 1972) 20.

[203]

When this experiment to produce Irish plays for Irish people came to an end, various groups were inspired to continue its mission of establishing an Irish national drama and give it a more grassroots identity. Members from the nationalist women's group, the Daughters of Erin, from the Hermetic Society associated with George Russell and from the Fay Brothers' theatre company, joined forces in 1902 to perform Yeats' play *Cathleen ni Houlihan* and George Russell's *Deirdre*. This loose co-operation was first called W.G. Fay's National Dramatic Company, but placed itself on a firmer footing in August 1902. They also changed the name into the Irish National Theatre Society and invited Yeats to be president. They wanted their plays to be a *representative* platform not just *for* but also *of* Irish people. From December 1904 onwards, the company called itself after the hall which they had then acquired, the Abbey Theatre.

In 1903, however, a group of politically active members of the INTS, including Maud Gonne, Máire Quinn and Dudley Digges, left the original society in order to concentrate on what they believed to be their more important propagandist work. For this purpose they established a rival company called The National Players. They were dissatisfied with Yeats' artistic control over the society and the lack of political interest in the theatre company. They continued to stage plays as part of wider nationalist projects, but slowly faded into anonymity for want of good actors, good playwrights and funds. This group was responsible for the first controversy over names and titles, when in April 1904 Máire Quinn, Dudley Digges, P.J. Kelly, Charles Caulfield and Elisabeth Young of the National Players travelled to the World Fair at St. Louis to perform a few plays from the Irish dramatic revival. The political conviction of its nationalist actors already became clear on the boat trip across the ocean: at one of the banquets in the middle of the Atlantic Ocean, they refused to sing the official British national anthem 'God Save the King' when it was requested by some guests.[4]

At the World Exhibition, however, more serious arguments arose over Irish identity. On arrival, the company was forced to co-operate with a very successful actor, Patrick Tuohy, who won all the laughs with his genuine stage-Irishman slander of Irish vice and virtue. After his far from captivating joke that 'it takes the Irishman thirty days to observe St Patrick's Day—one day to celebrate and twenty-nine to get over it,' one of the Irish National Players ended up in a fight with the farcical actor. As a result, half of the company was discharged. The other half refused to ignore this 'travesty on the Irish race' and discontinued its performances.[5] The controversy was faithfully reported by the Irish expatriate press in the States, and the manager of the fair, Myles Murphy, clarified his point of view that 'only a supersensitive individual could take offence. These Dublin folk are of that class.'[6]

However, as the National Players performed plays that were originally the property of the INTS, the two companies were easily mixed up in the heat of the

4 *Gaelic American* (1 May 1904) 4.   5 *Gaelic American* (11 June 1904) 5.   6 Ibid.

argument. In reaction to this confusion, Yeats wrote the above quoted letter to the editor of the American expatriate Irish journal, *The Gael*, but the editor responded with an interesting justification of the borrowing of the term 'Irish National Theatre':

> It is true that the theatre in the Irish section at the St. Louis World's Fair has been named The Irish National Theatre, but we are assured that it was so named because of the intention to present there a series of typical Irish plays truly National in spirit and sentiment, and not with any idea of trading on the fame of the original society in Ireland ... The fact that a National Theatre Society has just been formed in Cork indicates that the word national is not considered the exclusive property of any organization, even in Ireland.[7]

The other group whose name caused Yeats' indignation, was The Ulster Branch of the Irish Literary Theatre, set up by admirers of the original INTS in 1902. They brought over some of the new Irish plays to Belfast in 1903 and 1904, for which they received help from other INTS members—not surprisingly Dudley Digges and Máire Quinn. First they performed Yeats' *Cathleen ni Houlihan* along with James Cousins' short play *The Racing Lug*, and the second time Yeats' play was accompanied by George Russell's *Deirdre*. Their second performance with solely Ulster actors was widely recorded in the national press, but as soon as Yeats found out, he denied them first of all the rights to perform his play *Cathleen ni Houlihan* and secondly the right to use the name of the Irish Literary Theatre. Though initially a great blow to the society, this break proved to be beneficial to the new theatre company. 'Damn Yeats', said Bulmer Hobson, one of its founding members, 'we'll write our own plays,' and these prophetic words announced the beginning of the Ulster Literary Theatre in 1904.[8]

As I have already indicated, these arguments were more than just 'ripples' in the history of the Irish National Theatre. Addressing the question *why* Yeats reacted so vehemently against the two companies, opens up a wide range of intricacies and alterations within the walls of the INTS. It is important to remember that when the INTS was first established in 1902, it was through the combined efforts of members from political, nationalist, social, philosophical and artistic circles. Each of them had different expectations of an Irish national theatre, but believed that their new venture could function as a tolerant and representative home for all of these ideals and expectations. Within a complex web of artistic collaborations and competing egos, differences of opinion arose that inevitably led to disruptions in the amateur society.

7 *Gael / An Gaodhal* (June 1904) 234.   8 Quoted in Sam Hanna Bell, *The Theatre in Ulster* (Dublin: Gill & Macmillan, 1972) 1.

However, Yeats' increasingly authoritarian artistic control over the INTS narrowed the scope of the repertoire and concentrated on an apolitical repertoire of Irish peasant plays and poetic drama. The culmination of this aestheticization of the Irish National Theatre is illustrated in statements such as 'art for art's sake' in the company's 1904 issue of *Samhain*, and in Yeats' declaration in 1905 that his theatre was one in which 'the fiddler calls the tune.' Borrowing the words of Bulmer Hobson from the Ulster Literary Theatre, during the years 1902-6 the INTS 'like a snake shed its skin—its political skin.'[9] As a result, many of the original members left the society during those years, and established 'alternative' companies in order to realize what *they* believed to be the true function of a national theatre. The National Players, for example, were more outspoken in their political agenda, while the Ulster Literary Theatre concentrated on satirical and realist drama and addressed sectarian issues rather than avoid them.

The growing discrepancy between political and aesthetic ideals in the INTS makes it easier to answer the question *why* possible confusion between the National Players, the Ulster Branch of the Irish Literary Theatre and the INTS was such a worry to Yeats. The National Players were closely associated with political organizations such as the Cumann na nGaedhal (one of the precursors of Sinn Fein) and the Ulster Literary Theatre was set up by members of the Protestant National Association in Belfast. These associations could harm the prestigious and indepen-dent artistic status Yeats was striving for, especially now he was negotiating with the wealthy Annie F. Horniman who offered to buy them a hall—the Abbey Theatre—and provide them with funding. In addition, the theatre's successful English tours in 1903 and 1904 had secured them an outstanding reputation as an arts theatre.

Yeats' obsessive, protective reaction signals not only a new phase in the internal management of the INTS, but also in the nature and function of a national drama in general. Referring back to the Irish Literary Theatre of 1899-1901, this brief exper-iment was the first manifestation of the demand for a National Theatre in Ireland. This demand had already revealed itself in other European nations such as Norway and Germany, and also England and France were trying to follow this example. Throughout the nineteenth century, theatres had given themselves 'national' status on the basis of their prestige, even if the productions in that theatre bore no relevance to the nation itself. The Theatre Royal in Dublin, for example, had displayed itself in the 1870s as Ireland's National Theatre, even if the theatrical fare consisted mainly of visiting English, French or Italian opera and melodramatic companies.[10]

However, near the end of the nineteenth century, this changed and a new interpretation came to the foreground: that of a national theatre as a fundamental *institution* for a modern nation, in which the drama was representative *of* and *for*

---

9 Memoirs by Bulmer Hobson in Margaret McHenry, 'The Ulster Theatre in Ireland' (Philadelphia, unpublished thesis, 1931) 82.   10 *The History of the Theatre Royal, Dublin, from its Foundations in 1821 to the Present Time* (Dublin: Edward Ponsonby, 1870)

the nation.[11] The important issue of 'representation' includes various aspects: first of all, the national theatre is now expected to give a representative portrayal *of the nation* on the national stage, one that holds the mirror up to nature. Secondly, the theatre has to *summon* the entire nation as its audience, or a representative cross-section of it. Thirdly, the theatrical staging needs to be representative *for the nation*. In other words, a theatre must show how the nation *should* be, rather than how she really is.

This triple function of a National Theatre is responsible for the various rows and controversies over plays that were or were not supposed to be truly Irish, such as Yeats' *The Countess Cathleen* in 1899, Synge's *In the Shadow of the Glen* in 1903 and his *Playboy of the Western World* in 1907, and later on the plays by Sean O'Casey. A nation is never a monolithic collection of individuals; therefore disagreements over the nature and function of a national theatre are countless.

The Irish Literary Theatre was thus the first Irish theatre to shift the emphasis from *prestige* to *representation*, even if the prestige issue was never totally absent. Next, the Irish National Theatre Society carried that representational function even further. They adopted the name of 'Ireland's National Theatre' mainly for its *descriptive* features, acknowledging the complexity of this term. Inevitably, however, the more conflicts arose over the various realizations of a national theatre, the more *prescriptive* the concept became. Every important individual, newspaper, artist or politician in Ireland believed they had a right to dictate what an Irish national theatre should be like. For example, when the INTS became less political in its programme, nationalists denied the theatre its national status; and when the INTS presented the Irish peasant as immoral or adulterous, plays such as *In the Shadow of the Glen* would be re-written in the *United Irishman* in a more virtuous form and provided with the title *In a Real Wicklow Glen*.[12]

The above changes are not surprising, but the evidence described in this essay suggests that very soon after the establishment of the Irish National Theatre, the concept experienced another transformation: this time the title became a *possession*, a *property* that was in need of protection against theft, borrowing or damage. I refer again to the editorial in the American journal *The Gael*, which illustrates the conflict between the descriptive interpretation of a national theatre and the application of the term as a corporate trademark: 'the word national is not considered the exclusive property of any organization'.

The two controversies referred to are not the only manifestations of this change; they are symptomatic of an underlying change in the organization of the theatre. In fact, the abandonment of the political national ideal of the society was paralleled by a structural transformation. Between 1902 and 1906, Yeats was moving the INTS from a coalition of enthusiastic amateurs into a professional

11 Loren Kruger, *The National Stage* (Chicago and London: Chicago UP, 1992) 3-29   12 *United Irishman* (24 October 1903) 4.

business producing Irish drama. In 1904 they acquired their own theatre space, and at the end of 1905 the INTS was transformed into a company of limited liability with three directors and a numbers of employees. The original INTS members were no longer a collective of actors, designers or stage managers, all united by the wish to create a national drama. Instead, they would now become employees of the INTS, Limited. Yeats, Lady Gregory and Synge were its sole directors. This structural change was inevitable in the professionalization of the company, but the more this theatre became an institution with a corporate logo, with a patent on its products and a clear staff hierarchy, the more it was removed from its original ideal of being a theatre 'representing the Irish nation'.

'Great Hatred, Little Room': The Writer, the University and the Small Magazine

DAVID WHEATLEY, UNIVESITY OF HULL

In 1955 a three-way exchange took place in the pages of *Studies* magazine between Denis Donoghue, Donald Davie and Vivian Mercier. In the course of his contribution, Davie, who was then teaching at Trinity College, Dublin, offers the following remarks on the differences between Ireland and England:

> while the critic as such has never been much esteemed in England, yet England has had critics, even a continuous tradition of literary criticism; while nothing is more striking in the Anglo-Irish literary tradition than the absence of any true critic at all, certainly of any critical tradition.[1]

There were Goldsmith's 'pot-boilers', he goes on, and more recently John Eglinton, Daniel Corkery and Yeats' 'one contribution' to the genre, the preface to his *Oxford Book of Modern Verse*, but otherwise nothing. The consequence of this critical vacuum is that 'any degree of objectivity in criticism is impossible', leading to the dismal introspection Davie finds 'all but universal'[2] in the Dublin of *Dead as Doornails* then regnant at the other end of Grafton Street from Trinity College.

Though writing as a visiting Englishman, it is not Davie who emerges from the debate accused of cosmopolitan insouciance. On the contrary, Vivian Mercier uses Davie's article against Denis Donoghue, urging him to apply his reading of Kenneth Burke and William Empson to home grown writing: 'only by daring to do this can he hope to found an Irish school of criticism.'[3] A significant resource

---

1 Donald Davie, 'Reflections of an English Writer in Ireland', *Studies* 44 (Winter 1955) 440. 2 Ibid. 441. 3 Vivan Mercier, An Irish School of Criticism?', *Studies* 45 (Spring 1956) 87.

in fostering Irish criticism was the presence of a journal like *Studies*, in which debates of this kind could be held. In his *Decolonization and Criticism* Gerry Smyth has surveyed the intellectual outlets of this period, which is still a byword for stagnation. Though an affiliated journal with a Catholic ethos, *Studies* at least succeeds in transcending the arid disengagement Smyth finds in *Eriu*, the magazine of the Royal Irish Academy: 'A discursive universe is implied in which writer and reader belong to an initiated community, but one which bears no relation to any community outside this particular universe.'[4] But with the demise of *The Bell* in 1946 the role of a truly independent review was filled not by *Eriu* or *Studies* but the *Dublin Magazine* and *Kavanagh's Weekly*, alternately embodying and fulminating against the genteel amateurism of the period.

The divide between professionalised scholarship and belle-lettristic amateurism is not unique to 1950s Ireland, but a regularly recurring symptom of anxiety about the nature of cultural production. Writing twenty years after Davie, Mercier and Donoghue, Anthony Cronin judged the real division in contemporary poetry to be 'not between left and right, formalists and anti-formalists, realists and romantics ... It is between academics and the rest', a stand-off Cronin characterizes as 'a war'.[5] In language behind which we can dimly make out Pádraig Pearse's rage against 'The Murder Machine', Cronin contrasts those whose response to art remains 'natural' and the academic bureaucrats 'who have so subjected themselves to the process as to be incapable of responding to poetry in any other way than the process dictates'.[6] When commentators invoke the organic community, Raymond Williams observed, the one thing certain was it was always gone. Cronin worked on *The Bell* with Peadar O'Donnell, and though he doesn't claim that it spoke to a natural audience for poetry that has since disappeared, to make this claim would be to forget how much time *The Bell* spent attacking Ireland for failing to produce just this audience. In fairness to Cronin, attempts to produce this elusive entity, rather than just arguments deploring its absence, would quickly lead us back to Wordsworth's preface to *Lyrical Ballads* and beyond.

In the absence of this organic unity, more and more we are used to the writer and the academic bureaucrat being one and the same person, a development which either enables a fully integrated radical poetics, if you're an American $L=A=N=G=U=A=G=E$ poet, or the final abandonment of poetry's 'natural audience', if you're Dana Gioia or Les Murray. In recent years Cronin's musings on the academy have been taken up with particular vehemence by the Australian poet, who goes beyond the Irishman's misgivings into outright hysteria. 'Who reads poetry? Not our intellectuals; / they want to control it', he writes in his collection *Conscious and Verbal*, though the line could come from any of his

4 Gerry Smyth, *Decolonization and Criticism: The Construction of Irish Literature* (London: Pluto, 1998) 126.   5 Anthony Cronin, 'The Muse in Captivity', in Dermot Bolger (ed.), *Letters from the New Island* (Dublin: Raven Arts, 1986) 170.   6 Ibid. 171-2.

books.[7] Surfing a riptide of indignation, Murray denounces the academy's collusion with totalitarian political correctness: 'she loves this new goddess for whom abortion is orgasm'.[8] The orgasm of fatuous denunciation is scarcely less intense. The fact that Murray has been feted by academic critics around the world only intensifies the comedy of what, laughing aside, is a shabby and obscurantist copout.

I've lingered over the example of Murray as someone who has made strenuous efforts to keep alive the notion of the writer and the university as implacable enemies. Central to his tactics is the presentation of academic criticism as mono-lithically in thrall to an aloof radical consensus. For Murray the threat to poetry comes from multiculturalism, literary theory and other academic *patois* hostile to the organic substance of literature. I'm less interested here in the small detail of Murray's argument than in its recurrence throughout the twentieth century and into the twenty-first, and how flexible the distinctions have proved between the presumed organic tradition and the radical threat to its integrity. To put Murray's tirade in perspective, in 1976 John Carey published an essay titled 'The Critic as Vandal',[9] arguing that much of what we call criticism is in reality nothing more than wilful assault on literature. Unsurprising, you might think, coming from the rearguard author of *The Intellectuals and the Masses*, but for the fact that the critic-vandals he cites are ... William Empson, C. S. Lewis and Christopher Ricks! Innocent times, 1976. A list of modern critics denounced in their time as renegades from tradition would also include T. S. Eliot, F. R. Leavis, Frank Kermode, Denis Donoghue (as we've seen) and Harold Bloom: a virtual rogue's gallery for those orgasmic abor-tionists of Les Murray's contemporary academy.

If the interaction between the academy and poetry's 'natural audience' is a source of confusion, suspicion and misunderstanding, I'd like to suggest that one of the most valuable buffer zones between the two is the world of literary jour-nalism and the small magazine. Literary journalism is one of the most elusive of genres. After the failure of his career Hazlitt considered he 'declined into a jour-nalist', but in the fifteen years before his death he produced over three million words of journalism: even after Tom Paulin's welcome revival of Hazlitt, how many people will ever read more than a tiny fraction of it? Much of T. S. Eliot's critical prose remains uncollected even today, stillborn on the pages of *The Athenaeum* and *The Egoist*. The difference between these scattered, transitory pieces and how they end up in volumes of *Collected Prose* can often be crucial to our understanding of how writers work. Academics working in this field however are encouraged to be less diffuse in their publishing habits than some of their subjects. Yeats' most throwaway piece of journalism is the object of scholarly attention, but academics at the mercy of a Research Assessment Exercise do not

7 Les Murray, 'The Instrument', *Conscious and Verbal* (Manchester: Carcanet, 1999) 24. 8 'Sidere Mens Eadem Mutato', *Selected Poems* (Manchester: Carcanet, 1986) 38. 9 Revised as John Carey, *Wording and Re-Wording: Paraphrases in Literary Criticism* (Oxford: OUP, 1977).

have the luxury of publishing their findings in outlets as fugitive as *The Freeman's Journal* or the old *Daily Express*.

Besides, the journal culture Hazlitt and the young Yeats epitomize has been dead a long time, or so we're told: John Gross' classic study, *The Rise and Fall of the Man of Letters*, itself thirty years old, charts the tradition's trickling to extinction in the pages of *Horizon* and *Scrutiny* several decades before that. All that survived, it seemed, was a form of impotent whimsy and trifling. In his *Enemies of Promise*, Cyril Connolly reminds us of the now sadly neglected career of one Walter Savage Shelleyblake. This diligent scribe's first book, *Vernal Aires*, got him a job as reviewer on *The Blue Bugloss*, where he made his debut with a sparkling piece on the Nonesuch *Boswell*. His next review wasn't so good, and soon he'd declined into writing up the 'Shorter Notices' of books about famous Royal mistresses and the secrets of the Mayan jungle before disappearing entirely, sucked dry by his editor Mr Vampire.[10]

Connolly doesn't mention whether Shelleyblake was tempted to trade in Fleet Street for one of the university jobs still so easy to come by in his time—to become Amis' Lucky Jim, in short. In the quaint days before quality assessment audits, many academics were free to write as much, or as little as they wanted. In their history of Trinity College Dublin, R. B. McDowell and David Webb describe the culture of abject inertia that characterised the college in the early twentieth century, where large numbers of Trinity fellows 'produc[ed] little or nothing in the way of original scholarship', or followed a 'sadly provincial or muddled' vision of culture, whether writing pastiche Latin poetry or reciting Kipling to students after dinner.[11] Some idea of how late this culture persisted can be had, again from Gerry Smyth's book, in which he notes that of the 88 texts published by members of staff at Trinity College, Dublin, in the decade 1948-58, 43, or almost half were by Donald Davie—and this despite the fact that he didn't arrive in Ireland until 1950.[12] If academics are not given to publishing in small magazines today, it is for exactly the opposite reason: enforced publication, but in refereed professional journals. Since these are unlikely to pay, except in the obvious sense that appearance in their pages holds the key to appointments and promotions, academics in search of pocket money are likely to write for the books pages, the *TLS* or the *LRB*—anywhere but an amateur small magazine with a minimal circulation and no contributor's fee. So why do it?

Academics keen to boost their Research Assessment Exercise returns have nothing to gain from writing for a small magazine such as *Metre* but, equally, nothing to lose. Moving between academic publishing and writing for a magazine such as ours, is an excellent way of testing your work against utterly different sets of expectations and putting to the test its ability to communicate beyond any one coterie readership. Writing on Matthew Arnold recently, that byword for all

10 Cyril Connolly, *Enemies of Promise* (London: Penguin, 1961) 103-8.   11 R. B. McDowell and David Webb, *Trinity College Dublin* (Cambridge: CUP, 1983) 398-400.   12 Smyth 154.

that is insulated and patronising in English criticism, Terry Eagleton has pointed out how much more versatile he was than our caricatures of the hidebound elitist acknowledge. Arnold was 'neither an academic nor a commercial hack, but a writer who passes to and fro between poetry, criticism, periodical journalism and social commentary, and thus a voice within what could still be termed the public sphere.'[13] How many commentators today could boast as much? Given how embarrassingly *de rigueur* condemnations of him are in Irish Studies today, there is no small irony in how closely commentators like Eagleton himself or Tom Paulin approximate to a model of the public intellectual that we inherit from their nemesis Arnold.

To return to the example I gave at the outset of Donald Davie. Davie's denial of an Irish critical tradition, as I've already admitted, is a lot less than the full picture. It may even be culturally imperialist. Gerry Smyth would probably think so, commenting on how an article of Davie's on Synge:

> mirrors the typical structure of colonialist discourse with its initial reference to that which is to be dominated and marginalized ... recall[ing] the liberal mode of decolonization in which a formerly marginalized subject seeks equality with the metropolitan power, only to reconfirm, at the very moment of its 'success', the hierarchies on which the established structure of power and knowledge were based.[14]

I'd like to demur at the terms of Davie's treatment here. Mid-Atlantic Poundian though he was, Davie wrote prolifically on Berkeley, Yeats, Synge, Beckett, Heaney, Clarke, Padraic Fallon, doing as much as anyone to advance the reputation of the last two, wrote some of his best poetry about Ireland, its Georgian architecture, the Church of Ireland and military history, and achieved as fruitful an immersion in Irish culture as any twentieth-century English poet. He did the same for Polish, Russian and American culture too, which is more than most Irish critics get round to. But how many undergraduates, reading the words 'typical structure of colonialist discourse', would ever discover any of this? Why bother, when Davie has been unmasked as one more fall-guy for the useless liberal humanism whose persistence into the postcolonial era cannot be endured?

The erosion of the non-aligned, boundary-crossing commentator's place in intellectual life is one reason for our not knowing what to do with a figure like Davie any more. There are others. Among the principal enemies of promise for young scholars today is enforced overproduction of work whose main target audience is RAE panels. In despair at leaden academic verbiage John Gross has suggested that 'it might not be a bad idea if no one under thirty was allowed to undertake original research without special permission.'[15] Tactless though it may

13 Terry Eagleton, 'Sweetness and Light for All', *Times Literary Supplement* (21 January 2000) 15.   14 Smyth 135.   15 John Gross, *The Rise and Fall of the Man of Letters* (London: Penguin, 1973) 321.

be to say so in a book devoted to graduate research, this mightn't be such a bad idea if it at least forced universities to rethink their assumptions about what exactly research is for, and the reasons for the large dropout levels among students allowed to drift into it by departments which then overwhelm them with undergraduate teaching. Equally, it mightn't be such a bad thing if the link was broken between productivity and professional advancement, or at least the Gradgrind model of RAE points equalling prizes that we currently endure. The alternative, or complement to conventional scholarly publishing represented by a small magazine like *Metre* can make a contribution here.

What the small magazine represents, if this doesn't sound too Blairite, is a third way between the rough and tumble of newspaper reviews, in the few enough papers that still pay poetry any attention, and the straggling attentions of the academic reviews. Much of what makes a small magazine distinctive takes the form of neither /nor constructions like this. In the case of *Metre*, we are neither an academic journal nor are we willing to stop pestering academics to write for us. Despite our title we do not confine ourselves to metrical verse, trying to overcome static dichotomies of formal versus free writing, traditional versus experimental. *Metre* tries to make a point of publishing contributions that might have difficulties finding a home elsewhere: long poems, poems in translation, macaronic poems, essays, long reviews, prose poems. But the magazine is as much about the mix of contents, the pleasure of combining the familiar and the utterly unknown, about the individual contributions. But beyond that, what exactly constitutes a magazine's identity or legacy? Magazines are transitory things, but long after their contents have been absorbed into books or silently, charitably forgotten, the best live on as climates of opinion. Very few readers of contemporary poetry who didn't buy it when it came out will ever have seen Ian Hamilton's *The Review* but many will know it by hearsay, and many more again will have absorbed its ethos unconsciously through the influence it continues to have two decades on.

Another distinguishing feature of the small magazine is its essential precariousness, always threatening to run out of subscribers, not come out on time, go broke, and behave in a generally irresponsible way. Not the least of its charms is its proneness to technical disasters: crookedly printed pages, pages printed upside down, verses left out of poems, horrendous typos. One example of this last complaint that stands out in memory is our spicing up of the pastoral phrase 'I / no longer goad the stubborn beasts' with the strategic addition of a consonant, giving 'I /no longer goad the stubborn breasts'. At least in this case the poem made some sort of sense in its revised form, though our author decided against holding onto the change.

A central component of *Metre* has always been its review coverage. Only in a very few cases does criticism outlive its object: who would rather read Richard Savage's forgotten poetry than Doctor Johnson's brilliant 'Life of Savage'? But if any branch of criticism is unlikely to live on it is the mere review, the best of which are still 'only remembered for a fortnight', Cyril Connolly thought.[16] The closest most come to an afterlife is a line or two on the back of a paperback, unless one adopts what might be called the Erostratus approach to posterity. Realizing that none of his achievements would make him immortal, Erostratus decided to burn down the temple of Artemis instead to keep his name alive. It worked, and where poetry reviewing is concerned isn't always a dishonourable approach. This may not have been what Croker and Lockhart thought they were up to when they savaged Keats for the *Edinburgh Review* and *Blackwood's Magazine*, but few of their other claims to posterity have been as memorable.

Not all harsh reviewers are ignorant Crokers and Lockharts, of course, and some of the best are at their most enjoyable at their most acid. Resources may be permanently short for the small magazine but, as Ian Hamilton has observed (with Geoffrey Grigson's *New Verse* in mind) there is 'always more than enough vitriol to go round', or as Yeats more memorably put it: 'great hatred, little room', a phrase W. J. McCormack has suggested would make the perfect title for an anthology of Irish book reviews.[17] What reader blowing the dust off copies of Grigson's *New Verse* could resist the cracker-barrel invective, the exuberant bile with which Grigson denounces what he calls the 'poisonous and steaming Gran Chaco of vulgarity, sciolism and literary racketeering'?[18] Try to imagine the *New Verse* reviewers' comparison of Edith Sitwell to 'the scarecrow of an advanced fool farm' or Cecil Day-Lewis to 'the grease in the sink-pipe of letters' transferred to the pages of the *TLS*, or another anonymous scribe's verdict on George Barker: 'I have never attempted, I am certain, to review more nauseating poems, and I have never read more inept juvenilia.'[19]

Metre in its time has also published negative reviews whose tone has ranged from mild disapproval to Erostratian ferocity. Much of the hostile reaction to this has been directed as much at the editors as the reviewers, but *Metre* has never pursued a prescriptive editorial line, consoling though it may be to think otherwise. Nor does publication of a poem in the magazine guarantee favourable reaction to the book in which it eventually appears. There is something amusing, if predictable, in the way that X's demolition-job on a well-known Irish poet draws howls of protest from her Irish admirers while a savaging of some Australian experimentalists goes unremarked —in Ireland that is, unlike Australia, where the treatment of the experimentalists provokes outrage but no one could care less about X's views on the Irish poet.

Writing in our diaspora issue of *Metre*, Peter Sirr reminds us of the provincialism that is the norm, not just in Ireland but any culture where writing in translation receives so little attention:

16 Connolly 106.   17 W. J. McCormack, 'Honest Scribes and Sottish Reviewers', *Krino* (10, Autumn 1990) 90.   18 Quoted in Ian Hamilton, *The Little Magazines: A Study of Six Editors* (London: Weidenfeld and Nicholson, 1976) 83.   19 Ibid. 88, 91, 97.

An international poetry magazine is suddenly, miraculously, available in Dublin bookshops because it is an Irish issue. We will never see the German issue or the Italian issue, not to mention the Scottish, Welsh or English issue. I have a sense that the more we pat ourselves on the back for our newly discovered 'Europeanness' the more are we ensnared in our own theme park.[20]

Beyond prodding the conscience of a naturally inward-looking culture, what does negative criticism achieve? If intelligently querulous reviews achieve their aim of seeing off the second-rate only to be forgotten themselves, it's not such a bad bargain: you don't need to keep taking medicine for an illness that's been cured. And if the illness has been misdiagnosed—if the reviewer is wrong—there's still the element of comic enjoyment we get from Lockhart and Croker (though obviously rescuing the Temple of Artemis from Erostratus' summary verdict on it is a little more difficult). But to the accusation of programmatic negativity, I would answer that one good poem mixed in with any amount of harsh reviews is enough to make a poetry magazine an inherently cheerful occasion. Not that there's anything wrong with negativity: when David Lloyd ends his study *Nationalism and Minor Literature* with the claim that the present cultural moment is one in which 'the only possible position for the intellectual appears to be that of unrelenting negative critique',[21] it strikes me as a perfectly reasonable position. The true enemy is not Grigsonian acid, but blandness: bland or uncritical praise is far more damaging than any amount of intelligent hatchet-jobs, though obviously the writers on the receiving end may not agree. In 'Work Without Hope' Coleridge wrote that 'Work without Hope draws nectar in a sieve, /And Hope without an object cannot live.' In contemporary poetry it often seems to be 'Worth without Hype' that is doomed to draw nectar in a sieve, but if the small magazine culture does its job properly, hype, cut off from its objects of exploitation in the poetry-reading public, should find the going more difficult than it otherwise would. If this is all *Metre* achieves, it will have more than done its job.

20 Peter Sirr, 'Irish Poetry and the Diaspora', *Metre* 3 (Autumn 1997) 21.   21 David Lloyd, *Nationalism and Minor Literature: James Clarence Mangan and the Emergence of Irish Cultural Nationalism* (Berkeley: University of California P, 1987) 214.

Index